The Professional Caterer Series

Volume 2

Individual Cold Dishes
Pâtés - Terrines
Galantines and Ballotines
Aspics Pizzas and Quiches

Denis Ruffel

assisted by

Roland Bilheux and Alain Escoffier

under the direction of
Pierre Michalet

Translated by Anne Sterling

cicem

A copublication of
CICEM (Compagnie Internationale
de Consultation *Education* et *Media*)
Paris

and

Van Nostrand Reinhold
New York

Contents

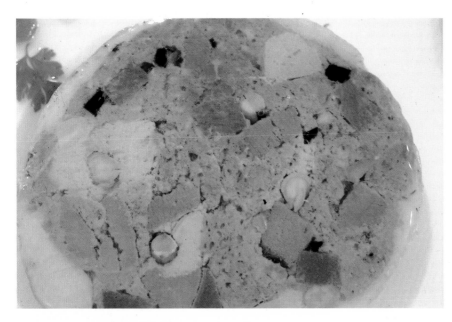

3

Introduction to the Six Chapters

The Basic Dishes of the Caterer's Repertoire

This volume includes the basic and most classic dishes in the repertoire of the Professional Caterer. All of these basic preparations are versatile and have many variations:

- from the most simple to very complex
- from economical to luxurious

These dishes adapt to the different methods of sale that involve the caterer:

- Specialty food store
- Small, informal restaurant
- Buffets and receptions
- Off-premise catering
- Supplying restaurants

The six chapters include basic preparations as well as innovative variations to encourage the caterer to be creative and expand his repertoire.

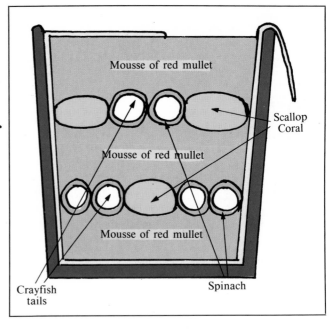

Valuable Visual Aids

In addition to the detailed description of each dish, the preparations are visually explained in two ways:
*1. **Cross-section,** (included where appropriate) is especially helpful in the chapter on terrines.*
*2. **Procedure Diagram,** at a single glance, the caterer will find step-by-step directions to illustrate the sequence of preparation to insure that each dish is completed on schedule.*

Chapter 1 – Individual Cold Dishes

These light, simple dishes are easy to prepare. They are easy to handle and are very colorful which makes them an ideal choice on a buffet or in the refrigerated case of a specialty food store. Appropriate as a first course or light main course, these cold individual dishes can be served in an informal restaurant and they transport easily for off-premise catering.

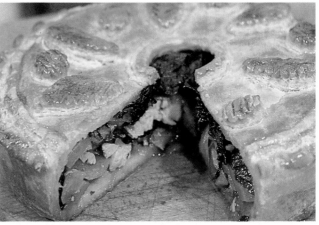

Chapter 2 – Pâtés

Pâtés are among the most classic offerings of the caterer. This group of dishes is extremely varied. Their common feature is the presence of a pastry crust or "pâte" in french.

These preparations range from the most simple to the very complex and they adapt to all methods of sale.

The caterer can augment many of these dishes with a sauce that is made specially for the pté, adding another dimension to express his culinary talents.

of " The Professional Caterer " (Volume 2)

Chapter 3 - Terrines

Like pâtés, terrines can vary widely. The choice of ingredients, from inexpensive to luxurious, provides a terrine for every budget.

Their common feature is the "terrine" mold in which they are baked.

Terrines made with meat are usually accompanied by tart pickles. Fish and vegeatable terrines, which tend to be more subtle in flavor, can be accompanied by a creamy sauce.

Chapter 4
Gallantines and Ballotines

The basic forcemeat used to make these dishes is similar to the mixtures for terrines. The assembly of these elegant preparations is more complicated and they are more difficult to serve and do not keep fresh as long as terrines. Therefore galantines and ballotines require a more advanced knowledge to prepare.

They are usually ordered in advance and are most often served during the holidays and for special occaions. Since they are more expensive to make than terrines, they are rarely sold in individual portions in a specialty food store.

Chapter 5 - Aspics

Aspics are as lovely look at as they are delicious to eat. These delicate dishes must be prepared with attention to the following:
• Use clear, full-flavored aspic.
• Choose the filling ingredients with great care.

They should be perfectly fresh and the color and taste should marry well with the flavor of the aspic.

These decorative dishes are suitable for all methods of sale.

Chapter 6 - Quiches and Pizzas

This is the most important group of dishes for the caterer. The preparations in this chapter is just a sampling of the many possible variations. Additional innovative recipes are described in Volume 3.

Although they are simple to prepare, quiches and pizzas can be very special when the caterer adds a personal touch.

These dishes are easy to serve in a restaurant and can be sold whole or by the slice in a specialty food store.

Chapter 1

Individual Cold Dishes

These dishes are simple to prepare and do not require an in-depth knowledge of cooking nor any special equipment.

These individual cold dishes are appropriate for various methods of sale: they may be purchased individually from the display case of a specialty food shop, they can be included in the lunch menu of a restaurant, as well as being served as a first course of a full meal or being featured at a catered buffet.

Certain dishes, such as the avo-cado and the grapefruit, are assembled in the "shell" made by the skin of the fruit. The artichoke bottoms make natural bases for other ingredients and the other dishes are often placed on toasted croutons, which makes serving and eating them easier. The dishes can be sold in clear plastic molds or unmolded on a plate with salad greens.

Ideally, these items are made using fresh seasonal ingredients, allowing the caterer to offer a varied assortment throughout the year. Sold individually, the sales price for these items will vary according to the price of the ingredients used and the type of sale.

- Avocado halves filled with crabmeat in cocktail sauce.

- Hollowed-out grapefruit halves, lined with lettuce and filled with refreshing ingredients dressed with soy sauce.

- Cooked artichoke bottoms, stuffed with mushroom duxelles, topped with a poached egg and coated with chaud-froid and glazed with aspic.

- Poached eggs in aspic prepared in either metal molds or clear plastic molds. Both preparations are garnished with flavorful ingredients in decorative shapes which are held in place with a layer of aspic.

- Shellfish, meat and vegetables set in molded aspic.

- Poached eggs napped with chaud-froid sauce, set on toasted "pain de mie" (enriched white bread) spread with foie gras mousse.

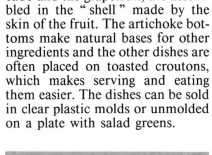

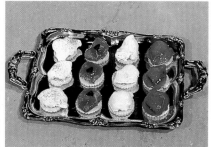

Avocado with Crab

Introduction

These avocados filled with crab make a lovely and appetizing first course and can be arranged with salad greens on a silver tray.

Level of Difficulty

The method for preparation is very simple, requiring no special techniques.

Be sure to choose ripe avocados, good quality crab meat and make a stiff mayonnaise.

Preparation Time

These items are quick to make. For a restaurant service, prepare the cocktail sauce and the crab separately, and combine them to order; likewise, cut the avocados only as you need them.

Profitability

Since preparation time for the dish is very short, it is not an important aspect of the cost. Avocados are available year-round from many different sources, therefore the most costly ingredient is the crabmeat, of which there are numerous grades and prices. The important thing is to always use the same size avocado and quantity of filling for which you have calculated the cost.

Equipment

Cutting board, flexible stainless steel knife, paring knife, serrated knife, small measuring cup, whisk, 3 small mixing bowls, 2 plates, small strainer, tablespoon

Ingredients

For 4 servings:

2 avocados
1/2 lemon
120 g (4oz) crabmeat

Sauce

1.5 dl (2/3 cup) mayonnaise
Few drops cognac
5 cl (1/4 cup) ketchup
4 black olives
4 cherry tomatoes or 1 small tomato
Lettuce leaves
Cayenne pepper or hot pepper sauce

Procedure

Remove the pit with a knife, taking care not to damage the fragile flesh.

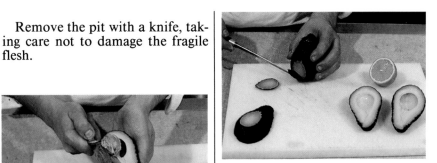

Using a stainless steel flexible knife to avoid discoloration, cut the avocado in half, by cutting

With the serrated knife, cut a thin slice from the underside of each avocado half so it will sit flat on the plate.

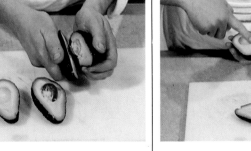

around the entire circumference, then pull the two halves apart.

Sprinkle the lemon juice on the avocado to keep it from discoloring.

Drain the crab meat and with your fingers, pick out any bits of shell.

9

Preparing the Sauce

Make the cocktail sauce: Start with a stiff mayonnaise and add the ketchup.

Add the cognac, blend with the whisk and season with a pinch of cayenne or a drop of hot pepper sauce.

Drain the crabmeat well and squeeze out any excess moisture so the sauce is not diluted. Add the crab and carefully combine it with the sauce using a spoon.

Taste and adjust the seasoning. Note: Be sure to taste the crabmeat before salting because canned crab is often very salty.

With the tablespoon, fill the hollow in the avocado half with crab and mound it slightly.

Use more or less filling depending on how the dish will be served and how much you are going to charge.

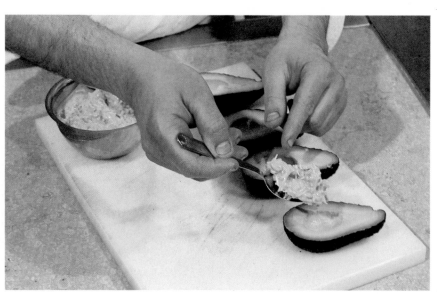

For an attractive presentation, garnish the avocado by topping it with a black olive and arranging the tomato wedges on the end. A decorative frilled wooden pick can be added as well.

The filled avocado halves may be displayed in the refrigerator case of a specialty food store or they may be made to order for service during a meal.

Grapefruit with Crab

Introduction

The presentation for this dish is both easy and very attractive, taking advantage of the hollowed-out grapefruit peel as a container for the salad.

They can be served any way the caterer needs – in a shop, at receptions for cocktails or lunch, as a first course for a dinner party.

Level of Difficulty

This simple to prepare dish rounds out the selection of individual cold first courses. A special knife makes segmenting the grapefruit easier.

Preparation Time

The few simple steps needed to make this dish are performed quickly and can be prepared in advance.

Preparing fresh crab will require more time than if canned crab is used. Bean sprouts purchased fresh usually need to be sorted and trimmed. The bean sprouts are also available ready to use in jars or cans.

Profitability

All the necessary ingredients are relatively inexpensive, except for the crab, which may be used in greater or lesser quantities. This allows the caterer to offer this popular and unusual dish at an affordable price.

Equipment

Cutting board, paring knife, serrated knife, grapefruit knife, 3 mixing bowls, strainer, 3 plates, small whisk, tablespoon, fork

Ingredients

For 6 servings:

3 grapefruits
1 small head leaf lettuce
150 g (5 oz) soy bean sprouts
120 g (4 oz) crabmeat
60 g (2 oz) corn kernels
18 small sweet peppers

Sauce

1/2 lemon,
8 cl (1/3 cup) oil,
1 cl (2 tsp) soy sauce, salt, pepper, ginger

Procedure

Using the serrated knife, cut a thin slice from the stem end and the opposite side of the grapefruit so the halves will sit flat on the plate.

Cut the grapefruit in half with the serrated knife. The segments of the fruit are now visible.

Using the special grapefruit knife, remove the segments of fruit by cutting around the inside of the membranes. The curved sharp blade will make this easy to do.

Cut out all the flesh and set aside in a bowl.

Using a tablespoon, remove the membrane from the peel.

The empty peels will be containers for the filling.

Pick through the crab meat and remove any bits of shell or membrane.

13

Use fresh or canned crab, of which there are numerous varieties.

Two types of grapefruit are available – pink and white. The pink ones are used in prepared dishes most often as they are sweeter and less bitter.

Drain the grapefruit segments so the juice doesn't dilute the sauce.

With a very sharp knife, cut the grapefruit segments into pieces, taking care not to crush them.

Lay the pieces of fruit on a hand towel to thoroughly drain.

Combine all the prepared ingredients in a bowl that is large enough so everything can be easily mixed – the drained grapefruit pieces, the fresh or canned bean sprouts, the sorted and well-drained crab, the corn kernels and the little peppers that will add color to the dish.

Chill until ready to season.

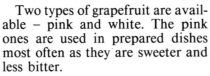

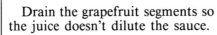

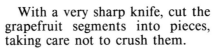

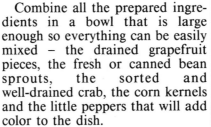

Making the Sauce

In a small bowl, combine the lemon juice, salt, pepper and a pinch of powdered or grated fresh ginger.

Whisk to dissolve the seasonings. Add a little soy sauce and then add the oil. Whisk well to combine.

Pour the sauce over the salad ingredients and carefully mix everything together, taking care not to crush the juice out of the grapefruit.

Line the inside of the grapefruit "shells" with some pretty lettuce leaves.

Fill the shell with the crab mixture so it is slightly rounded, taking care that all the five colorful elements of the salad are visible.

The salad is presented individually in the grapefruit shells or else in a salad bowl. The dish is appropriate for various methods of sale.

15

Artichoke Bottoms " St. Fiacre "

Introduction

Versatile and delicious, artichoke bottoms appear in many dishes. In this case, the artichokes are prepared using one basic technique to make two versions of this dish, one simple and the other more elaborate. This allows the caterer to offer the client a choice of prices.

The basic preparation is an artichoke bottom garnished with a layer of mushroom duxelles, topped by a poached egg.

Two versions may be made: a) simple: top the mushroom duxelles with some crab meat and coat the egg with herb chaud-froid sauce. b) elaborate: coat the egg with plain chaud-froid and top with a slice of smoked salmon, decorated with a truffle design.

Level of Difficulty

If using fresh artichokes, the bottoms must be shaped correctly. The eggs must be carefully poached so the yolks stay soft.

Although not extremely complicated, the dish requires close attention to all the elements.

Preparation Time

Five separate steps are necessary in the preparation of this dish. If using fresh artichokes, trimming the bottoms will take quite awhile, as will preparating the other ingredients. For efficiency, it is best to prepare each element separately then assemble the dishes systematically.

Profitability

These dishes have a relatively high food cost. Use the best quality artichokes available, as inferior grades will be stringy. The version of this dish using smoked salmon and truffles will of course be even more costly.

Ingredients

For 12 servings:

12 artichokes, 2 lemons, 5 L (5 qts)

water, 75 g (2 1/2 oz) salt, 10 black peppercorns, 10 coriander seeds, 1 dl (1/2 cup) olive oil, 150 g (5oz) flour

Mushroom duxelles:

45 g (1 1/2 oz) clarified butter, 45 g (1 1/2 oz) shallots, 300 g (10 oz) mushrooms, 1/2 lemon, salt, pepper, mayonnaise, 12 eggs (for poaching)

a) crab version: 180 g (6 oz) crab, herb chaud-froid sauce (1/4 L (1 cup) mayonnaise, 1/2 L (2 cups) aspic, chervil, tarragon, chives), 1/4 L (1 cup) aspic (for the final glaze)

b) salmon version: 4 slices smoked salmon, plain chaud-froid sauce (1/4 L (1 cup) mayonnaise, 1/2 L (2 cups) aspic), 1 hard-boiled egg white, 1 small truffle, 1/4 L (1 cup) aspic (for the final glaze)

Equipment

Cutting board, serrated knife, chef's knife, paring knife, lemon squeezer, soft-bristled brush, tablespoon, large saucepan, sauté pan with lid, skimmer, 5 mixing bowls, small whisk, strainer, measuring cup, plain pastry cutters, truffle cutters, hotel pan, stainless steel sheet pan, stainless steel cooling rack, 12 aluminum "shells"

Procedure

Trim the artichokes: with the serrated knife, cut off the artichoke stem. With a very sharp paring knife held against the side of the artichoke, cut off all the large bottom leaves, starting at the widest part of

the artichoke and turning. Trim away all the leaves in this manner, then neatly trim the bottom so it is even and flat on the underside.

Rub the entire surface with the cut lemon to prevent it from discoloring.

Keep the artichoke bottoms in a bowl of acidulated water until ready to cook.

Prepare a "blanc", a solution in which to cook the artichoke bottoms so they stay light in color, consisting of water and flour. The cooking time will vary with the size of the artichokes and can be tested by piercing them with the point of a knife.

Let the artichoke bottoms cool in their cooking liquid to prevent them from drying out or discoloring.

The artichoke bottoms must be carefully and thoroughly drained before using, taking care not to break them.

Use large eggs (55-60 g (about 2 oz)) that are very fresh, so that the white will wrap evenly around the yolk during poaching.

Poach the eggs in a mixture of 1 L (1 qt) water to 1 dl (1/2 cup) distilled white vinegar. Never add salt to the water, as this will prevent the white from coagulating.

When the poaching water is just simmering, break an egg in a small

bowl, then let the egg slide from the bowl into the water. Poach the eggs in batches of no more than six at a time in order to keep track of the cooking time.

Check for doneness by gently pushing the egg with your finger; the yolk must remain soft.

As soon as the eggs are cooked, remove them from the water with a skimmer and plunge them into a bowl of ice water.

When they are cool, remove them with your hands, taking care not to damage them.

Lay the eggs to drain on a hand towel. When the first side is dry, carefully turn them over so the other side dries. Chill until ready to use.

Preparing the Mushroom Duxelles

Peel the shallots and cut into very fine dice. Cook them in clarified butter until soft but not brown.

Trim the mushrooms, wash them and rub with lemon juice. Chop finely and add them to the shallots.

Season with salt and pepper. Cook covered at first to draw out the liquid in the mushrooms, then continue cooking without the lid to let the moisture evaporate. Pour onto a tray and leave to cool.

Assembling the Artichoke Bottoms

After draining the artichoke bottoms carefully, remove the fibrous choke using a spoon.

If necessary, trim the edge with a paring knife. Rinse to remove any small fibers.

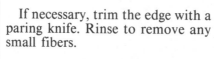

Turn the artichoke bottom over on a hand towel to let them drain completely.

When the mushroom duxelles are cool, add them to the mayonnaise and mix well with a wooden spoon.

Fill each artichoke bottom with a spoonful of the mushroom duxelles. For the version with the herb chaud-froid, sprinkle a little crabmeat over the mushrooms.

Trim any ragged edges of the poached eggs with scissors, then place an egg on top of the artichoke bottom.

Chill the artichoke bottom so they can be more easily coated with sauce.

For the herb chaud-froid sauce, using a chef's knife, carefully cut the chives.

Chop the tarragon and chervil very finely.

Combine the mayonnaise and the aspic in the proportion of 1 part mayonnaise to 2 parts aspic. Combine with a whisk, but do not whisk so vigorously that you make any foam, which would ruin the smooth finish of the sauce.

19

Put the bowl of chaud-froid sauce over crushed ice and stir slowly until the sauce begins to thicken slightly. Take the eggs from the refrigerator and using a large spoon, coat them with sauce as shown. Repeat if necessary to get a smooth even coat.

Lay the thin slices of smoked salmon on a cutting board and with a plain round pastry cutter, stamp out rounds that are approximately 2/3 the diameter of the coated egg.

Lay the salmon on each egg and brush with a thin coat of aspic.

Chill the artichoke bottoms again, then carefully brush on a final coat of clear aspic to help them keep fresh longer and to make them shine.

For the version with the salmon, follow the same procedure, omitting the herbs.

With a knife, cut thin strips of truffle, then using the truffle cutters, stamp out designs and arrange them on the salmon.

The final coat of aspic will seal and protect the chaud-froid sauce and decoration as well as protecting the egg from contact with the air and will keep the dish looking shiny and brilliant.

Keep refrigerated until sale, and be sure to advise the client on the best methods for storage and service.

Repeat this step with the egg whites to finish the decoration. Brush again with aspic.

Separate the leaves from the head of lettuce, rinse and dry them.

Remove the thick central rib. Lay a leaf in each aluminum "shell" or on each plate.

21

Eggs in Aspic

Introduction

These little dishes can be made in numerous ways and degrees of sophistication. Too often, however, they are made with too little of the main ingredient or flavorless and rubbery gelatin. Nonetheless, with the right ingredients and proportions, eggs in aspic can be delicious. Three examples are presented in this section.

Preliminary Advice

Eggs in aspic are presented in two ways for carry-out sales. They may be prepared in metal molds, then unmolded on a platter or small cardboard plate, or they may be prepared and displayed in a clear plastic mold, which allows the customer to see the egg and the other ingredients.

This second method also protects the egg during transport. To unmold, the customer simply dips the plastic mold in warm water for a few seconds just before service.

Level of Difficulty

This dish poses no particular problems. Follow the guidelines for poaching eggs. Use an aspic that has a lot of body, without being rubbery. Allow the aspic to set completely after the application of each layer. Always chill the ingredients well.

Preparation Time

Always organize your work logically and efficiently. If you prepare the ingredients correctly ahead of time, the eggs in aspic dishes can be made very cost-effectively. When properly stored, they can be made up to five days in advance.

Profitability

You can use ingredients at all different price levels, therefore you can tailor your food cost to fit the client's budget.

Notes on Poaching Eggs

Equipment

Saucepan, measuring cup, small bowl, skimmer, mixing bowl, hotel pan

Procedure

Fill the mixing bowl with ice water to chill the cooked eggs.

Fill the saucepan with water and add vinegar in the amount of 10 % of the volume of the water. Never add salt, as this will prevent the egg white from coagulating.

Break an egg into the small bowl, then let the egg slide gently from

the bowl into the water that is just simmering.

Poach the eggs in batches of no more than six at a time in order to control the cooking time.

The yolk must remain soft.

Remove the egg with the skimmer.

Plunge the egg in the ice water to stop the cooking and chill the egg.

When the eggs are cold, take them from the water with your hands so the yolk does not break.

Lay the eggs on a hand towel to dry. When the first side is dry, carefully turn them over to dry the other side.

1 – Eggs in Aspic with Ham

Introduction

Eggs in aspic with ham is the most classic of the three preparations discussed in this chapter. A bit of decoration completes the presentation. The food cost of this item is quite low, although if truffles are used in the decoration, the cost must be adjusted accordingly.

Ingredients
6 poached eggs
2 slices boiled or baked ham
1 hard-boiled egg white
1/4 cooked red pepper
6 dl (2 1/2 cups) aspic, flavored
   with port, madeira or sherry

Procedure

Cut the ham into ovals using the metal molds as a guide.

These will be layered between the egg and the aspic. Cut the trimmings into large stips, which will decorate the aspic.

Cut thin round slices of egg white and stamp out designs using a special cutter. Do the same with the cooked red pepper.

Chill the molds so the aspic will set.

Pour a thin layer of aspic in the bottom of the chilled mold and let it set slightly.

Arrange the decorations in an attractive pattern on the bottom. Pour on another layer of aspic and chill again.

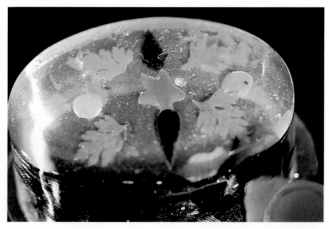

The clear aspic allows the decoration to show through.

Lay an oval slice of ham in the mold.

Pour a little aspic on top and chill.

Trim the well-dried egg so it fits neatly in the mold and place it on top of the ham.

Arrange the strips of ham around the egg. Fill the mold with aspic just to the rim.

Chill until ready to unmold. Depending on how the eggs are to be

presented and sold, dip the metal molds quickly in warm water and unmold onto lettuce leaves on a platter or a plate, or else invert the clear plastic mold onto a platter so the decoration is visible.

Serve very cold.

2 – Eggs in Aspic "à l'Indienne"

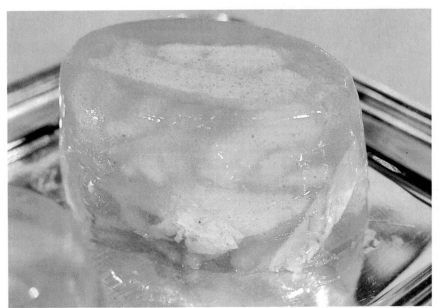

Introduction

This is a less classic presentation of eggs in aspic that is equally easy to prepare and again uses inexpensive ingredients, allowing the caterer to offer a nice variety of affordable items to the client. Eggs in aspic "à l'indienne" (in France, the name usually designates a dish with curry or chutney) is very versatile and the slightly unusual ingredients are always appreciated by customers, especially at a buffet offering more exotic food.

Ingredients

For 6 servings:

6 poached eggs
1/2 banana
1 small apple
1 slice pineapple
1/2 lemon
1 chicken breast, poached in chicken stock
6 dl (2 1/2 cups) aspic
Pinch of curry powder

Melt the aspic in a bain-marie and add the curry powder, which provides flavor as well as a golden color.

Procedure

Prepare the fruit garnish: peel the banana and apple and rub them with the cut lemon to prevent discoloration. Use fresh or canned pineapple.

Cut the chicken breast into thin strips. Cut the trimmings into small cubes.

Using a stainless steel knife to avoid discoloring the fruits, cut the banana, apples and pineapple into short julienne.

Chill the molds so the aspic will set. Pour a thin layer of curried

aspic in the bottom of each mold and chill again to set, then place a strip of chicken in the bottom of the mold.

Pour over another thin layer of aspic and chill again.

Sprinkle a little of the prepared fruits into each mold.

Pour on a little more aspic and chill again.

While the aspic is setting, trim the well-dried poached egg with a pair of scissors, if necessary, to fit neatly in the mold. Lay an egg in the mold when the aspic is ready.

Add more fruit and the small pieces of chicken around the egg. Fill the molds just to the rim with aspic. Chill.

This, like the other eggs in aspic, is a very popular product. When served with an appropriate salad, it makes a nice light supper or after-theater meal.

3 – Eggs in Aspic "Luculus"

Introduction

This is the most elaborate and luxurious preparation of the eggs in aspic, reserved perhaps for a holiday celebration or a very special buffet.

The method of preparation is simple, taking only as much time as the other eggs in aspic already discussed. However, the foie gras and truffles used in this presentation make the food cost quite high.

Ingredients

For 6 servings:
6 poached eggs
90 g (3 oz) foie gras
30 g (1 oz) truffles
100 g (3 1/2 oz) good quality baked ham
6 dl (2 1/2 cups) aspic with Port

Procedure

Slice the ham, trim away the fat and cut into short julienne.

Cut the foie gras and the truffles in short julienne approximately the same size as the ham (the truffles should be slightly smaller).

Lay the ingredients on a plate so they are ready to use for garnish.

Melt the aspic in a bain marie and flavor it with some port; madeira, sherry or sauternes would be good also.

Chill the molds, then pour in a thin layer of aspic and chill again until set.

Lay the three ingredients in an attractive pattern on the bottom of the mold.

Pour in a little more aspic just to cover the ingredients, then chill until set.

Trim the poached egg if necessary to fit neatly in the mold. Lay an egg in each mold. Arrange the rest of the garnish around the egg. Fill the mold just to the rim with the aspic and chill.

For these, as well as the other eggs in aspic, make sure the aspic is well-set before unmolding. Only take the molds from the refrigerator at the last minute, and try to work in a cool place. To loosen the eggs, run the point of a small knife around the edge of the mold, keeping the edge of the blade toward the side of the mold.

Dip the mold quickly into warm water. Turn the mold over in your hand and shake lightly so the aspic releases from the mold.

Arrange on a cold platter or plate.

Eggs in aspic are simple to make, and when made carefully with the right proportions, they are quite delicious.

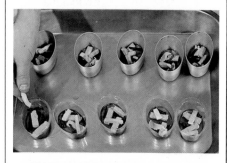

The aspic should be well-flavored and not too stiff. The amount of gelatin in the aspic should be adjusted according to the temperature of the season in which they will be made.

The amount of other ingredients should be appropriate for the size of the mold. Too much aspic with too little garnish is not a successful combination.

The type of presentation depends on how the eggs in aspic are being sold and on the customer's specifications.

A green salad makes an appropriate accompaniment.

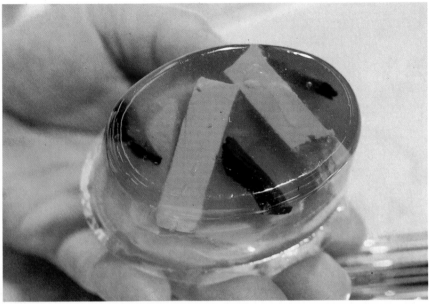

Aspic Molds

Introduction

Like eggs in aspic, aspic molds are prepared by layering many different kinds of ingredients with different flavors of aspic. The base for the aspic can be fish, meat or poultry and flavorings range from various wines and spirits to spices and other condiments.

These aspic molds adapt easily to any type of catering function.

Level of Difficulty

The aspic molds are not difficult to produce, but thoughtful attention to the originality of the ingredients is all important.

Always use the correct proportion of gelatin in the aspic for the weather and temperature.

Prepare the garnishes carefully and attractively.

Choose ingredients that combine well together and are appropriate to the season.

Preparation Time

The time required to make these dishes varies, but their preparation will always be quicker and more cost effective if the work is systematic and well organized.

Profitability

As with anything a caterer makes, the choice of ingredients depends in large part on the client's budget.

For special parties or holiday celebrations, the client may be more inclined towards buying expensive products, but the caterer must decide what is appropriate to offer.

Preliminary Advice

Aspic molds can be made large enough to serve several people or in individual portions. They may be prepared in metal molds, to be unmolded for presentation, or they may be prepared and displayed in clear plastic molds, which allows the ingredients to be visible for an attractive display in a specialty food shop.

In this book, we address the individual aspic molds; large aspic preparations are discussed in Volume 3 of this series.

The following three versions are presented here:

- vegetable aspic molds

- seafood aspic molds

- smoked salmon aspic molds

1 – Aspic Mold with Vegetables and Basil

Introduction

Five different vegetables give this dish a bright and colorful look, while a poached quail's egg enhances the center. A fine julienne of fresh basil perfumes all the ingredients.

This version can be made year-round using different combinations of seasonal vegetables, however, fresh basil can be hard to find and quite expensive in winter, bringing the food cost up. Excellent canned corn is available and is a good choice.

Ingredients

For 6 servings:

45 g (1 1/2 oz) green beans
100 g (3 1/2 oz) peas
45 g (1 1/2 oz) carrots
45 g (1 1/2 oz) corn
45 g (1 1/2 oz) zucchini
1 small bunch basil
6 quail's eggs
6 dl (2 1/2 cups) aspic

Procedure

After choosing and weighing the vegetables, wash, peel and cut them into very small even dice.

Cook each vegetable separately in salted boiling water; the vegetables should remain firm but not crunchy.

As soon as they are cooked, refresh them in ice water and drain.

Green vegetables are ideally cooked in an unlined copper pan that has first been cleaned with a mixture of salt and vinegar.

The vegetables may be steamed rather than boiled. A couscous steamer or bamboo steamer works very well.

If steaming the vegetables, simply salt them lightly before cooking, then cover with a damp hand towel when they are cooked.

Assembly

The assembly is generally the same as the eggs in aspic.

Make sure to "fluff up" the julienne of basil so that it can be evenly distributed throughout the mold.

To finish, fill the molds to the rim with aspic and chill again to set thoroughly.

The vegetables are arranged in alternating layers with the aspic, chilling to set after each successive layer.

Unmold and plate the aspics in the manner appropriate to their presentation.

Keep refrigerated until ready to serve.

In this version, the quail's egg is placed in the center of the mold, which makes the mold look pretty when it is cut open.

2 – Seafood Aspic Molds

Introduction

This lovely, refreshing and delicious dish is always very popular.

It takes quite a while to prepare.

Three types of shellfish are used: mussels, crayfish and scallop coral (if the latter is not available, use bay or sea scallops, or for color use fresh salmon).

As for the vegetables, it is important to choose a combination that will be refreshing with the seafood: carrots, cucumbers, corn kernels, julienne of lemon and lime zest.

The food cost for this dish is higher than for the other aspics.

Ingredients

For 6 servings:

500 g (1 lb) mussels
3 pieces scallop coral
3 salt water crayfish
150 g (5 oz) cucumber
150 g (5 oz) carrots
45 g (1 1/2 oz) corn kernels
1 tsp green peppercorns in brine
Zest from 1/2 lime.
Zest from 1/4 lemon.

Procedure

The Shellfish

The Mussels

Wash and scrub the mussels and cook them " à la marinière " (steam them open with a little dry white wine, chopped onions and shallots).

Do not overcook or they will become tough. After cooking, let the mussels cool, then remove them from their shells and pull off the dark rim or " beard ".

The Scallop Coral

Scallop coral is used because of its bright color, rather than the taste, which is quite bland. (The scallop itself is the flavorful part.) Poach the coral gently in a court bouillon or light fish stock. Do not overcook.

Leave to cool in the poaching liquid.

The Crayfish

If the price of large crayfish makes the food cost too high, you may substitute small shrimp instead.

Remove the shell and the " vein " and poach in court bouillon or light fish stock. Leave to cool in the poaching liquid.

The Vegetables

The carrots and cucumbers are prepared in the same manner, but they are cooked separately because their textures are very different. Rinse and peel the vegetables. Using a tiny melon baller, scoop out little balls.

Cook the vegetables in boiling salted water or steam them. Refresh in ice water after cooking.

The preparation is the same for both the julienne of lemon zest and lime zest, but they must be cooked separately because the lime zest is tougher and more bitter than the lemon zest.

Using a vegetable peeler, pare large strips of zest from the lemon and lime, avoiding the white pith.

Cut the pared zest into very fine strips and put them in a saucepan with cold water. Bring the water to

a boil and boil 3-4 minutes, drain in a fine strainer, then refresh with cold water. Do this twice for the lime zest so it becomes soft and less bitter.

Drain the green peppercorns and the corn kernels separately.

Assembly

Follow the guidelines for using aspic given in the preceding recipes. Blend the colors of the seafood and the vegetables so they look attractive in the transparent aspic.

Between each layer of ingredient, pour a layer of aspic and chill until set.

Fill the mold just to the rim and refrigerate until ready to unmold.

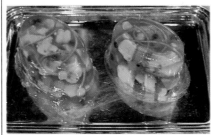

Unmold and arrange according to the method of sale.

3 – Smoked Salmon Aspic Molds

Introduction

This aspic can be offered in any season because the ingredients are available year-round.

Their cost, however, is quite high, but the preparation is simple, therefore this aspic is easy and convenient to produce.

Ingredients

For 6 servings:

2 slices smoked salmon
60 g (2 oz) salmon eggs
1 avocado
3 cl (2 tbsp) heavy cream
1 leaf gelatin (optional)
1/2 lemon
Sprig of fresh dill
6 dl (2 1/2 cups) aspic
Salt, cayenne pepper

Procedure

Assemble all the ingredients and then start by making an avocado mousse.

Choosing the right avocado is very important – an unripe one is hard, with an unpleasant bitter taste and will not work for the mousse. In contrast, an over-ripe avocado is too soft and dark, therefore select only perfectly ripe avocados.

Cut the avocados in two, remove the pit with the tip of a knife, then with a spoon, scoop out the flesh.

Sprinkle with lemon juice to prevent discoloration. Pass through a fine sieve to make a purée.

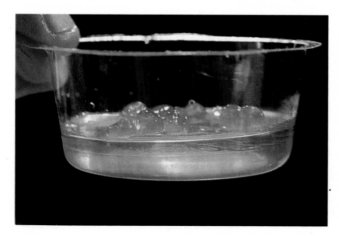

Add a little heavy cream and mix well.

If the purée is too loose, you may add the softened and melted gelatin to give the mousse a little body.

The mousse may be mixed in a bowl set over crushed ice to keep it very thick.

Assembly

Pour a thin layer of aspic in the molds and chill to set. Lay a sprig of dill in the mold then sprinkle with salmon eggs.

Pour a thin layer of aspic over the decoration and chill to set.

Cut the sliced smoked salmon in pieces that will fit into the molds.

With a pastry bag and a plain medium tip, pipe some avocado mousse in the center of the mold.

Top the avocado with some more salmon eggs and some strips of smoked salmon.

Carefully pour on more aspic to fill the mold just to the rim.

This is an elegant and attractive aspic mold, which may be accompanied by a small salad. It can be served in the same way as the preceding aspics.

Glazed Eggs

Introduction

This is an unusual way of using poached eggs that is valuable to the caterer, as it is quick, easy and inexpensive to produce.

The " glaze " can be made from numerous sauces with different tastes and colors, which produces a very pretty platter that is appealing on a buffet table.

Recipe

Basic Ingredients

Eggs
" Pain de mie "
   (enriched white bread)
Melted butter
Liver purée

Sauces

Sauce A

Curry Chaud-froid

Mayonnaise
Aspic
Curry
Salt and pepper

Sauce B

" Perigueux " Sauce

Madeira sauce
Demi-glace
   (reduced brown sauce)
Truffle juice
Cooked roux
Gelatin
Salt, pepper
Truffle

Sauce C

Herb Chaud-froid Sauce

Mayonnaise
Sherry
Aspic
Tarragon
Chives
Chervil

Sauce D

Tomato Sauce

Ketchup
Gelatin
Tarragon
Tomato paste
Aspic

Be sure to poach the eggs far enough in advance so they are completely cold before glazing.

Follow the previous guidelines for poaching eggs using unsalted water and distilled white vinegar. Refresh the eggs in ice water. Drain them thoroughly and dry them on a hand towel.

Make the croutons by cutting out rounds of bread using a pastry cutter approximately the same diameter as the poached eggs.

Brush the bread lightly with melted butter, then toast in the oven until the croutons are crisp and golden brown.

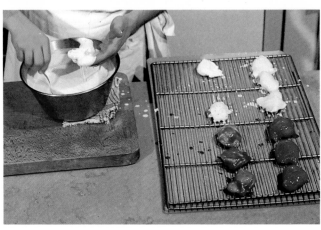

Work the liver purée until it is soft and spreadable. Set aside until ready to put on the toasts. The liver purée will help hold the eggs in place.

Make the desired sauces to glaze the eggs.

Prepare any decoration-curry powder, truffles, herbs and melt a little aspic to be used for a final glaze.

At right
(from top to bottom)

1. Glazed eggs with curry chaud-froid sauce

2. Glazed eggs with "Perigueux" sauce

3. Glazed eggs with herb chaud-froid sauce

4. Glazed eggs with tomato sauce

Chapter 2
Pâtés

In this chapter we present a wide range of pâtés, from the simplest to the most elaborate.

The pastry casings are shaped in different ways and filled with a variety of ingredients including meats, poultry, fish, vegetables, with carefully selected seasonings and garnishes.

The flavor is further enhanced with marinades that marry well with the taste of the other ingredients.

The price of each pâté varies according to the price of the ingredients and the work involved in preparation.

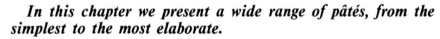

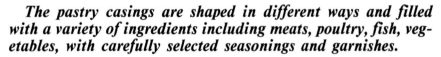

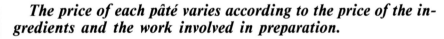

Introduction to Pâtés

Fundamental Principles of Pâtés

A pâté by definition is always wrapped in some sort of pastry, regardless of the other ingredients or techniques used in its preparation. The pâté filling may include a forcemeat made of ground lean and fatty meats which helps bind all the ingredients. Many of the dishes included in this chapter are not bound with a forcemeat, however, but use other preparations to hold the fillings together, such as the custard in the Tourte Lorraine or the béchamel sauce in the Ham and Spinach Pithiviers.

The finished product will be delicious, in part because all the different flavors in the ingredients have been trapped by the pastry wrapping.

The Meats

The pâtés may be assembled in various ways: the forcemeat may be layered with meat filets, strips of fat or ham or other ingredients such as pistachios, hazelnuts, and truffles. Other additions include pieces of meat or variety meats or colorful vegetables.

No matter what ingredients or which method of assembly, it is crucial to choose a well-balanced combination of ingredients to produce a savory, delectable pâté which even the most discriminating client will enjoy.

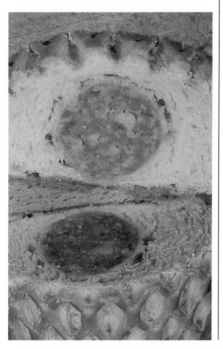

The Pastry Doughs

Many different kinds of dough can be used and the caterer should use the recipe that works best in his or her operation. The most frequently used and appropriate doughs are:

- " pâte à pâté " (pâté pastry)
- " pâte brisée " (pie pastry)
- " pâte feulletée " (puff pastry)
- " pâte à brioche " (brioche dough).

The pâté pastry is pie pastry which is made sturdier with extra egg and sometimes oil or lard. This pastry is usually easier to press into the molds and holds up well during cooking.

In some cases, two doughs are used to make an attractive pastry casing, for example, brioche with a lattice of puff pastry.

Cooking the Pâtés

Cooking pâtés requires a lot of effort and strict adherence to the rules. The larger the pâté, the longer the cooking time. In this case, the temperature must be lower so that the heat penetrates to the center of the pâté without overcooking the pastry.

If a very moist filling is used, a " chimney " can be made in the top crust to allow the steam produced during cooking to escape so it does not make the pastry soggy.

If the pâté is to be reheated before serving, the caterer must take care not to overcook it initially so that it can be reheated without becoming too dry.

Adding an Aspic Finish to Cold Pâtés

Allow the pâté to cool thoroughly (making sure the center is cool as well). Stir the aspic over ice until it thickens slightly and just begins to set. Pour the aspic over the top of the pâté so it completely fills any cracks or spaces. The aspic should be made from a stock that is appropriate to the pâté and it may be flavored with various wines or fortified wines. Fruits, truffles or other colorful ingredients can be used as decorations which are held in place by the aspic.

Storage

Unlike meat terrines, pâtés cannot be stored for a long time. The pastry casing, which is an essential part of the pâté, must stay fresh and crisp.

The storage depends also on the ingredients used for the filling, as many meats and especially variety meats and fish can be quite perishable.

Terrines have the advantage of being protected by a layer of melted fat, which helps prevent spoilage. However, pâtés cannot use this method of conservation. Therefore, pâtés can be kept for only two to three days in the refrigerator.

Advice for Serving Pâtés

To serve cold and hot pâtés to their best advantage, the following points should be observed:

Cold pâtés should be eaten at the proper temperature, which is cool enough so the aspic remains firm and does not melt, yet not so cold that the flavors of the pâté are diminished. They are delicious served with pickled condiments such as " cornichons " (tart gherkins) or pickled onions.

Hot pâtés should never be reheated while wrapped in foil, because the steam created will make the pastry soggy.

They should be reheated in a moderate oven so the heat penetrates slowly, heating the pâté through to the center without drying or burning the crust. Some may be enhanced by a sauce. Generally the sauce is offered seperately so the guests can serve themselves and the crust does not become soggy from sitting in sauce.

Denis Ruffel's Selection of Pâtés

1. Veal and Ham Pâté in Aspic

Dough	Filling	Presentation
Pâté pastry	Blade end of pork, pork jowl, fat back, foie gras, ham, sirloin tip of veal	Aspic, truffle

2. " Pantin " Pâté

Dough	Filling	Presentation
Pâté pastry and puff pastry	Blade end of pork, pork jowl, fat back, foie gras, ham, sirloin tip of veal	Hot

3. Tourte of Rabbit with Hazelnuts

Dough	Filling	Presentation
Puff pastry	Rabbit, fat back, foie gras, hazelnuts	Hot, with " Poivrade " sauce

4. Tourte Lorraine

Dough	Filling	Presentation
Pâté pastry, puff pastry	Pork tenderloin, sirloin tip of veal	Hot cream sauce added at the end of cooking

5. Tourte of Sweetbreads and Morels

Dough	Filling	Presentation
Pâté pastry, puff pastry	Sweetbreads, morels, vegetables	Hot, with sauce from braising liquid

6. Ham and Spinach " Pithiviers "

Dough	Filling	Presentation
Puff pastry	Crêpes, spinach, ham, béchamel sauce	Hot

7. Sausage in Brioche

Dough	Filling	Presentation
Brioche, puff pastry	Sausage	Hot, with " Perigueux " sauce

8. Pâté of Duck à l'Orange in Aspic

Dough	Filling	Presentation
Pâté pastry	Duck, pork jowl, foie gras	Aspic, sliced oranges

9. Salmon Koulibiac

Dough	Filling	Presentation
Brioche, puff pastry	Salmon, crêpes, eggs, spinach, rice, mushrooms, béchamel sauce	Hot, with cream sauce

Pâté Forcemeat

General Advice

These forcemeat stuffings are the basic component of many charcuterie preparations: pâtés, terrines, galantines and ballotines.

Most of the forcemeats made with meat, poultry or game also use fat, in varying quantities from different sources: shoulder of pork, pork jowl, fat back.

Saltpeter is an optional ingredient which is added to maintain the rosy color of the meats.

For the best taste and consistency in the pâté, the meat used as the base for the forcemeat is prepared by marinating it in various wines with spices and other seasonings.

The meat is then ground and bound with eggs. Foie gras or goose liver purée can be added, as it binds well, tastes delicious and lends a very smooth texture to the mixture.

Preparing the Garnish

The garnish ingredients can be marinated also. They are layered with the forcemeat.

After assembling the forcemeat with the garnish, the mixture is wrapped in pastry, either shaped by hand or lined in a mold. After cooking, the pâtés are eaten either hot or cold with a sauce or aspic accompaniment.

The Meats

To make the forcemeat, three pork products are necessary: blade end, jowl and fat back.

Blade End of Pork

This cut of meat is found at the top of the shoulder. It has a pleasant taste with a slightly stringy texture and moderate amount of fat.

Boning the Blade End

The blade end is a flat cut that is attached to the bone in an open V-shape.

Using a well-sharpened boning knife, cut the meat from the bone along one side. Cut under this bone and work the knife out to the other side where the meat is attached to the flat rib bones.

Cut from the top of the bone, cutting away the meat and working gradually downward, taking care to scrape the meat from the bone so the maximum amount of meat is removed.

Turn the piece over and make a small cut along each rib to loosen the meat.

Once each rib is cut, cut the meat above the rib and cut down toward

the other side where the meat is already cut away.

Set the meat aside and scrape off any bits of meat that remain on the bone.

Cut the meat into cubes approximately 4-5 cm (about 2 in) on each side.

The Jowl

Also called neck fat, the pork jowl has no bone. It is found just below the pig's head running into the body. This cut is rather fatty, which will add richness and moisture to the forcemeat.

Skinning the Jowl

Cut the pork jowl into large strips. Remove the skin by cutting it with a stiff-bladed knife, taking care to angle the knife blade toward the skin so no fat is missed.

Reserve the skin for other preparations, such as stock for aspic. Small amounts of skin can be added to various stocks to add gelatin and body. It can be frozen. Always blanch it before use.

At this stage, we have two components of the forcemeat – a lean cut, the blade end, and a fatty cut, the jowl. To balance the recipe, it is sometimes necessary to add a small proportion of fat back. Remove the skin of the fat back and cut into 2 cm (3/4 in) cubes.

The Sirloin Tip of Veal

This is one of the basic components of many pâté fillings, located between the top round and the shank. It is a very good cut of veal. The French name for the cut (noix pâtissière) comes from the fact that it is often used in making pâtés. It is a plump cut, which is very thick with few tendons and therefore is ideal for cutting into slices or small strips to be used along with the ground forcemeat in the filling for the pâté.

Preparing the Sirloin Tip of Veal

Using a thin-bladed knife, cut away the silver skin and remove the few tendons. Cut into thick slices, then into small strips.

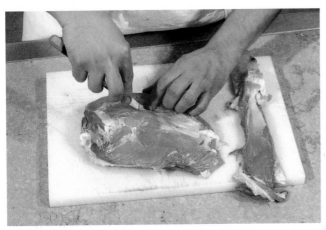

Ingredients

The Meats

3.8 kg (8 lb 8 oz) blade end of pork with the bone yields 3 kg (6 lb 8 oz) of boned meat (approximately 20-23% loss)

3.2 kg (7 lb) pork jowl yields 3 kg (6 lb 8 oz) after removing the skin (5-8% loss)

850 g (1 lb 12 oz) untrimmed fat back yields 800 g (1 lb 10 oz) after removing the skin (4-5% loss)

2 kg (4 lb 8 oz) untrimmed sirloin tip of veal yields 1.7 kg (3 lb 12 oz) after removing the tendons (10-25% loss)

The Marinades

The three pork cuts (blade end, jowl, and fat back) are marinated together and the veal is marinated separately.

*Marinade for the Forcemeat
(blade end, jowl, fat back)*

per 1 kg (2 lb) meat:

4 shallots (approximately 120 g
   (4 oz))
4 cloves garlic (approximately 45 g
   (1 1/2 oz))
45 g (1 1/2 oz) clarified butter
1 dl (1/2 cup) white wine

12 g (approximately 2 1/2 tsp)
   salt
2 g ground pepper
2 g allspice
3 g saltpeter
pinch thyme
2 small bay leaves
2.5 dl (1 cup) white wine
2 dl (3/4 cup) madeira
1.5 dl (2/3 cup) cognac

Making the Marinade

Peel the garlic, cut in half to remove the green "sprout", crush
with the flat of a chef's knife and
chop finely.

Melt the clarified butter in a
small sauté pan. Add the shallots
and garlic and cook until soft but
not brown.

Deglaze the pan with white wine,
then bring it to a boil and boil until
reduced by half.

Transfer the mixture to a bowl
and leave to cool.

Season the meats (blade end,
jowl, fat back) with the herbs and
spices. Add the cooled shallot and
garlic mixture and combine well
with a wooden spoon.

Add the white wine, madeira and
cognac and mix well.

Cover the meats with plastic film
and marinate in the refrigerator approximately 24 hours.

*Marinade for the Sirloin Tip of
Veal*

per kg (2 lb) meat

12 g (approximately 1/2 oz) salt
2 g ground pepper
2 g allspice
3 g saltpeter
pinch of thyme
2 small bay leaves
3 dl (1 1/4 cup) white wine
1.5 dl (2/3 cup) cognac

Mix all the ingredients together.
Cover with plastic film and marinate in the refrigerator for approximately 24 hours.

Making the Forcemeat

When the meats have marinated for one day, make the forcemeat.

First, remove the bay leaves from the marinated ingredients, as their very strong flavor would overwhelm the other ingredients if ground with the meats.

Put the pork cuts (blade end, jowl, fat back) through a meat grinder with a medium or fine disk and set aside in a bowl.

Fatty cuts of meat usually need to go through a medium disk before being ground finely because forcing the fat through the fine disk first often creates heat which may melt the fat.

Gradually work in the purée of foie gras, if using, and 6 eggs. When combined, return the mixture to the refrigerator until ready for use.

Once the forcemeat is mixed and the veal strips are cut, all that remains is to shape the pâtés. This may be the " Pantin " type of pâté, made with a rolled out sheet of puff pastry, " pâté pastry " or " pâte brisée " (basic pie pastry). These are served hot, possibly accompanied by a sauce. The other type of pâté is a molded pâté, encased in pastry and baked in a mold with pastry decorations. This type of pâté is eaten cold.

Veal and Ham Pâté with Aspic

Introduction

This beautiful and delicious pâté can be made in molds of many shapes, most often lined with pâté pastry or pie pastry. The interior is made of a forcemeat layered with strips of veal. Strips or slices of ham may be added to the alternating layers, as well as layers of foie gras. After cooking and cooling, this pâté is glazed with a meat aspic flavored with wine, port, madeira or sherry.

To make this pâté more appealing to customers, decorate the top to make it both attractive and original. Truffles and sprigs of chervil make good decorations, as well as cornichons and olives, though the latter is not as refined.

Notes

This pâté can be made in various shapes and sizes, ranging from sizes to serve only three to four people up to large ones for 20-24 people. They are assembled in hinged molds which allow for easy unmolding.

Equipment

Pâté molds, round or rectangular baking sheets, pastry crimper, tablespoon, pastry cutter, rolling pin, brush, pastry brush, aluminium foil, chef's knife, cutting board

Ingredients

Forcemeat, marinated veal strips, ham, foie gras, truffle (optional), aspic

Pâté pastry recipe

1 kg (2 lb) flour, 500 g (1 lb) butter, 20 g (about 1/2 oz) salt, 2 dl (3/4 cup) water, 1 egg

Shape the dough into a ball and flatten it slightly with the rolling pin, keeping the round shape.

Using your fingers, make an indentation in the circle of dough. Dust the indentation generously

with flour, then fold it in half, as shown, forming a pocket.

Using the rolling pin, gently roll out the dough to the shape of the mold.

When the dough is the right size, open the pocket and shape it using the end of the rolling pin.

Lining the Pâté Molds

It is best to use a dough that has been made well in advance so that it has had ample time to rest. In this case, however (especially if the pastry was made the day before), be sure to take the pastry from the refrigerator early enough to let it warm up slightly and become malleable. Butter the molds.

Lining Small Round Molds

Turn the rolling pin up so the pastry is set on the top. Slide the mold over the pastry, making sure it fits snugly. Turn the pastry and mold over onto the work surface and remove the rolling pin.

Finish pushing the pastry into the mold using your fingers.

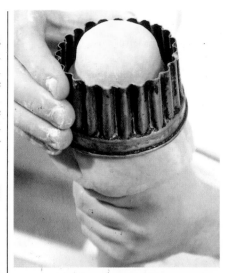

When the mold is completely and evenly lined with the pastry, cut off the excess pastry with a pair of scissors, leaving a 6 mm (1/4 in) border above the rim of the mold. Smooth out the border with your fingers, then crimp it with the pastry crimper to make a neat decorative edge.

Note: To make an even, regular pastry lining: do not roll the pastry too thin, which will be fragile and may break after cooking. However, if the pastry is too thick, it will cook unevenly and will ruin the balanced taste of the finished product. Remember that the pastry on the pâté serves as a base and the right balance of pastry and meat filling is crucial.

Shape a piece of dough into a rectangle and flatten it slightly with the rolling pin, keeping its rectangular shape.

With your fingers, make a long indentation in the dough. Dust it generously with flour, then fold in half, forming a pocket. With the rolling pin, carefully roll out the dough to the size and shape of the mold.

Open the pocket and slide it into the mold. Using the end of the rolling pin, carefully push the dough all the way into the mold. Finish pushing the pastry into the mold using your fingers. The pastry should conform perfectly to the shape of the mold.

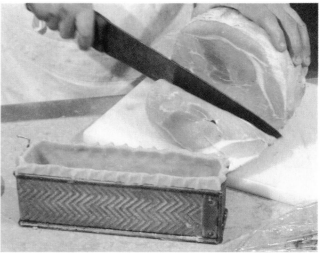

Cut off the excess pastry using a pair of scissors, leaving a 6 mm (1/4 in) border above the rim of the mold.

Even out the border and then crimp it by pinching with your fingers.

Assembling the Pâtés with Aspic

The method of assembly depends on several factors, notably the height of the mold, which will determine the possible number of layers of different ingredients.

Another important factor is the food cost. Depending on the de-

sired sales price, truffles can be included along with the strips of veal, ham, purée or mousse of foie gras or duck liver. For all methods of assembly, it is important to arrange each different ingredient layer by layer.

Assembling a Large Rectangular Pâté

Using a spoon, spread an even layer of the forcemeat in the bot-

tom of the pastry-lined mold.

Place the strips of veal on the forcemeat, then spread on another layer of forcemeat.

Cut the ham into 4-5 mm (3/16 in) slices and cut into strips the same width as the mold. Arrange them on the forcemeat.

Cut the foie gras mousse into slices about 1 cm (3/8 in) thick and the same width as the mold and lay them on the ham.

Add more forcemeat and spread in an even layer. Add another layer of veal strips.

Finish the assembly with another layer of forcemeat, bringing the filling just to the bottom of the pastry border.

Assembly of Small Round Pâtés

Using a spoon, spread an even layer of forcemeat in the bottom of the pastry-lined mold.

Arrange a layer of veal strips on the forcemeat. Add another layer of forcemeat.

Stamp out a piece of ham using a pastry cutter the same size as the mold and lay it on the forcemeat layer.

Lay a layer of foie gras mousse on the ham.

Finish the assembly with another layer of forcemeat.

Finishing the Pâtés

There are two possible ways to finish these pâtés. Regardless of the shape of the molds, a layer of pastry can be placed on top. In this case, it is not necessary to shape and crimp the border of pastry when the mold is first lined, as long is it is evenly trimmed. After the pâté is assembled, brush the inside of the pastry border with egg glaze. Roll out a thin sheet of pastry just larger than the mold and place it on the filling. Seal the two thicknesses of pastry by pinching with your fingers.

Cut off the excess pastry with a pair of scissors to form a border about 6 mm (1/4 in) above the rim of the mold.

Even out the border, then crimp it with a pastry crimper or your fingers.

This method of finishing the pastry is used less and less frequently for several reasons. First, in terms of taste, it produces too much crust. Second, it is more interesting and attractive to show the top of the pâté with decorations through a layer of aspic. Therefore the following method of finishing is recommended.

Cover the forcemeat with a piece of unbuttered aluminum foil. To protect it during cooking, fold the foil so it has several thicknesses. Position it carefully so that it completely covers the forcemeat but does not cover any of the pastry crust.

Cooking the Pâtés

Generally, the mold used for this kind of pâté has no bottom, so it is placed directly on a round or rectangular baking sheet. There are specially designed baking sheets for this purpose. They consist of two layers of metal, the top layer being perforated so any grease or juice from the marinade dripping from the pâté can drain away.

The oven should be set at about 180 C (350 F). This moderate temperature is crucial since the pâté forcemeat contains lots of fat which will separate out if the temperature is too high. This would make the pâté too dry and the forcemeat would shrink too much. Furthermore, this temperature allows the forcemeat and the pastry to cook at the same rate.

Cooking Time

Cooking time depends on the size of the pâté. For small round molds, an average time would be 35-40 minutes. For a rectangular mold, count on 1-1 1/4 hours. To cook a very large pâté, lower the oven temperature by 5-10 C (41-50 F).

Cooling

After cooking, leave the pâté to cool to room temperature in its mold.

Place a weight on top to help it keep its shape.

When the pâté has reached room temperature, transfer it to the refrigerator and leave to chill thoroughly.

Preparing the Aspic

When the pâté is completely cold, prepare the meat aspic that has been flavored with port, sherry, madeira or other wine. Stir the aspic gently over a bowl of crushed ice, using a spoon or a pastry brush, and taking care not to incorporate any air bubbles.

Glazing the Pâté with Aspic

Be sure the aspic is cold and beginning to set, yet still liquid. Pour it over the cold pâté filling so that it flows evenly to fill any gaps or holes. Do not use warm aspic because it will melt the fat in the meat, which will then cloud the aspic and look unattractive. Pour in enough aspic just to cover the forcemeat.

Return the pâté to the refrigerator.

When the aspic has set, remove the pâté from the refrigerator and decorate with the slices of truffle. Apply a little more aspic to cover the truffle.

The pâté may be left undecorated, simply with a shiny coating of aspic. Other ingredients that may be used for decoration include hard-boiled egg white, leek greens, peppers and chervil sprigs.

Unmolding the Pâté

Remove the pâtés from the molds very carefully to avoid damaging the crust. Many rectangular molds are fitted with hinge-pins, which makes it easier to take out the pâté.

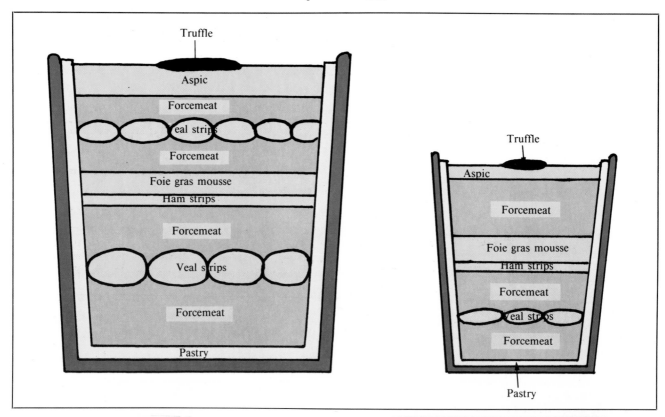

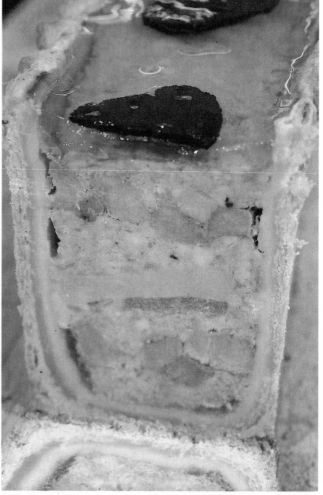

Storage

If you are producing a large number of pâtés, it is best to apply the delicate aspic to order.

Glazed aspic pâtés should be kept in a refrigerator or refrigerated display case at 4 C (40 F) for a maximum of two days. After this period, the aspic tends to dry out from contact with the air and becomes rubbery. If this happens, the aspic on top of the pâté may be peeled off and replaced with a fresh layer. This procedure may be repeated every two days in order to keep the pâté looking and tasting its best. At 4 C (40 F) the pâtés may be kept for four to five days without problem.

Presentation

For sale in a delicatessen or specialty food shop, large pâtés may be sold by the slice. Be sure to cover the cut end of the pâté with plastic wrap so it stays perfectly fresh and so the customer can see what is inside.

Large pâtés may also be sliced and arranged on a platter. In this case, each slice should be coated with a thin layer of aspic to protect it from drying out and to enhance its appearance.

The platter may be decorated with salad greens, chopped aspic and perhaps some "roses" shaped from strips of tomato peel.

The pâtés may be served as described above in either individual slices or small portions served in disposable containers. They can also be included on a lunch menu served with a small salad.

They can be very attractively displayed on a buffet table as well.

Be sure to tell the client that these pâtés should be kept refrigerated and served cold.

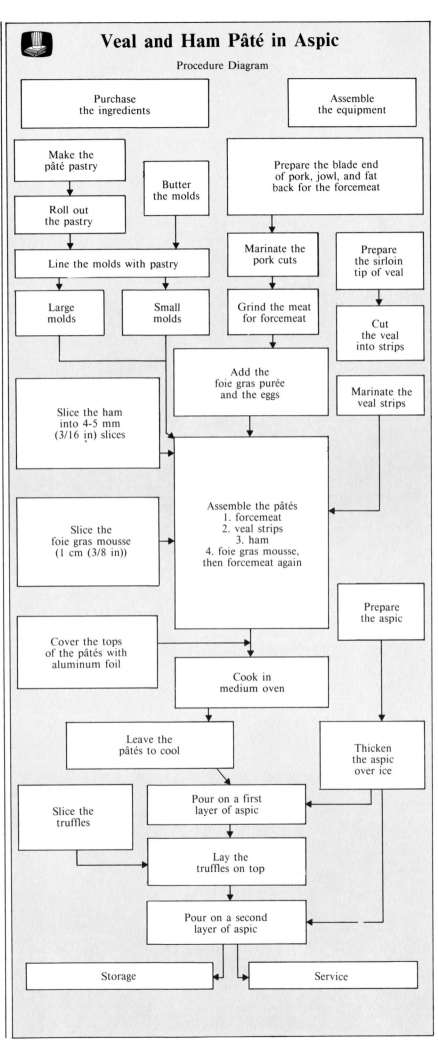

Veal and Ham Pâté in Aspic
Procedure Diagram

Purchase the ingredients

Assemble the equipment

Make the pâté pastry

Butter the molds

Prepare the blade end of pork, jowl, and fat back for the forcemeat

Roll out the pastry

Line the molds with pastry

Marinate the pork cuts

Prepare the sirloin tip of veal

Large molds

Small molds

Grind the meat for forcemeat

Cut the veal into strips

Slice the ham into 4-5 mm (3/16 in) slices

Add the foie gras purée and the eggs

Marinate the veal strips

Slice the foie gras mousse (1 cm (3/8 in))

Assemble the pâtés
1. forcemeat
2. veal strips
3. ham
4. foie gras mousse, then forcemeat again

Prepare the aspic

Cover the tops of the pâtés with aluminum foil

Cook in medium oven

Leave the pâtés to cool

Thicken the aspic over ice

Slice the truffles

Pour on a first layer of aspic

Lay the truffles on top

Pour on a second layer of aspic

Storage

Service

" Pantin " Pâté

Introduction

A " Pantin " pâté is eaten hot. It is shaped into a rectangle, with the pastry completely enveloping the meat filling. The pastry crust can be made from puff pastry, pâté pastry or pie pastry or a combination of two pastry doughs.

The filling for these pâtés is made of the pork forcemeat de-scribed on the preceding pages, lay-ered with ham strips and mari-nated veal strips. Truffles cut in slices or large julienne may be added.

In the following example, the pâté filling will be wrapped with pâté pastry and then covered by a thin layer of puff pastry.

Equipment

Round or rectangular baking sheets, rolling pin, brush, pastry brush, ridged rolling pin, pastry wheel, aluminum foil, cutting board, chef's knife, paring knife, small round pastry cutter, fluted pastry cutter, ruler, sharpening steel, tablespoon, spatula

Ingredients

Pâté forcemeat
Marinated veal strips
Ham
Truffle (optional)

Quantities for the " Pantin " Pâté

Estimate an average of 75-80 g (about 2 1/2 oz) of forcemeat and 30 g (1 oz) of garnish (marinated veal, ham and truffles) per person.

The thickness of the pastry will vary slightly with the size of the pâté. For the pâté shown here the pastry is rolled out to a thickness of 3 mm (1/4 in).

For the garnish, use a good quality boiled or baked ham.

Assembling the " Pantin " Pâté

Roll out a sheet of pâté pastry to a rectangle, using a rolling pin or sheeter.

Place the sheet of pastry on a lightly floured work surface, preferably marble.

Trace a rectangle in the center of the pastry to use as a guide for placement of the filling. With a spoon, spread an even layer of the forcemeat on the rectangle, making sure the thickness is uniform so the pâté will look neat when sliced.

On the whole surface of the layer of forcemeat, arrange alternating strips of marinated veal and ham that have been cut to the same length.

Cover with a second even layer of forcemeat.

Place another layer of alternating veal and ham strips on the forcemeat. The alternation of the veal and ham will make the sliced pâté look prettier.

Complete the assembly with a final layer of forcemeat.

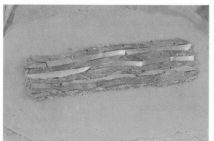

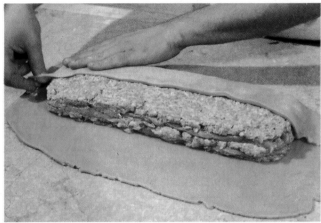

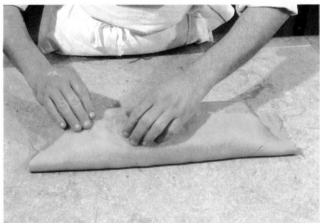

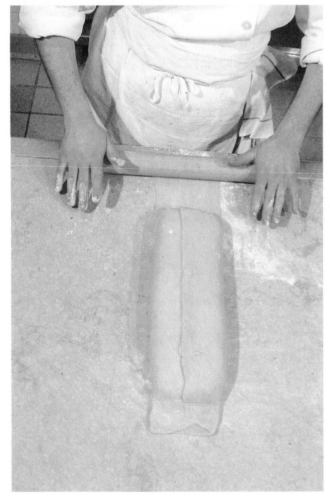

Assembling the Pâté, continued

Using a pastry brush, brush the entire border of the pastry with egg glaze.

Fold up one long edge of pastry to half cover the filling. Brush both long edges with egg glaze.

Fold up the other long edge so it amply overlaps the first edge, and therefore will completely cover the filling even if the pastry shrinks during cooking.

With the back of a chef's knife, press lightly on the juncture between the pastry and the filling, as shown, so the pâté keeps its neat rectangular shape and the filling stays separate from the pastry.

With a rolling pin, roll out the two ends of the pastry until they are quite thin, taking care not to tear them. Dust the pastry with flour if necessary.

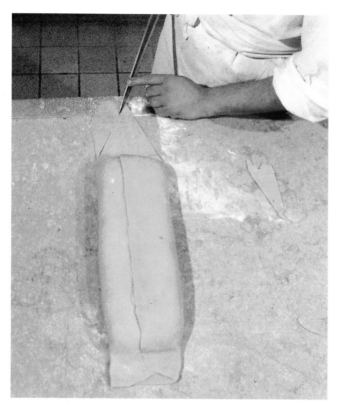
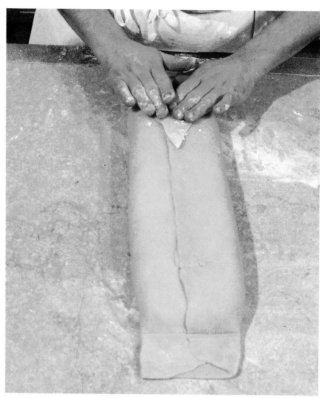

Trim the two flattened ends to long points so there will not be too much pastry on the bottom of the pâté. Brush each point with egg glaze and fold them up. Each point should cover about 1/3 of the length of the pâté.

Reshape the pâté with the chef's knife so it keeps a neat rectangular form with sharp right angles. Turn the pâté over onto a heavy baking sheet and brush on a coat of egg glaze. Leave it to rest in the refrigerator.

With a rolling pin, roll out a piece of puff pastry to a thin sheet, then roll over the pastry with a ridged rolling pin (usually made of metal and often used for candy making) to make linear indentations.

Using the ruler, measure the pâté exactly and cut the puff pastry sheet to a size that can be draped over the pâté to cover the top and most of the sides. Use the pastry wheel to cut the puff pastry to add a decorative fluted edge.

Brush the pâté with a second coat of egg glaze.

Carefully roll up the sheet of puff pastry onto the rolling pin then unroll it onto the pâté, taking care not to stretch or tear it. Gently brush off any excess flour.

Brush two coats of egg glaze on the layer of puff pastry.

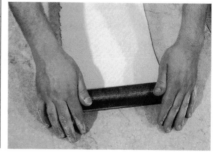

Decorating the Pâté

Using the small round pastry cutter or a large pastry tip, cut out one to three holes, depending on the length of the pâté, which will serve as chimneys to release steam. The holes can be made decorative by ringing them with a circle of puff pastry cut with the fluted pastry cutter.

Complete the decor with leaves stamped from the pastry using a fluted oval cutter. Brush the decorations with egg glaze, then score small lines in the leaves with a paring knife.

To make the actual chimneys, roll up a piece of parchment paper or aluminum foil around a small tube, the end of a sharpening steel

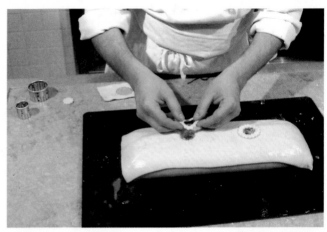

or the handle of a small whisk, then insert the tubes into the holes in the pastry. The chimneys will allow the steam to escape during cooking, which will prevent the crust from becoming discolored and soggy.

Leave the pâté to chill at least one hour before cooking, to avoid shrinkage of the pastry.

Procedure for Volume Production

The fillings for this pâté can be made in advance in a variety of sizes and kept refrigerated or frozen.

Measure out the ingredients for the size of pastry to be made, using the per person quantities given previously. Assemble the pâté on a sheet of plastic film.

Begin with a layer of forcemeat, spread evenly into a neat rectangle. Cover with a layer of alternating veal and ham strips.

Cover with another layer of forcemeat and repeat until the filling is finished, wrap in plastic, then chill or freeze the filling until ready to use.

Prepare the pastry then complete the assembly as described on the preceding pages.

Cooking the "Pantin" Pâtés

As with other pâtés in pastry, the Pantin pâtés take a long time to cook.

As a rule, start the cooking in a high oven (around 210 C (400 F) so the puff pastry can rise and color,

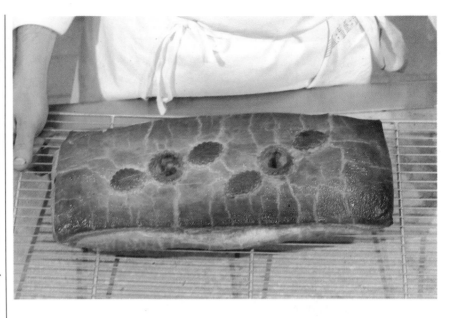

then lower the temperature to about 180 C (350 F) to finish.

The exact cooking time will vary with the size of the pâté.

Cooking Time

At first, the cooking is judged by the color of the pastry, then by the look of the meat filling. Since the meat is not visible under the pastry, look through the chimneys.

During cooking, the fat in the meat will melt and begin to boil.

You can determine when the meat is cooked by checking these fatty juices - when they are clear, the pâté is cooked.

The meat can also be tested by inserting a metal skewer through the chimney, removing it and checking its temperature with your fingers.

As soon as the pâté is cooked, transfer it to a cooling rack, using a long palette knife. Do not leave the pâté to cool on the baking sheet because moisture will condense on the bottom and make the crust very soggy.

Storage

Store in the refrigerator at about 4 C (40 F) or in the refrigerated display case of a delicatessen or specialty food store.

Maximum storage period is 2-3 days as long as the temperature is carefully controlled.

The Pantin pâté is almost always sold whole, because they are designed to be eaten hot and it is difficult to successfully reheat a single slice of this pâté.

Reheating the " Pantin " Pâtés

The caterer must stress to the client that these pâtés should not be reheated wrapped in aluminum foil. The pâté will produce more steam when reheated, which would be trapped in the foil and would make the crust soggy and unpleasant.

The " Pantin " pâté should be reheated in a moderate oven so the heat can penetrate to the center without drying out or darkening the pastry.

Presentation

Once the pâté is hot, slice it and arrange the slices on a platter for service as a first course. Some madeira sauce or " Perigueux " sauce (brown sauce flavored with truffles) would be a delicious accompaniment.

The sauce should be served in a sauceboat so each diner can pour on the desired amount.

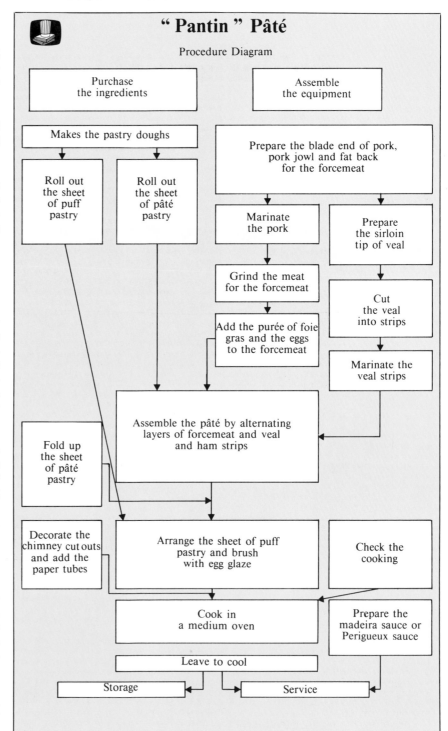

" Pantin " Pâté

Procedure Diagram

Rabbit and Hazelnut Tourte

Introduction

This is a hot first course suitable for any season, which would be equally appropriate as a light lunch or as part of a full dinner menu.

The distinctive taste of the rabbit can be complemented by wild thyme which would lend a hint of "woodsiness".

Accompanied by a "Poivrade"

sauce, this dish is refined and delicious.

The pastry must be of very good quality.

Ingredients

A 1.6 kg (3 lb 8 oz) rabbit, cut-up, will make 3 24 cm x 2.5 cm (10 in × 1 in) tourtes, each one serving 8 people, for a total of 24 portions.

This size rabbit yields:

500 g (1 lb) carcass + 45 g (1 1/2 oz) nerves and trimmings

400 g (14 oz) (filets and meat from thighs + kidneys (to be used as garnish)

650 g (1 lb 5 oz) meat + liver + legs (to be used as the forcemeat)

Use also:

600 g (1 lb 3 oz) fat back with the skin (75 g (2 1/2 oz) skin and 200 g (7 oz) fat for the garnish, 325 g (11 oz) fat for the forcemeat
2 shallots (about 45 g (1 1/2 oz))
15 g (1/2 oz) clarified butter
5 cl (1/4 cup) white wine
200 g (7 oz) liver purée
2 eggs
reduced rabbit stock
salt (12 g (about 1/2 oz) per kilo (2 lb) of meat) saltpeter (2-3 g per kilo (2 lb) of meat) pepper, coriander seeds, wild thyme (if not available, use ordinary fresh or dried thyme), mace
2 dl (3/4 cup) white wine
8 cl (1/3 cup) cognac
150 g (5 oz) hazelnuts

Equipment

Cutting board, sharpening steel, chef's knife, fish fileting knife, paring knife, roasting pan, hotel pan, mixing bowls, plates, strainer, measuring cup, sauté pan, large saucepan, scissors, pastry brush, pastry crimper, small whisk, ladle, spoon, fork, spatula, spice mill, round baking sheets, pastry rings, grinder, pastry cutter, rolling pin, brush, aluminum foil

First Day's Work

Preparation of the Meats

Boning the Rabbit

Lay the rabbit, back side up, on a cutting board with its four legs spread flat.

Using a very sharp paring knife, make an incision the length of the back bone, which is located by feeling with your fingers.

Starting just below the head at the shoulder, angle the knife blade toward the bone. Cut away the meat from the backbone, then from the rib cage. Continue cutting down to the joint of the hind leg and cut the filet free at each end. Turn the rabbit over and cut away the triangular flank section of meat that runs from under the rib cage to the hind leg.

Twist the thigh at the joint and detach it. This yields the front leg, the filet, the flank and the hind leg. Repeat the procedure for the other side. Turn the carcass with the back to the board to remove the two "filets mignons" on either side of the backbone.

Remove the kidneys, which will be used for the garnish along with the filets and the thigh meat.

Scrape the carcass to remove any bits of meat clinging to the bones.

Trimming the Meats

Each piece of meat is trimmed to remove tendons and skin. The legs are carefully boned and the tendons removed.

Remove the "noix" (the main piece at the top of the thigh) from each rear leg, and reserve for use as the garnish.

The remaining meat from the thighs, flanks, cheeks, legs, and the liver will be used for the forcemeat.

The tendons are kept along with the bones, cartilage and the rest of the carcass to make the stock.

Weigh each of the types of meat for the garnish and for the forcemeat.

Preparation of the Fat Back

The net amount of fat back (skin removed) is half the weight of the rabbit meat (removing the skin

from the fat back will result in a loss of about 5%).

Preparation of the Meat for Marinating

Cut the garnish meats in even 1 cm (3/8 in) cubes - the filets, the thigh meat, and half of that weight in skinned fat back, as well as the kidneys from which the outer membrane has been peeled using a small knife.

Set all the cubes aside on a tray for seasoning. The meat to be used in the forcemeat is cut into larger chunks, along with half its weight in skinned fat back. Set these aside on another tray.

Cooking the Shallots

Peel two shallots and cut them

into very fine dice. In a small saucepan, heat 15 g (1/2 oz) clarified butter and add the diced shallots.

Cook gently until soft but not brown.

When the shallots are very soft, with the consistency of a compote, deglaze the pan with 5 cl (1/4 cup) white wine. Reduce by half then set aside to cool.

When cool, add half of the compote to each marinade mixture.

Preparation of the Marinade

The forcemeat and garnish meats are marinated in the same way.

Seasoning the Marinades

Each batch of meat to be marinated, along with the shallot compote, is seasoned with salt, saltpeter, freshly ground pepper, freshly ground coriander seed (note that freshly ground spices always have more flavor and aroma than preground ones), mace (which is the ground hull of the nutmeg), a pinch of crumbled wild thyme.

The wild thyme goes especially well with rabbit. This wild plant, similar in appearance to ordinary thyme, is gathered at the end of summer and dried. It retains its flavor and aroma well.

Sprinkle each batch with the white wine and cognac.

Mix the ingredients well.

Cover each batch of meat with plastic film and place in the refrigerator to marinate for at least 12 hours.

Making the Rabbit Stock

Ingredients

500 g (1 lb) carcass, bones and trimmings

20 g (about 1/2 oz) clarified butter or 2 cl (about 1 tbsp) oil
1/2 onion (about 30 g (1 oz))
1 shallot (15 g (1/2 oz))
1 clove garlic
1/2 carrot (45g (1 1/2oz))
5 cl (1/4 cup) white wine for deglazing
1 dl (1/2 cup) white wine for the liquid
1 branch fresh thyme
1/4 bay leaf
5 parsley stems
1 leek green
1/2 stalk celery
5 peppercorns
5 coriander seeds
salt
1 L (4 cups) reduced stock

Preparation of the Bones and Carcass

Using a mallet or cleaver, break up the bones and carcass.

Coat a roasting pan with a little oil or clarified butter, add the bones, carcass and trimmings and put them in a moderate oven for 10-15 minutes to brown.

During this stage, when the bones are just lightly colored, add the aromatic vegetables - diced onion, shallot cut in half, clove of garlic in its skin, and roughly chopped carrot.

Continue browning until the vegetables are golden brown.

When this step is completed, drain everything in a strainer to remove any grease, which would give an unwanted flavor to the stock.

Deglaze the roasting pan with the white wine and scrape well with a whisk or wooden spoon to dissolve the caramelized "brown bits" stuck to the pan. These are very important for the flavor of the stock.

Cooking the Stock

Put the drained carcass, bones and trimmings and the aromatic vegetables into a large saucepan. Add the wine from deglazing the pan.

Add the rest of the white wine, bring to a boil and cook for a few

minutes to boil off the excess acidity of the wine.

Make a bouquet garni by wrapping the thyme, bay leaf and parsley stems into the leek green and tying securely into a little bundle.

A stalk of celery and a tomato cut in half may be added as well

(the tomato will give the stock more color).

Season with coarse salt, which brings out the flavors in the stock, and peppercorns and coriander seed tied up in cheesecloth.

Add the stock to cover by half and bring to a boil.

Leave the stock to cook gently over a very low heat for 1 1/2-2 hours. The stock should be skimmed occasionally during cooking to remove fats and impurities that would mar the taste and appearance of the stock.

After cooking the recommended amount of time, taste the stock, it should taste like rabbit.

Remove the bouquet garni, the spices in cheesecloth and the stalk of celery.

Pass the rest through a fine-meshed conical strainer.

Press on the solid ingredients to squeeze out all the flavorful liquid.

Degrease the stock with a spoon.

Make the rabbit glaze by slowly reducing the stock. Monitor the reduction and stop when the liquid has thickened to a syrupy consistency.

Chill the rabbit glaze until ready to mix with the forcemeat. This is an important ingredient that will make the filling full-flavored and moist.

The Second Day's Work

Preparation of the Other Garnish Ingredients

Remove the skins from the hazelnuts by putting the nuts in a pastry ring on a round baking sheet (or in a cake pan) and cooking in a moderate oven.

When the skins start to split from the nuts, remove from the oven and rub them around in a sieve to remove the skin.

Return the skinned hazelnuts to the oven to thoroughly toast them. Pay close attention to this step so the nuts are golden brown and perfectly cooked. If they are too pale, they will be soft and flavorless; too dark, they will be bitter and unattractive.

Making the Rabbit Forcemeat

Put the forcemeat ingredients

through a grinder fitted with a fine disk.

In a mixing bowl, combine the ground meat, the liver purée, whole eggs and the rabbit glaze.

With a spatula, stir all the ingredients thoroughly to form a smooth mixture.

Adding the Garnish Ingredients

In a large mixing bowl, combine all the ingredients - the forcemeat,

the marinated cubes of meat and the hazelnuts. Blend, pan-fry a spoonful of the mixture, taste and adjust seasoning.

Preparation of the Tourtes

The shell for these tourtes is made by lining a pastry ring, 2-2.5 cm (about 1 in) high and any diameter, with pastry. The method of lining the mold is similar to the method for lining a tart mold, except that the excess pastry is not trimmed off; when the top layer of pastry is added, the two layers of pastry are trimmed and crimped together.

When the pastry for lining the mold is rolled out, the pastry for the top should be prepared as well. Roll out a round sheet of pastry, cover well to protect it from drying out and chill until ready to use.

The pastry used for these meat pies is usually " demi-feuilletage " (puff pastry with trimmings incorporated into the dough on the sixth turn).

Some versions may be made with pie pastry or pâté pastry.

Filling the Tourtes

Fill the pastry-lined mold 3/4 full with the forcemeat, marinated meat garnish and the hazelnuts

(the nuts can be added one by one for even distribution).

Smooth the top of the filling with a pastry scraper or the back of a spoon.

Brush the overhanging edges of the pastry with egg glaze.

Place the top layer of pastry on

the tourte and gently press the edges to seal.

Cut away the excess pastry with a pair of scissors, leaving a 1 cm (3/8 in) border.

Turn up the border and crimp it neatly, using either your fingers or a pastry crimper.

In the center of the pastry, cut a hole using a pastry cutter approximately 2 cm (3/4 in) in diameter.

Make a chimney by rolling up two thicknesses of aluminum foil and insert it into the hole. This will allow the steam to escape during cooking; the tourte would otherwise crack or become soggy.

Brush the surface of the tourte with a coat of egg glaze.

Decoration of the Tourte

Roll out a thin sheet of puff pastry and let it rest so it loses its elasticity. Cut out shapes from the pastry using different shaped pastry cutters, and arrange them attractively on the pie.

Brush on a second coat of egg glaze, then score the decorative shapes with the point of a knife to embellish the design.

Preparation of the Vegetables

Carefully wash and peel the vegetables and cut them into "mirepoix" (very small dice).

In the sauté pan, cook the vegetables over low heat in the clarified butter until they are slightly softened, then increase the heat to brown them.

Strain through a fine-meshed conical sieve or cheesecloth to remove excess grease. Return the strained vegetables to the sauté pan and deglaze with the wine vinegar.

Slowly reduce the mixture by 1/4.

Add the red wine, the parsley, thyme and bay leaf and slowly reduce again by 1/4. (Because the sauce will be carefully strained at the end, it is not necessary to tie up the herbs in a bouquet garni.)

Making the "Poivrade" Sauce

This delicious and slightly spicy sauce is a perfect partner for the rabbit pie, yet its versatility makes it useful for many other dishes.

The sauce can be made in a separate operation from the pie. It can be stored 2-3 days in a well-covered container at 4 C (40 F), therefore it is possible to make it ahead.

Equipment

Cutting board, paring knife, chef's knife, vegetable peeler, sauté pan with lid, tablespoon, ladle, pastry scraper, mixing bowls, plates, measuring cup, spatula, fine-meshed conical strainer

Ingredients

30 g (1 oz) clarified butter
150 g (5 oz) carrots
120 g (4 oz) onions
1.5 dl (2/3 cups) wine vinegar
3 dl (1 1/4 cup) full-bodied red wine
8 parsley stems
1 branch thyme
1/2 bay leaf
Salt
Reduced stock
Black peppercorns
Cooked roux (optional)
500 g (1 lb) cold butter

When the sauce has reduced, add the demi-glace and the crushed pepper corns. (To crush the peppercorns, put them in a hand towel and crush with a heavy rolling pin or the bottom of a heavy saucepan.) Add a little salt and leave to reduce by 1/2, skimming occasionally during reduction.

When the sauce has reduced, taste and adjust the seasoning if necessary. Pass the sauce through a fine-meshed conical sieve or a cheesecloth into a clean saucepan, extracting as much liquid as possible without pressing too hard on the solids, which would squeeze out too much vegetable juice and alter the taste of the sauce. Mount the strained sauce with butter.

Mounting with Butter

Add the butter bit by bit to the hot sauce while shaking the pan constantly to incorporate. The butter will make the sauce rich tasting, with a smooth and glossy texture.

Storage

Chill the sauce immediately and store in a non-reactive well-covered container at 4 C (40 F) for up to three days.

The sauce can be sold in small disposable containers to accompany many dishes.

An average portion of sauce is 5 cl (1/4 cup) per person.

Serving

The sauce is reheated to serve in a sauceboat or poured around a slice of the tourte, enhancing the dish by its rich color, sheen and flavor.

Cooking

Let the assembled tourte rest in the refrigerator long enough to allow the pastry to lose it elasticity. The time will vary depending on the pastry, but an average time is

1 1/2-2 hours after rolling it out and lining the mold.

Put the tourte in a high oven (210 C (400 F) so the top of the tourte starts to brown, then lower the heat to 180 C (350 F) to finish the cooking so the meat has a chance to cook and the pastry does not burn.

Tourtes with more or denser fillings need a longer time in a lower oven to cook correctly.

Cooking Time

Insert a metal skewer or trussing needle into the center of the tourte, it should come out clean and hot (about 80 C (175 F)).

The juices that run from the chimney should be clear.

Cooling

Immediately transfer the tourte to a cooling rack, to prevent the crust from becoming soggy.

Storage

The cooled tourte should be stored at 4C (40F). For longer storage, wrap it in plastic film or aluminum foil to keep the meat fresh and the crust from drying out. The maximum storage time is 2-3 days.

Presentation

These tourtes are always eaten warm. They should be reheated just before service in a low oven so they heat through without browning too much.

They are generally presented whole and cut into slices at the table.

Individually sized tourtes are a nice alternative.

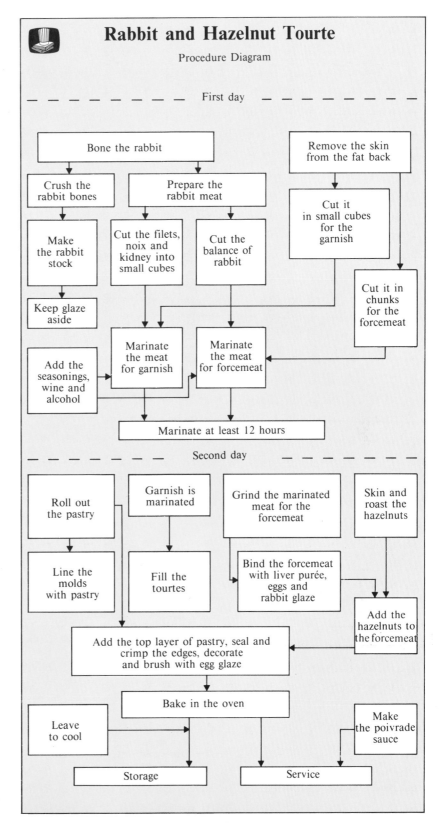

Rabbit and Hazelnut Tourte

Procedure Diagram

— — — — — — — First day — — — — — — —

Bone the rabbit

Remove the skin from the fat back

Crush the rabbit bones

Prepare the rabbit meat

Cut it in small cubes for the garnish

Make the rabbit stock

Cut the filets, noix and kidney into small cubes

Cut the balance of rabbit

Keep glaze aside

Cut it in chunks for the forcemeat

Add the seasonings, wine and alcohol

Marinate the meat for garnish

Marinate the meat for forcemeat

Marinate at least 12 hours

— — — — — — — Second day — — — — — — —

Roll out the pastry

Garnish is marinated

Grind the marinated meat for the forcemeat

Skin and roast the hazelnuts

Line the molds with pastry

Fill the tourtes

Bind the forcemeat with liver purée, eggs and rabbit glaze

Add the hazelnuts to the forcemeat

Add the top layer of pastry, seal and crimp the edges, decorate and brush with egg glaze

Bake in the oven

Leave to cool

Make the poivrade sauce

Storage

Service

Tourte Lorraine

Introduction

As indicated by the name, this tourte is a specialty from the region in eastern France, Alsace-Lorraine.

The light meat (pork and veal) filling is bound at the end of cooking with a custard that complements nicely both taste and appearance.

This tourte is notable because it is made with two types of pastry - the base is made of pâté pastry and the top of puff pastry.

This tourte is served all year, but it is especially appropriate during colder seasons.

Ingredients

As this tourte does not rely on specific seasonal ingredients, it can be made year-round. Always use top quality meats.

1.2 kg (2 lb 8 oz) trimmed pork tenderloin
700 g (1 lb 7 oz) trimmed sirloin tip of veal
4 shallots (75 g (2 1/2 oz))
salt, saltpeter, ground pepper
2 dl (3/4 cup) white wine

Equipment

Cutting board, sharpening steel, chef's knife, paring knife, fish fileting knife, plates, mixing bowls, hotel pans, round baking sheet, pastry ring, pastry crimper, pastry brush, rolling pin, soft-bristled brush, measuring cup, whisk, spatula, pastry scraper, aluminum foil, pastry cutter, tablespoon, food processor (optional), funnel

First Day's Work

Preparing the Meats

The two types of meat are prepared separately and combined for marinating.

Pork tenderloin is used for its " finesse "; it is very tender with few tendons, therefore it is easy to prepare with minimal weight loss.

Put the pork on a cutting board, and using a sharp knife trim away any silver skin and nerves.

Cut the trimmed meat into strips approximately 4 cm × 1 cm × 1.5 cm (1 3/4 in × 3/8 in × 1/2 in).

Set aside in a mixing bowl until ready to combine with the veal.

Prepare the veal in the same way, taking care to trim away any bits of fat, tendons, veins or cartilage that will mar the taste and texture.

Cut the veal into strips the same size as the pork strips.

Add the veal to the bowl with the pork.

Preparing the Ingredients for Marinating

Seasoning

Season the mixed meats with salt, saltpeter (to set the color), and freshly ground white pepper (which will blend in with the color of the light meats).

Flavorings

Peel the shallots and cut them into fine dice. Add them to the seasoned meats. Add the white wine to moisten.

Using a spatula, mix all ingredients thoroughly so the marinade is evenly distributed.

Cover the bowl with plastic wrap and place it in the refrigerator to marinate for at least 12 hours.

Second Day's Work

Making the Tourte Pastry Base

The tourte base is formed in the same way as a tart, using a buttered pastry ring 2-2.5 cm (about 1 in) high.

The buttered pastry ring is placed on a round baking sheet and the circle of dough placed inside so it forms a perfect right angle at the base of the ring.

The excess pastry is left hanging over the ring until the second layer of pastry is placed on top of the filled tourte.

After rolling out the pastry and lining the ring, roll out the puff pastry for the top layer to a circle a little larger than the diameter of the ring.

Use puff pastry with 6 turns or puff pastry with 6 turns and the trimmings incorporated before rolling out.

Filling the Tourtes

It is best to roll out the two pastry layers in advance, so they both will have rested enough to reduce elasticity and avoid shrinkage when baking.

Wrap the puff pastry round with plastic film to keep it from drying out, and chill until ready to use.

Note:

The pastry may be rolled out, the rings lined the night before and kept chilled and covered until use.

Stir the marinated meat again to mix, then fill the pastry-lined ring 3/4 full. An average is 90 g (3 oz) filling per person.

Smooth out the filling.

Brush the overhanging pastry edges with egg glaze.

Lay the sheet of puff pastry on top of the tourte and gently pinch the edges to seal.

Trim the excess pastry with a pair of scissors, leaving a 1 cm (3/8 in) border. Turn up the pastry border above the rim of the ring.

Crimp the pastry with your fingers or a pastry crimper to completely seal the two layers of pastry and to give the tourte a decorative appearance.

Cut a hole in the center of the tourte using a pastry cutter about 2 cm (3/4 in) in diameter.

Make a chimney by rolling up two thicknesses of aluminum foil and insert it into the hole.

The outside of the hole may be ringed with a circle cut from the puff pastry and fixed in place with egg glaze.

79

Brush a coat of egg glaze over the top of the tourte, and if you wish, decorate with cut out shapes of puff pastry.

Leave to rest in the refrigerator from 30 minutes to an hour, depending on the elasticity of the dough and the amount of time the rolled out pastry rested before the filling was added. Brush on a second coat of egg glaze and score a design in the top with the tip of a paring knife.

Cooking

Cook the tourte in a high oven (210 C (400 F)) for about 5-10 minutes to brown the pastry, then lower the temperature to 180 C (350 F) and continue cooking.

Three-quarters of the way through the cooking time, the tourte is filled with the custard.

Making the Custard

Ingredients

1/2 L (2 cups) heavy cream
2 tbsp chopped parsley
salt and pepper
4 eggs

Procedure

Measure out the heavy cream.

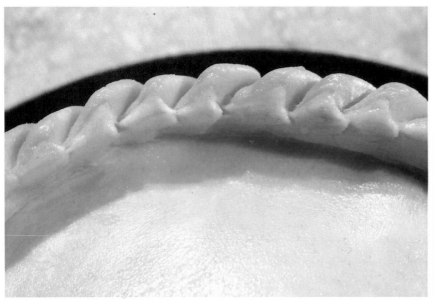

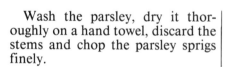

Wash the parsley, dry it thoroughly on a hand towel, discard the stems and chop the parsley sprigs finely.

Put the cream in a bowl. Add the eggs and beat well with a whisk without letting the mixture get frothy.

Season with salt and pepper. Taste and adjust seasoning.

Lastly, add the chopped parsley.

Filling the Tourtes

Take the partially baked tourte from the oven. Remove the aluminum foil chimney.

Using a funnel or ladle, carefully pour the custard into the hole, letting it seep into all the gaps in the meat filling.

To make sure the sauce spreads evenly throughout the tourte, it may be necessary to lift the top pastry crust slightly by inserting the handle of a fork and gently prying it up.

Finishing the Cooking

Return the filled tourtes to the oven. At this stage several tourtes can be placed in the same oven.

Since the custard is poured into the hot interior of the tourte, it will cook quickly, count on about 10-15 minutes more.

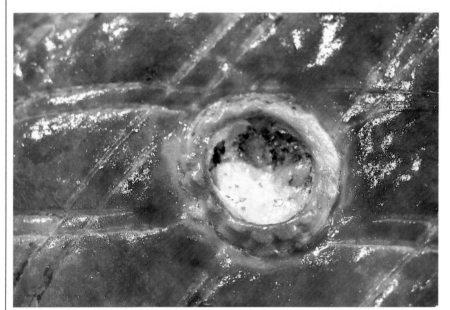

Checking the Cooking

The pastry should be a deep golden brown and thoroughly cooked and crisp. The custard is set and the meat is thoroughly cooked.

Cooling

Immediately transfer the tourte to a cooling rack to prevent the pastry from becoming soggy.

Presentation

If serving the tourte immediately, put it on a platter lined with a paper doily.

These Tourtes Lorraine should be eaten warm. Reheat them just before serving in an oven set at 170 C (325 F).

Storage

The tourte Lorraine can be kept at 4 C (40 F) for 2-3 days.

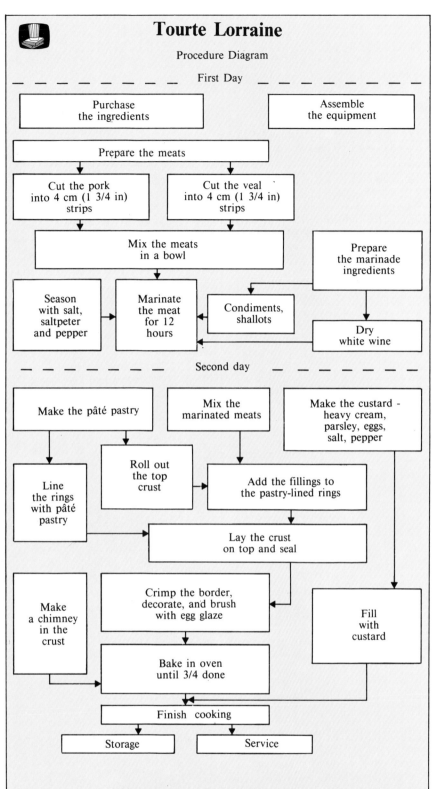

Tourte Lorraine

Procedure Diagram

First Day

Purchase the ingredients

Assemble the equipment

Prepare the meats

Cut the pork into 4 cm (1 3/4 in) strips

Cut the veal into 4 cm (1 3/4 in) strips

Mix the meats in a bowl

Prepare the marinade ingredients

Season with salt, saltpeter and pepper

Marinate the meat for 12 hours

Condiments, shallots

Dry white wine

Second day

Make the pâté pastry

Mix the marinated meats

Make the custard - heavy cream, parsley, eggs, salt, pepper

Line the rings with pâté pastry

Roll out the top crust

Add the fillings to the pastry-lined rings

Lay the crust on top and seal

Make a chimney in the crust

Crimp the border, decorate, and brush with egg glaze

Fill with custard

Bake in oven until 3/4 done

Finish cooking

Storage

Service

Tourte of Sweetbreads and Morels

Introduction

The ingredients in this tourte make it appropriate for serving at even the grandest dinner. The combination of flavors will please the most discriminating palate.

The tourte can be made year-round. It uses ingredients that are easily available yet quite luxurious-morels, sweetbreads, truffle juice-therefore the food cost is quite high.

They can be made in large or individual sizes and served as a first course for a lunch or dinner. They are equally appropriate for sale in a delicatessen, specialty food shop or as part of lunch or buffet.

Equipment
Cutting board, chef's knife, paring knife, vegetable peeler, sharpening steel, 2-pronged fork, pastry brush, rolling pin, tablespoon, fork, whisk, spatula, kitchen twine, drum sieve, hand towels, measuring cup, ladle, skimmer, slotted spoon, mixing bowls, plates, hotel pans, cooling rack, sheet pan, strainer, fine-meshed conical sieve, high-sided sauté pan with lid, copper bowl, round baking sheets, pastry rings, pastry cutter, aluminum foil

Ingredients

For 3 22 cm (9 in) tourtes, serving 6-8 people each, for a total of 18-24 portions:

1.5 kg (3 lb 5 oz) trimmed sweetbreads
100 g (3 1/2 oz) clarified butter
5 cl (1/4 cup) oil
romaine lettuce
400 g (14 oz) carrots
300 g (10 oz) leeks (white part only)
100g (3 1/2 oz) shallots
45 g (1 1/2 oz) garlic
45 g (1 1/2 oz) dried morels
1 sprig thyme
2 small bay leaves
8 parsley stems
salt, freshly ground pepper
1/4 L (1 cup) white wine
1/4 L (1 cup) madeira
3/4 L (3 cups) reduced stock

1/4 L (1 cup) heavy cream
roux (optional)
45 g (1 1/2 oz) cold butter

Preparation of the Sweetbreads

Since sweetbreads are a variety meat, they must be degorged by soaking in several changes of cool water. Alternatively, leave them under cold running water. The

water will draw out any particles of blood or impurities remaining in the sweetbreads.

After degorging, the sweetbreads

should be trimmed of membrane and fat.

Note: The quantity in the list of ingredients is for trimmed sweetbreads, therefore allow for loss from trimming, which will vary depending on the quality and condition of the sweetbreads themselves.

After trimming and weighing the sweetbreads, leave them to dry thoroughly on a hand towel.

Preparation of the Morels

If dried morels are used, soak them for four or five hours in warm water or overnight in cold water until they swell and soften.

Dried morels are used more frequently, as fresh ones are not available in every season.

Fresh morels must be meticulously washed in several changes of water to remove all the sand and grit.

Preparation of the Vegetables

Peel the carrots and rinse them in cold water. Cut the white part from the leek and carefully wash and drain it. Wash the leek greens and save them for another preparation such as a bouquet garni, decorations or clarifying aspics.

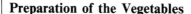

Peel the shallots and garlic and cut the garlic in half to remove the green "sprout" present in more mature garlic cloves.

Cut the carrots and leeks in diagonal slices.

Sort the morels by size - cut the large ones in half so they will all cook at approximately the same rate.

Cut the shallots into fine dice. Crush the garlic cloves, then chop finely with the chef's knife.

Arrange each separate ingredient on a plate.

Make a bouquet garni: tie the thyme, bay leaf and parsley stems together with kitchen twine.

Preparation of the Cooking Fats

A mixture of clarified butter and oil is used. The butter gives a golden color and the oil raises the smoking point of the butter so it will not burn at high temperatures.

Preparation of the Lettuce Leaves

Romaine lettuce is used because of its large crisp leaves that are bright green with white center ribs. Cut out the central core from the head and separate the leaves without breaking them.

Wash the leaves carefully one by one.

Blanching the Leaves

Fill a large pot, or an unlined copper bowl that has been cleaned with salt and vinegar, with water, add salt and bring to a boil.

Blanch the leaves one by one by holding them under the water with a slotted spoon for about 10 seconds.

Remove them and plunge immediately into a bowl of ice water to stop the cooking.

The leaves should just be softened by this blanching process, not actually cooked.

Draining the Lettuce Leaves

Carefully remove the leaves from the ice water after a few seconds and lay on a drum sieve to drain partially, then on a cooling rack covered with a hand towel to dry.

Removing the Large Ribs

Lay each drained leaf on a cutting board and with a sharp knife, cut along each side of the central rib and remove it.

Return the trimmed leaves to a dry hand towel so they dry completely.

Browning the Sweetbreads

Put the clarified butter and the oil in a large sauté pan and heat until very hot, but not brown.

Place the sweetbreads in the pan in a single layer so they brown evenly.

When the first side is browned, carefully turn them over and brown the second side, then transfer to a strainer to drain.

If the oil and butter left in the pan is not burned, use it to cook the vegetables; if it is burned, discard and replace with fresh oil and clarified butter.

Preparing the Liquid Ingredients

Use a dry white wine. A sauvignon type is recommended for its flavor and affordable price. The madeira will highlight the other flavors; also use reduced veal stock.

Preparation of the Seasonings

Use salt and freshly ground pepper.

The sweetbreads should be lightly seasoned with salt and pepper on each side before cooking.

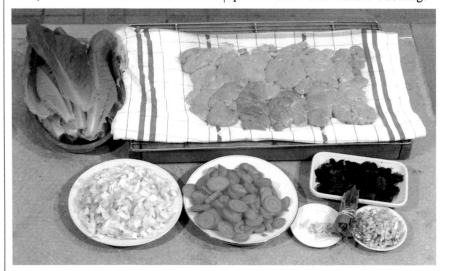

Cooking the Vegetables

Add the shallots, carrots and leeks to the hot oil and butter in the sauté pan. Cook gently until soft but not brown.

Next add the prepared morels, the garlic and the bouquet garni. Continue cooking 3-4 more minutes.

Braising the Sweetbreads

Lay the cooked sweetbreads on the bed of vegetables. Add the white wine and bring to a boil to deglaze the pan and dissolve all the caramelized juices from the meat and vegetables on the bottom of the pan. Boil for 1 minute to cook off some of the wine's acidity. Add the madeira and return to a boil.

Add the stock to cover the sweetbreads by 1/2 (not completely), so they can be braised. Season lightly with salt and pepper, but remember the seasoning will concentrate as the liquid reduces. Seasoning

can always be corrected at the end of cooking.

Cover the pan and put it in a medium-high oven (200 C (375 F)). Cooking time will depend on the thickness of the sweetbreads, an average time is 10-15 minutes. The ingredients will not be fully cooked at this stage, as they will be cooked a second time when the tourte is baked.

When the braising is finished, remove the ingredients separately: carefully remove the sweetbreads with a 2-pronged fork; remove the vegetables with a slotted spoon and put them in a strainer. Discard the bouquet garni.

Pass the braising liquid through a fine-meshed conical sieve and reserve it to make the sauce that accompanies the tourte.

Cutting the Sweetbreads

Cut each drained piece of sweetbreads into escalopes with a very sharp knife. Set the escalopes aside to chill thoroughly before assembling the tourtes.

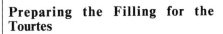

Preparing the Filling for the Tourtes

Make sure all the elements are ready:

- the blanched romaine leaves

- the drained and cooled vegetables, divided into two batches

- the cooled sweetbreads cut in escalopes

Making the Tourte Pastry Base

The tourte bases are made by lining 2.5-3 cm (1-1 1/4 in) high pastry rings with a sheet of pastry.

Pay attention to the following points when lining the rings: the rings should be clean and lightly buttered and the pastry rolled to a circle about 3-5 mm (about 1/8 in) thick, depending on the size of the tourte (the larger the tourte, the thicker the pastry). Make sure the pastry is at an even right angle to the base of the ring and the excess pastry hangs over by about 2 cm (3/4 in).

Roll out a round sheet of pastry slightly larger than the diameter of the circle, to use as the top crust. Cover with plastic film and chill until ready to use.

The pastry for the tourtes is left in the refrigerator to rest until it is time to add the filling.

Garnishing the Tourtes

Line the pastry with the lettuce leaves so they cover the base entirely and exceed the diameter of the circle by enough to fold over the filling and completely cover it.

Spread half of the vegetables in an even layer on the bottom.

Lay the escaloped sweetbreads on the top so they cover the vegetables but are not overlapping each other too much.

Spread the other half of the vegetables over the sweetbreads.

89

Fold the lettuce leaves over to cover the filling.

With a pastry brush, brush a coat of egg glaze on the pastry border.

Lay the top crust on the tourte. Pinch gently with your fingers to seal the edges.

Trim the excess pastry with a pair of scissors, leaving a 1-1.5 cm (about 1/2 in) border.

Turn up the pastry border above the rim of the ring. Crimp the border with your fingers or a pastry crimper to completely seal the two layers of pastry and to give the

tourte a decorative appearance.

Cut out a hole in the center of the tourte for a chimney, using a pastry cutter about 2 cm (3/4 in) in diameter.

Brush on a coat of egg glaze.

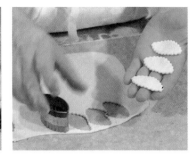

Decorating the Tourte

Decorate the top of the tourte, either with shapes cut from a sheet of pastry and applied with egg glaze or by scoring a design in the pastry with the tip of a paring knife.

Leave to rest in the refrigerator for about 30 minutes so the pastry loses its elasticity, then brush on a second coat of egg glaze and finish any decoration if necessary.

Make a chimney by rolling up two thicknesses of aluminum foil and insert it in the hole, with the aid of a whisk handle or metal tube.

Cooking

After letting the tourte rest adequately, put it in a high (210 C (400 F)) oven for about 10 minutes so the pastry browns, then lower the heat to 180 C (350 F) and continue cooking. When the tourte is an even golden brown and is cooked all the way through, remove from the oven and transfer to a cooling rack immediately so the pastry does not become soggy by condensation.

Remove the foil chimney, taking care not to damage the pastry, which may stick to the foil.

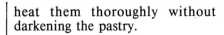

Presentation

Present the tourte on a platter covered with a paper doily.

If the tourtes are cooled, they may be reheated in a low oven to heat them thoroughly without darkening the pastry.

Storage

The cooled tourtes can be kept at 4 C (40 F) for 2-3 days.

Making the Sauce

These tourtes with sweetbreads and morels are often served with a warm sauce.

Reduce the reserved cooking liquid by half, then add some reduced heavy cream.

This sauce should have a coating consistency, i.e. it should be slightly thick. Depending on the thickness of the demi-glace used, additional thickening with a little cooked roux may be necessary.

A little truffle juice will greatly enhance this sauce (3-5 cl (2-4 tbsp) for the amount of sauce in this recipe), the combination of truffles, morels and sweetbreads being especially delicious.

Pass the sauce through a fine-meshed conical sieve into a small saucepan.

Taste and adjust the seasoning if necessary.

Enriching the Sauce with Butter

Add the cold butter to the hot sauce bit by bit and incorporate it by shaking and swirling the pan. Do not use a whisk, which would incorporate air into the sauce and make it less glossy.

The sauce may be stored in a well-covered container at 4 C (40 F) for 3-4 days.

Serving

Reheat the sauce in a bain marie without beating it (so it keeps its shine), then pour it in a sauceboat. Do not allow the sauce to reduce or boil during reheating.

Estimate 3-5 cl (2-4 tbsp) of sauce per person.

For sale in specialty food shops, serve the sauce in small disposable containers.

Tourte with Morels and Sweetbreads

Procedure Diagram

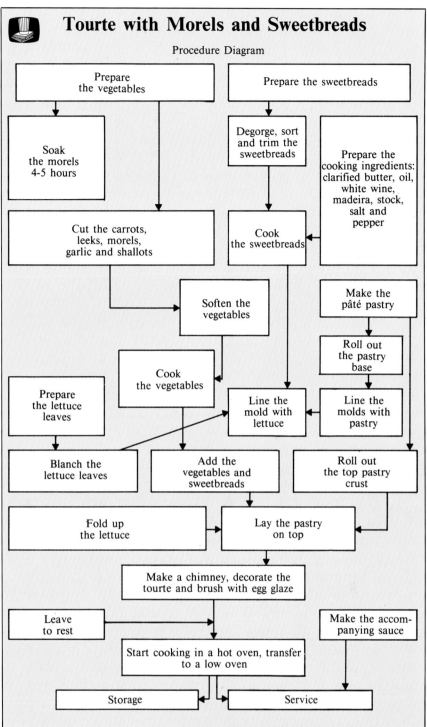

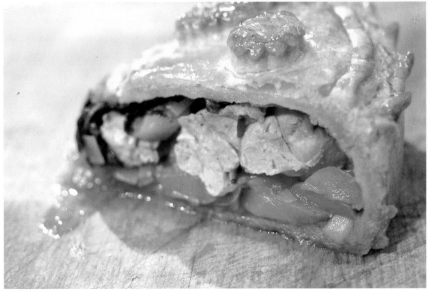

93

" Pithiviers " of Ham with Spinach

Introduction

This is an unusual and well-received dish that is straightforward to produce. The name " Pithiviers " designates a round filled pastry with a scalloped edge and a curved spoke design scored on the top.

It can be made in one day, but the procedure includes several important steps.

The flavors of the ingredients marry well for a delicious result.

As the ingredients are available year-round, it is possible to offer this for occasions in any season.

The Pithiviers can be made in large or small sizes. It is served hot without a sauce, as the filling includes a béchamel sauce.

Ingredients

For 3 26 cm (10 in) Pithiviers, each serving 8, for a total of 24 portions:

2.5 kg (5 lb 8 oz) of puff pastry with 6 turns

6 slices of boiled ham about 20 cm (8 in) in diameter and 3-4 mm thick

egg glaze

Vegetable Crêpes

Crêpe Batter

150 g (5 oz) flour, 2 eggs, 3 dl (1 1/4 cup) milk, 45 g (1 1/2 oz) melted butter, salt, pepper

Vegetable " Brunoise "

30 g (1 oz) clarified butter, 75 g (2 1/2 oz) onions, 150 g (5 oz) carrots, 30 g (1 oz) celery root, 100 g (3 1/2 oz) mushrooms, salt, pepper

Spinach and Béchamel Filling

Spinach

30 g (1 oz) clarified butter, 750 g (1 lb 8 oz) spinach, 10 leaves sorrel, 30 g (1 oz) butter, salt, pepper, nutmeg

Béchamel Sauce

3/4 L (3 cups) milk, 60 g (2 oz) butter, 60 g (2 oz) flour (for a roux), 3 egg yolks, 8 cl (1/3 cup) heavy cream (to bind), salt, pepper, nutmeg

Equipment

Cutting board, hotel pan, mixing bowls, measuring cup, paring knife, vegetable peeler, chef's knife, fish fileting knife, 2-pronged fork, palette knife, ham slicer (optional), spatula, whisk, pastry scrapers, tablespoons, spouted spoons, skimmer, plates, mandoline (optional), rolling pin, brush, pastry brush, sauté pan with lid, strainer, large saucepan with lid, round baking sheets, turntable (optional), frying pan, sheet pan

Preparing the " Brunoise " of Vegetables

Sort, peel and wash the vegetables carefully and drain. With a very sharp knife, cut the vegetables into " brunoise ", or very fine dice.

The carrots and celery root may be sliced first with a mandoline, then cut into dice with the knife.

Cooking the Vegetables

The vegetables are cooked in their own juices in a covered pan. Put a little clarified butter in a saucepan or sauté pan with a lid and add the finely diced vegetables.

Cook over medium heat to draw out the water.

Stir occasionally as the vegetables cook.

Cook until all the moisture has evaporated so that excess moisture does not dilute the crêpe batter.

Remove and leave to cool before thoroughly combining with the crêpe batter.

Make a classic crêpe batter by mixing together in a small bowl with a whisk the sifted flour, eggs, milk and lastly the melted butter.

Preparing the Vegetable Crêpes

Season with salt and pepper.

Pass the batter through a fine-meshed conical sieve to eliminate any lumps and make the mixture perfectly smooth. Add the cooked vegetables.

Cover the bowl with a cloth and leave to rest.

In a non-stick pan, or a pan reserved only for making crêpes and rubbed with a little clarified butter, fry crêpes the same diameter as the Pithiviers.

Put the crêpes in two stacks and cover with plastic film so they do not dry out.

Preparing the Spinach and Béchamel Garnish

Preparing the Spinach and Sorrel

Carefully sort the greens and discard any wilted leaves. Wash them in several changes of water.

With the help of a paring knife, remove the stems and the thick part of the central rib.

Drain the leaves well in a colan-der and then on a hand towel to dry them completely.

Cooking the Spinach and Sorrel
The cooking is done in two stages. First, put some clarified butter in a large saucepan with a lid.

Add the spinach and sorrel leaves, cover and cook over medium heat to draw out the water from the spinach.

Season lightly with salt and pepper and stir occasionally with a two-pronged fork to separate the leaves.

Remove the lid to finish cooking and let all the moisture evaporate.

Drain the spinach and sorrel in a colander and squeeze gently to remove excess liquid.

Next, in a sauté pan, heat some butter until it turns light brown and smells "nutty". This butter will give the greens a rich flavor.

Add the greens and stir gently with a two-pronged fork to separate the leaves and help evaporate any excess water.

When the spinach and sorrel give off no more liquid, transfer to a tray and leave to cool.

Making the Béchamel

Make a classic béchamel sauce: in a saucepan, melt the butter, add the sifted flour and mix well with a whisk to form a roux.

Warm the milk and add to the

roux, whisking constantly to avoid lumps.

Bring to a boil and let the sauce reduce until it is slightly thickened. Season with salt, pepper and nutmeg.

Take from the heat. Whisk together a mixture of egg yolks and heavy cream to use as a liaison with which to bind the sauce. Pour it into the béchamel in a thin stream, whisking constantly to incorporate so the yolks do not overcook and form lumps.

Cook over a low heat for a few minutes.

Taste and adjust seasoning if necessary.

Pour the sauce into a hotel pan and rub a little butter on the top to prevent the formation of a crust.

Leave to cool completely.

Transfer the sauce to a bowl and add the cooked spinach and sorrel. Mix well with a spatula.

Slicing the Ham

Cut the ham with a sharp knife or on a slicer. Cut two large round slices, 3-4 mm (about 1/8 in) thick per Pithiviers.

Assembly of the Pithiviers

The procedure is as for a classic Pithiviers: roll out two rounds of puff pastry with 6 turns. Estimate 80-100 g (about 3 oz) of pastry per person. The round to be used on the bottom may be slightly smaller than the one for the top.

Place the bottom round on a lightly buttered and moistened round baking sheet. Brush egg glaze all around the edge of the pastry.

Arranging the Garnish

In the middle of the pastry round, lay a vegetable crêpe. Spread a 6 mm (1/4 in) layer of the spinach mixture on top.

Place a slice of ham that is about the same size as the crêpe on the spinach. Spread a second layer of spinach mixture on the ham; do not spread all the way to the edges.

Lay over the second slice of ham, then spread on a third layer of spinach mix.

Finish the assembly with another vegetable crêpe.

Note: The crêpes should always go under and over the rest of the garnish. In this way, they can absorb the moisture rendered by the spinach and ham during cooking which helps to keep the pastry crisp.

Final Assembly

Turn over the second pastry round and lay it on top of the filling, making sure it follows the domed shape of the filling without trapping any air inside.

Press gently with the side of your hand on the edge of the pastry to seal it.
Brush on a second coat of egg glaze.

Score the Pithiviers with the tip of a paring knife in either a diamond or leaf design or else in the classic curved "spoke" pattern, which decorated both the original

Pithiviers that was a pâté and still adorns the " gâteau pithiviers ", the almond cream filled pastry we know today.

Complete the decoration with a few strokes of the back of the knife in the opposite direction of the " spokes ".

Prick all the way through the top crust 4 or 5 times to let the steam escape, which would otherwise make the crust soggy and uneven or cracked.

Chill another 30 minutes to let it rest.

Cooking

As with the classic Pithiviers, start cooking in a high oven (210 C (400 F) for 4-5 minutes) so the puff pastry has a chance to begin rising and browning. Then lower the heat to about 180 C (350 F) to finish.

Estimate 35-45 minutes for a Pithiviers for 8 people (bear in mind that the Pithiviers will most likely be reheated, so do not overcook).

Immediately transfer the cooked pithiviers to a cooling rack.

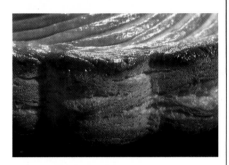

Checking the Cooking

The Pithiviers is done when the pastry is a deep golden color and is firm to the touch.

Storage

Ham and spinach Pithiviers can be kept 2-3 days at no more than 6 C (43 F).

Serving

These Pithiviers are eaten hot. They should be reheated at the last minute in a low oven. Given the fact that they have a dense filling, reheating takes quite a while.

They are usually served whole on heated platters, which keeps them piping hot until cut at the table, when all the delicious aromas will be released.

Ham and Spinach Pithiviers

Procedure Diagram

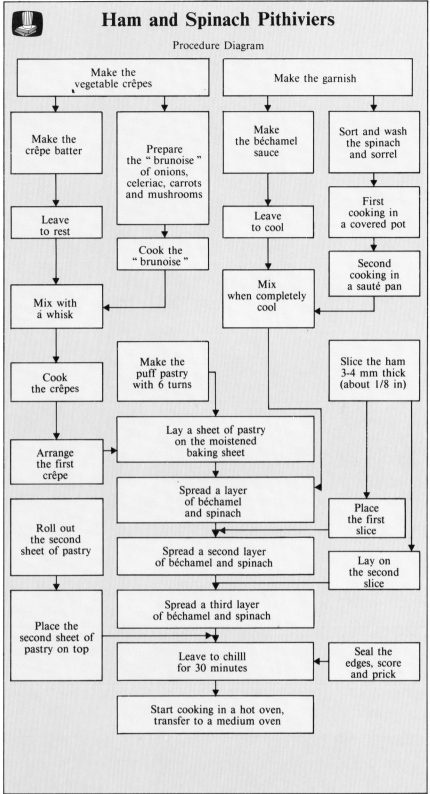

Sausage in Brioche

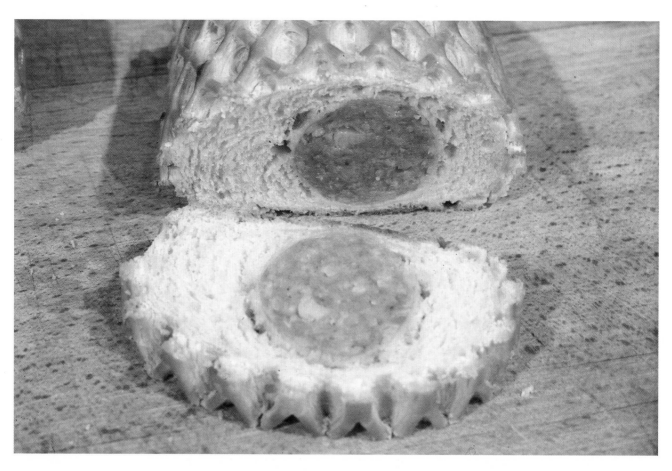

Introduction

Sausage in brioche is originally from the region around the French city of Lyon; it is also sometimes called sausage " à la lyonnaise ". Truffles and pistachios may be incorporated in the sausage meat.

These preparations are fairly simple to make and can be served year-round.

They are ideal for the caterer, as they are easy to transport and they can be served for many types of occasions - as a hot first course, on a buffet table, for restaurant service, for a small reception or dinner, or as an accompaniment to aperitifs or cocktails.

Sausage in brioche is a classic dish that is always popular.

Equipment

Cutting board, vegetable peeler, paring knife, chef's knife, forks, mixing bowls, hotel pan, kitchen twine, parchment paper, thermometer, skimmer, plates, aluminum foil

Ingredients

For 4 sausages serving 6 people each, for a total of 24 portions:

Weight of each piece: approximately 300 g (10 oz)

3 L (3 qts) light stock (use white veal or chicken stock or leftover liquid from poaching other sausages, plus water)

Aromatic Vegetables

100 g (3 1/2 oz) leeks, 45 g (1 1/2 oz) celery, 100 g (3 1/2 oz) carrots, 60 g (2 oz) onions, bouquet garni (thyme, bay leaf, 6 parsley stems)

Salt, pepper

Preparing the Aromatic Vegetables

Thoroughly wash the leeks, celery and carrots in several changes of cold water. Peel and quarter the onion.

Preparing the Sausages

Select nice, evenly shaped sausages.

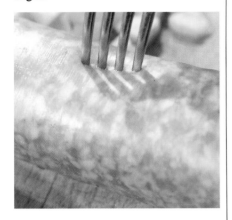

Prick the sausages with a fork at even intervals about 3 mm (1/8 in) deep.

Preparing the Bouquet Garni

With kitchen twine, tie up the thyme, bay leaf, parsley stems and, if you like, leek green.

Cutting the Vegetables

Cut the vegetables into small dice about 1 cm (3/8 in), so they can be cooked during the relatively short poaching of the sausages.

Preparing the Poaching Liquid

Use a light veal or chicken stock or the poaching liquid used for other sausages.

If using left over poaching liquid, be sure to degrease it and dilute it slightly with water so it is not too strong.

Poaching the Sausages

This first step is important in order for the dish to taste its best. The sausages can be poached ahead of time and frozen until ready for assembly or refrigerated at 4 C (40 F) for a short period of time.

In a saucepan large enough to hold all the sausages to be poached, put the cold stock or poaching liquid, the sausages, the vegetables, the bouquet garni, pepper and a little salt (not too much, as the sausages will already be quite salty).

Heat to the right temperature. Note: The goal is just to lightly

poach the sausages, so the temperature must be monitored closely and kept just around 85 C (185 F). It is best to use a thermometer.

Checking the Cooking
For sausages weighing 300-500 g (10 oz-1 lb), count on 20-25 minutes of cooking at 85 C (185 F).

As you become more experienced, you will be able to judge when the sausages are done simply by touching them.

Leave the sausages to cool in the liquid.

Before they are completely cool, remove the sausages and take off the casing by slitting with a paring

knife. This is done more easily when the sausages are still slightly warm.

The skinned sausages are rolled up in aluminum foil and put in the freezer so they get thoroughly chilled and firm before being rolled in the brioche. They may stay frozen for several days.

Because the sausages are cold, they are easier to work with and they will not cause the brioche dough to rise prematurely.

Preparing the Sausages

Remove the aluminum foil. With a pastry brush, coat the sausage

with egg glaze, then roll it in flour.

Remove any excess flour, leaving just a thin film around the sausage.

This will help the brioche dough to cling to the sausage and avoid any gaps between the cooked brioche and the sausage.

Keep the prepared sausages chilled until ready to use.

Preparing the Dough

Ingredients

For 4 sausages serving 6 people each (length 20 cm (8 in), weight 300 g (10 oz)): 1.2 kg (2 lb 8 oz) brioche dough, 600 g (1 lb 3 oz) puff pastry, flour, egg glaze

Equipment

Cutting board, hotel pans, pastry brush, rolling pins, lattice cutter, soft-bristled brush, round or rectangular baking sheets, paring knife, chef's knife, cooling racks, hand towel, ruler

Note: The two pastry doughs are best if prepared the day before. The basic pastry (the brioche) should be of excellent quality, using 600-700 g (1 lb 3 oz-1 lb 8 oz) butter per 1 kg (2 lb) flour).

The puff pastry is usually " demi-feuilletage " with trimmings incorporated in the last turn.

Rolling Out the Pastry

Brioche Dough

Using the least amount of flour possible while still preventing the dough from sticking, roll out an even sheet of dough about 6 mm (1/4 in) thick, depending on the size of the sausages.

The sausages may be trimmed so they are exactly the right size to

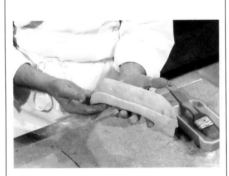

yield a specific number of portions (as a first course, count 45 g (1 1/2 oz) per person). Each rolled out sheet should be large enough to completely cover the number of sausages to be used.

Keep the rolled out sheets on a baking sheet or parchment paper in the refrigerator until ready to use.

Puff Pastry

Roll out an even sheet of puff pastry about 3 mm (1/8 in) thick and large enough to completely cover the sausage once it has been wrapped in brioche.

Cut the sheet of pastry with the lattice cutter. This delicate operation is performed more easily with two people, so that one person can hold down the edges of the pastry, while the other cuts. Alternatively, lay a heavy ruler along one edge to keep the pastry in place.

If a lattice cutter is not available, the sheet of pastry can be slit with a knife, though the result is not as neat.

This sheet of pastry is also chilled until ready to use.

It is important to allow the dough enough time to rest so it loses its elasticity by the time it is applied to the sausages.

Shaping

Cut the chilled brioche sheet so it is wide enough to wrap around the sausage 1 1/4 times and long enough to have 5 cm (2 in) excess at each end.

Brush away any excess flour.

Brush a coat of egg glaze over the entire surface of the dough.

Roll the sausage up tightly in the dough and press on the seam to close it securely. Shape the ends of the dough by pressing with your thumbs as shown to seal the dough.

Using a generously floured rolling pin, roll out the dough at either end. With a chef's knife, cut the ends into long points. Turn the sausage seam side up. Brush the two ends with egg glaze and fold them over the seam, smoothing them out so the layer of pastry is not too thick.

Place the sausage seam side down on the baking sheet. Brush the entire surface with egg glaze. (Note: several of the steps described above are pictured on the preceding page.)

Place the prepared puff pastry on the sausage in brioche, pulling lightly to open out the latticework.

Tuck the long edges of the lattice pastry neatly under the sausage in brioche, using the back of a chef's knife.

Trim the short edges into a point and neatly fold them under also.

Brush on a very light coat of egg glaze, taking care not to let the glaze drip down the sides of the cuts in the lattice, which would make the pastry rise unevenly.

Cooking

The sausage in brioche should be cooked right away, as the brioche dough must not start to rise before it goes into the oven or else it will pull away from the sausage.

Start the cooking in a high oven (210 C (400 F)) and then reduce the heat to around 180 C (350 F) to finish cooking.

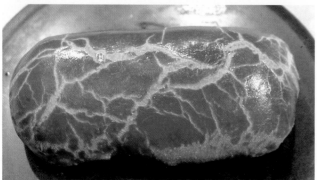

Checking the Cooking

The cooking of the sausage in brioche is judged mainly by looking at the color of the pastry - when done, it should be an even golden color. As soon as the pastry is cooked, the dish is cooked because the sausages were poached ahead of time. Do not overcook, since the sausage in brioche will be reheated before serving.

Cooling

Immediately transfer to a cooling

rack to prevent the pastry from becoming soggy through condensation.

Storage

Sausage in brioche can be stored at 6 C (43 F) for 2-3 days.

Service and Presentation

Heat the sausage in brioche whole so the pastry does not dry out too much, then cut into slices when ready to serve. If the sausage in brioche is sliced ahead of time, wrap the slices in aluminum foil to reheat.

The sliced sausage in brioche may be presented on a tray, arranged on a plate for lunch or dinner service, included on a buffet table, or sliced very thinly to serve with cocktails or aperitifs.

A madeira or " Perigueux " sauce is a nice complement to the sausage in brioche.

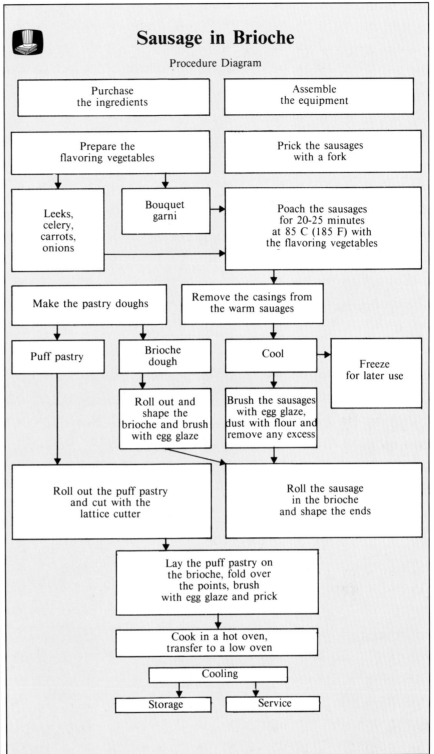

Sausage in Brioche

Procedure Diagram

- Purchase the ingredients
- Assemble the equipment
- Prepare the flavoring vegetables
- Prick the sausages with a fork
- Leeks, celery, carrots, onions
- Bouquet garni
- Poach the sausages for 20-25 minutes at 85 C (185 F) with the flavoring vegetables
- Make the pastry doughs
- Remove the casings from the warm sauages
- Puff pastry
- Brioche dough
- Cool
- Freeze for later use
- Roll out and shape the brioche and brush with egg glaze
- Brush the sausages with egg glaze, dust with flour and remove any excess
- Roll out the puff pastry and cut with the lattice cutter
- Roll the sausage in the brioche and shape the ends
- Lay the puff pastry on the brioche, fold over the points, brush with egg glaze and prick
- Cook in a hot oven, transfer to a low oven
- Cooling
- Storage
- Service

Pâté of Duck à l'Orange in Aspic

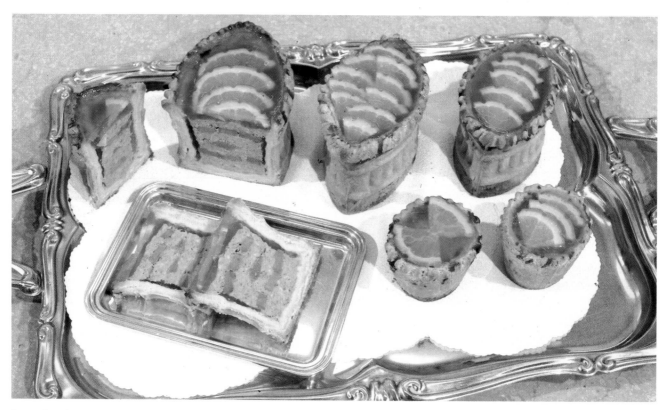

Introduction

Appropriate year-round, this pâté is made using the same techniques as other pâtés in aspic. The work is spread over two days. This classic dish is as delicious to eat as it is beautiful to see. There is a perfect balance between savory and sweet flavors. Popular with everyone, the pâté of duck à l'orange in aspic is extremely versatile and can be served for a variety of occasions: as a first course for a dinner or lunch, on a buffet table, for a light lunch main course or even an after-theater supper.

Equipment

Cutting board, chef's knife, paring knife, vegetable peeler, cleaver, palette knife, scissors, channel cutter, pastry brush, spoon, fork, pastry scraper, mixing bowls, plates, hotel pan, roasting pan, skimmer, ladle, spatula, electric meat grinder, sauté pan, large saucepan, fine-meshed conical sieve, kitchen twine, colander, pâté mold, aluminum foil, paper towels, plastic film, rolling pin, soft-bristled brush, rectangular or round baking sheet

Ingredients

1 large duck (about 2.1 kg (4 lb 8 oz)

For the Garnish

2 boneless breasts of duck (200 g (7 oz) × 2 = 400 g (14 oz)
2 cl (4 tsp) cognac

For the Seasoning

Salt, saltpeter, pepper, coriander, allspice, thyme, bay leaf, 6 oranges (peeled and cut in segments)

For the Forcemeat

700 g (1 lb 8 oz) duck meat (thighs, wings and trimmings), 700 g (1 lb 8 oz) pork jowl, 15 g (1/2 oz) clarified butter, 45 g (1 1/2 oz) shallots, 3 cl (2 tbsp) white wine for deglazing, 2 cl (4 tsp) white wine, 2 cl (4 tsp) cognac, 4 cl (3 tbsp) port, zest of 1/2 orange, salt, saltpeter, pepper, coriander, allspice, thyme, bay leaf

For Binding the Forcemeat

150 g (5 oz) duck liver purée, 150 g (5 oz) cold butter, 2 eggs, 1.5 dl (2/3 cup) reduced duck stock

For the Decoration

Fluted orange slices, aspic flavored with port

First Day's Work

Preparing the Duck

The work scheduled for the first day is identical to the initial steps for the duck with green peppercorn terrine, except that the pâté of duck à l'orange in aspic does not use the fat back. Please refer to the terrine recipe for a detailed explanation of the steps summarized below.

Preparing the Pork Jowl

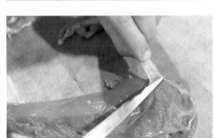

Preparing the Meats

Preparing the Shallots

Making the Duck Stock and the Duck Glaze

109

Marinating the Meats for the Filling

Put the forcemeat meats and the boneless duck breasts in two bowls with the marinade ingredients and chill until ready to use.

Second Day's Work

Lining the Mold

The most commonly used molds are oval shaped; they are available in many sizes. As a variation, the pâtés may be made in round or small individual molds.

The pastry used is pâté pastry.

Lightly butter the inside of the mold.

Roll out the pastry to a " bell " shape: Take a piece of pastry that is the right size for the size of the mold and shape it into a ball. (Estimate 50 g (about 1 1/2 oz) of pastry per person.) Using your fingers, make an indentation in the middle of the ball. Generously flour the indentation and fold over the pastry to form a pocket. Flatten it slightly with your hand.

Turn the open side toward you and with a rolling pin, roll out the " bell " shape, making sure that the two layers of pastry do not stick together. Dust with more flour if necessary.

Roll the pastry evenly to the size that will just fit the mold and allow the formation of a pastry rim. For a mold to serve 6-8 people, the pastry should be about 6 mm (1/4 in) thick.

Brush away any excess flour and place the pastry into the mold , tak-ing care not to stretch it, which would cause it to shrink during baking. Make a pastry rim by crimping it evenly with your fingers or with a pastry crimper.

Let the lined molds rest in a cool, but not too cold, place so the pastry can completely relax.

Making the Pâté Forcemeat

Remove the bouquet garni from the marinated duck and pork. Pass the meat through a meat grinder fitted with a medium disk.
Set aside in a bowl.

Preparing the Orange Zest

Wash and dry the orange, and peel off the zest from half of it using a vegetable peeler. Be sure to only remove the orange part and none of the white pith which is bitter.

Put the zest in a small saucepan with cold water, bring to a boil and boil for 2-3 minutes.

Drain the blanched zest and chop it very finely before mixing it with the forcemeat.

Preparing the Binding Ingredients

If using canned duck liver purée, soften it. Alternatively, use additional butter, which will give the same smooth texture but will not add the same amount of flavor, or else sauté and purée fresh duck livers with butter.
Weigh the butter, and check the consistency of the duck glaze.

Mixing the Forcemeat Ingredients

In the mixing bowl combine the ground meat, orange zest, eggs, liver purée, butter, duck glaze.

Mix all the ingredients together well with a wooden spatula. Taste and adjust seasoning if necessary. Cover and set aside until ready to assemble.

Preparing the Duck Breasts

Remove the bay leaf from the marinated duck breasts.
Drain the meat, then cook it just

a few seconds in clarified butter in a sauté pan. This will sear the duck, making it firm and preventing it from shrinking too much during the cooking of the pâté.

Drain the duck breasts and lay them on paper towels to absorb all the fat. Slice them into long strips (" aiguillettes ") and set them aside on a plate to cool.

The Sequence of Steps for Assembling the Pâté

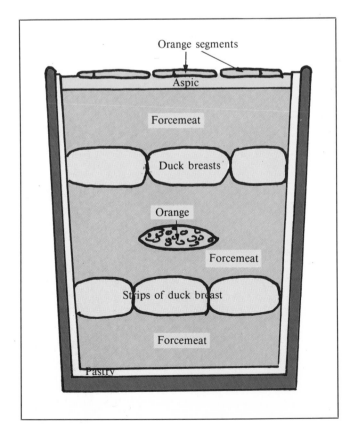

Orange segments

Aspic

Forcemeat

Duck breasts

Orange

Forcemeat

Strips of duck breast

Forcemeat

Pastry

Preparing the Orange Slices

With a paring knife, peel all the skin and pith from the oranges.

Cut out the orange segments from the membrane using a very sharp flexible knife. Cut away any remaining membrane.

Lay the trimmed orange segments on a hand towel to drain completely.

Note: The orange segments are optional, however they do contribute something special to the dish with their fresh flavor and the contrast of sweet and savory.

Assembling the Pâtés

When filling several pâtés at once, place the lined molds on baking sheets and add the filling by layers. The size of the mold will determine how many layers of filling and what order they are arranged.

For example, for a large pâté, serving 6-8 people: spread a 2 cm (3/4 in) layer of forcemeat in the bottom, evening it out with the back of a spoon.

Arrange a layer of duck breast strips on top of the forcemeat.

Repeat the layer of forcemeat then add a row of orange segments. Repeat with a layer of forcemeat and a layer of duck breast strips.

Finish with a smooth layer of forcemeat.

The filling should come to within 1 cm (3/8 in) of the top of the pastry rim.

Cover with a double layer of aluminum foil. This will keep the filling from drying out during cooking.

Cooking

Set the oven at 180 C (350 F).

Cooking time varies with the size of the pâté, but estimate 40-45 minutes for a pâté to serve 6-8 people.

Checking the Cooking

When the pâté is done, the pastry rim will be golden and the juices coming to the surface will be clear.

Insert a metal skewer into the center of the pâté; after a few seconds, remove it - it should be hot and clean with an even temperature along the surface that was inserted.

As soon as the pâté is cooked, transfer it to a cooling rack and set a weight on top until it is partially cool. This can be done by cutting a piece of cardboard to the shape of the pâté, laying it on the pâté and placing a heavy object on top. The larger the pâté, the heavier the weight should be. The aim of the weight is to compact the pâté slightly.

Preparing the Decoration

Preparing the Aspic

Use either a duck or chicken aspic. If the aspic is set, melt it in a bain marie until liquid but still cold.

Flavor the aspic with port.

Chill it over a bowl of crushed ice until it thickens slightly and is almost set, but still liquid enough to pour over the pâtés.

Preparing the Oranges for Decoration

Choose unblemished, seedless oranges. Wash and dry them; trim off the ends.

Cut regularly spaced decorative flutes in the orange peel with a channel cutter.

Cut the oranges in even 2-3 mm (about 1/8 in) slices. Set aside on a plate.

Decorating the Pâtés in Aspic

The decoration is usually done at the last minute.

Unmold the cold pâtés. Pour over a thin layer of the prepared aspic, which should be cold enough to set immediately.

Arrange the orange slices, whole or cut, in a pretty pattern on the aspic.

With a pastry brush, coat the orange slices with a thin layer of aspic.

Storage

The pâtés of duck à l'orange in aspic may be stored at 4 C (40 F) for 3-4 days, preferably wrapped in plastic film; the aspic layer keeps these pâtés fresher slightly longer.

If transporting the pâtés, take care that the aspic does not melt.

Serving

The pâtés are sliced at the last moment and presented on platters or plates decorated with salad greens or chopped aspic. They are eaten cold.

This pâté is rarely served with accompanying condiments.

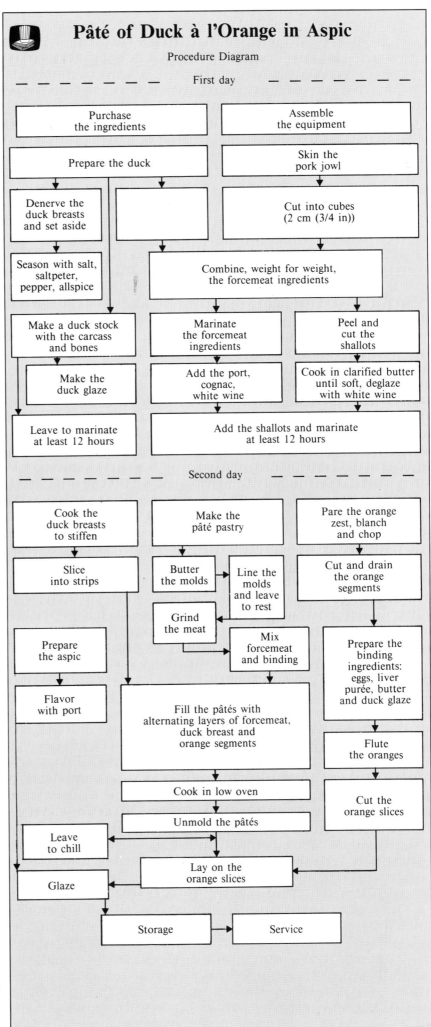

Pâté of Duck à l'Orange in Aspic

Procedure Diagram

— — — — — — First day — — — — — —

Purchase the ingredients

Assemble the equipment

Prepare the duck

Skin the pork jowl

Denerve the duck breasts and set aside

Cut into cubes (2 cm (3/4 in))

Season with salt, saltpeter, pepper, allspice

Combine, weight for weight, the forcemeat ingredients

Make a duck stock with the carcass and bones

Marinate the forcemeat ingredients

Peel and cut the shallots

Make the duck glaze

Add the port, cognac, white wine

Cook in clarified butter until soft, deglaze with white wine

Leave to marinate at least 12 hours

Add the shallots and marinate at least 12 hours

— — — — — Second day — — — — —

Cook the duck breasts to stiffen

Make the pâté pastry

Pare the orange zest, blanch and chop

Slice into strips

Butter the molds

Line the molds and leave to rest

Cut and drain the orange segments

Grind the meat

Prepare the aspic

Mix forcemeat and binding

Prepare the binding ingredients: eggs, liver purée, butter and duck glaze

Flavor with port

Fill the pâtés with alternating layers of forcemeat, duck breast and orange segments

Flute the oranges

Cook in low oven

Cut the orange slices

Unmold the pâtés

Leave to chill

Lay on the orange slices

Glaze

Storage

Service

115

Salmon Koulibiac

Introduction

The koulibiac is a delicious and popular dish that remains a classic in the caterer's repertoire. This historic dish originated in Russia.

The preparation of the koulibiac is not difficult, but is lengthy due to the number of separate steps.

The separate recipes that make up this elaborate dish can be made in advance and refrigerated individually or assembled and frozen, then wrapped in brioche just before baking. Therefore the components can be made in sizeable batches, then assembled to order, which makes the koulibiac more affordable for the client.

The koulibiac can be made large or small and can be decorated to suit the occasion, making an impressive dish when presented whole on a platter.

It can also be sliced, displaying the colorful layers, and served directly on plates accompanied by a beurre blanc (white butter sauce) which goes very well with the delicate components of the koulibiac.

Beurre blanc, however, is difficult to reheat, so for large dinners and buffets," crême fraîche " or sour cream flavored with lemon juice is an alternative sauce.

The brioche crust absorbs the juices from the ingredients inside, which makes the koulibiac moist and delicious.

It can be made all year round and is suitable for simple as well as elaborate occasions.

Equipment

Cutting board, paring knife, fish fileting knife, chef's knife, palette knife, spatula, 2-pronged fork, tablespoon, fork, ladle, skimmer, colander, whisk, mixing bowls, sieve, plastic film, hotel pans, plates, crêpe pan, large saucepans with lids, sauté pans with lids, kitchen twine, sheet pan, rolling, soft-bristled brush, lattice cutter, pastry brush, pastry cutter

Ingredients

(For 10 portions)
800 g (1 lb 10 oz) salmon filets
2 hard-boiled eggs
1 kg (2 lb) brioche dough
500 g (1 lb) puff pastry
Egg glaze

Crêpe Batter

125 g (4 oz) flour, 2 eggs, 3 dl (1 1/4 cups) milk, 45 g (1 1/2 oz) melted butter, 1/2 tbsp finely cut chives, 1/2 tbsp chopped chervil, 1/4 tbsp chopped tarragon, salt, pepper, nutmeg

Rice Pilaf

45 g (1 1/2 oz) clarified butter, 45 g (1 1/2 oz) onions, 150 g (5 oz) rice, 3.5 dl (1 1/2 cups) consommé, bouquet garni (thyme, bay leaf, parsley stems, leek green), salt, pepper

Mushroom Garnish

30 g (1 oz) clarified butter, 350 g (12 oz) mushrooms, 1 1/2 tbsp chopped "fines herbes" (chervil, tarragon, chives), salt, pepper

Spinach and Sorrel Garnish

30 g (1 oz) clarified butter, 1 kg (2 lb) spinach, 10 sorrel leaves, 15 g (1/2 oz) cold butter, salt, pepper, nutmeg

Béchamel Sauce (half for the rice, half for the mushrooms)

Roux (45 g (1 1/2 oz) butter + 45 g (1 1/2 oz) flour), 1/2 L (2 cups) milk, 15 g (1/2 oz) butter (to finish), salt, pepper, nutmeg

Procedure

Making the Herb Crêpes

Combine all of the ingredients for the crêpes (except the herbs), pass the batter through a fine-meshed conical sieve and set aside.

Trim and wash the herbs and dry them thoroughly on a hand towel.

Chop the chervil and tarragon finely. The chives are chopped separately as they should be cut in neat pieces from one end of the " stem " to the other with a chef's knife.

Cooking the Eggs

Bring a pot of lightly salted water to a boil and carefully add the eggs; cook at a simmer for 10 minutes.

Remove the eggs from the heat and stop the cooking by running cold water over them until they are cooled.

Remove the shells, rinse the eggs, then dry them on a hand towel.

Pass the hard-boiled eggs through a large-meshed sieve and reserve in the refrigerator, covered in plastic film, until ready to use.

Stir the prepared herbs into the crêpe batter.

In a preheated and " seasoned " crêpe pan, cook the crêpes without drying them out.

Keep the crêpes covered to keep them moist until ready to serve. If you are making them well in advance and refrigerating them, a

sheet of wax paper between each crêpe will help keep them from sticking to each other.

Preparing the Salmon

If you are working with a whole fresh salmon, take care to wash, scale and trim the fish properly.

Frozen filets of salmon can be used. In this case, defrost them slowly in the refrigerator for the best results.

Cut the filets of salmon in pieces the size of the koulibiac you are going to make.

For small or individual koulibiacs, the filets can be cut lengthwise in half to make them thinner.

Keep the prepared salmon in plastic wrap in the refrigerator until ready to assemble the dish.

Making the Rice Pilaf

Weigh out the rice needed for the size recipe you are making. Place this rice in a measuring cup, then measure out 1 1/2 this volume in chicken or veal stock. Put the stock in a pot and heat it slightly.

Preparing the Onions

Peel the onions and cut them into fine dice.

Make a bouquet garni with a branch of thyme, a bay leaf, a few stems of parsley and a leek green tied together with kitchen twine.

Cooking the Rice

Heat the clarified butter in a pan and cook the onions without browning them. Add the rice and stir over a low heat so that the rice absorbs the butter.

Pour the hot stock over the rice, add the bouquet garni, and season with salt and pepper. Bring to a boil, then cover with a tight-fitting lid.

Place the pan in an oven set at 180 C (350 F) and cook the rice for 20 minutes. The rice will absorb all of the cooking liquid during this time.

Remove the rice from the oven and stir in a little butter to keep the grains from sticking.

Cool the rice in a hotel pan.

Preparing the Mushroom Garnish

Using a paring knife, carefully trim the stems of the mushrooms which are often very sandy.

Wash the mushrooms in a large

basin of cold water, changing the water several times until there is no sand or dirt left.

Drain the mushrooms and dry them on a hand towel.

Rub the mushrooms with lemon to keep them from darkening. Cut the whole mushrooms in slices about 6 mm (1/4 in) thick. Sprinkle the slices with a little lemon juice and set aside.

Preparing the Herbs

Cut the chives and chop the chervil and tarragon as described in the preceding crêpe recipe.

Cooking the Mushrooms

Heat a little clarified butter in a pan and add the sliced mushrooms. Sauté the mushrooms over

high heat which will draw the moisture out of them. Continue to cook over high heat to evaporate this liquid. Stir the mushrooms as they cook to keep them from sticking to the pan.

Season with salt and pepper and add the prepared herbs. Put the cooked mushrooms on a plate or hotel pan and set aside.

Preparing the Spinach and Sorrel Garnish

Trim the spinach and sorrel, removing the stem and thick central rib from the leaves.

Wash the leaves thoroughly in several changes of cold water and dry them on a hand towel.

Cooking the Spinach and Sorrel Garnish

Melt a little clarified butter in a pan.

Add the spinach and sorrel and cover with a tight-fitting lid and cook over medium heat for a few minutes to draw the moisture out of the leaves.

Remove the cover and season with salt and pepper and continue to cook to evaporate the liquid, stirring constantly with a 2-pronged fork.

When the liquid has evaporated, remove the spinach and sorrel to a plate or hotel pan and set aside.

Making the Béchamel

In a pot, make a light roux by melting the butter and blending in the flour and cooking over a low heat.

Heat the milk in another pot,

then pour the warm milk into the roux stirring to blend thoroughly.

Over medium-high heat, bring the sauce to a boil, stirring constantly.

Reduce the heat and simmer the sauce to thicken it. Season to taste.

Pour the béchamel into a shallow pan to cool. With a piece of butter on a fork, pat the surface of the warm sauce to coat with melted butter to keep the surface from drying out and forming a skin.

Combining the Sauce and Garnish

With a wooden spoon, add the béchamel separately to the mushrooms and the rice.

Storage of the Filling Components

Up to this point, all of the separate steps can be prepared in advance and refrigerated until ready to assemble the koulibiac.

Make sure each component is carefully wrapped and stored properly.

Assembling the Koulibiac Filling

All of the prepared garnishes should be cooled completely before assembling the koulibiac as warm ingredients would cause the raw salmon to spoil.

To facilitate the assembly of the filling, line a baking sheet or tray with a sheet of plastic wrap large enough to cover the whole koulibiac.

The plastic wrap will help you to roll the crêpes tightly around the filling and in the case that you are making many koulibiacs in advance and freezing them, the plastic wrap will protect the assembled filling until ready to wrap in brioche and bake.

Note: Because it is recommended not to freeze the salmon twice, if you plan to freeze the assembled filling, do not use salmon that has already been frozen.

Remember that the size and form of the koulibiac can vary to suit any occasion.

Koulibiac to Serve 8-10

The koulibiac pictured here will provide 8-10 servings.

Start with crêpes, overlapping two crêpes in the center of the sheet of plastic wrap.

In the center of the crêpes, spread a rectangular layer of the spinach and sorrel about 3 mm (1/8 in) thick, leaving a border around the edge; make sure the layer is even and flat. With a spoon or palette knife, add a layer of the rice and béchamel mixture (6 mm (1/4 in)) as shown.

Next spread a layer of the mushroom and béchamel mixture on top.

Place a filet of salmon on top of the mushrooms. The chopped egg is then sprinkled over the filet of salmon.

A second filet of salmon is placed over the chopped egg.

On top of the salmon, repeat the layers of garnish starting with the mushrooms, the rice and finishing with a layer of the spinach and sorrel.

Wrap the crêpes around the sides of the filling. Trim two more crêpes to cover the top. The crêpes should completely cover the filling.

Cover the assembled filling securely in the plastic wrap. Press on the sides to form a neat rectangular "package".

Store in the refrigerator or freezer until ready to use.

Preparing the Pastry Casing

The Brioche Dough

The day before, make a classic brioche dough and chill it so that it is easy to roll out.

Roll out two sheets of brioche about 6 mm (1/4 in) thick, large enough to accommodate the assembled filling plus a border of about 5 cm (2 in).

Chill the sheets of dough, protected by plastic wrap, until ready to use.

The Puff Pastry

The puff pastry, which will be used for decorating the koulibiac can be a " quick " or " rough " puff pastry or one with trimmings incorporated during the 6th turn, as the pastry does not need to rise very much.

A single sheet of dough is needed to decorate each koulibiac and it should be rolled out 3 mm (1/8 in) thick and about the same size as the sheet of brioche dough. Place it on a sheet of parchment paper.

Cut the sheet of dough using a lattice cutter, with the help of another person or using a heavy ruler, as described in the sausage in brioche recipe.

It is important to chill the dough after it is cut into a lattice before it is placed on the koulibiac and baked so that it does not shrink during cooking.

Two Methods for Wrapping the Filling in the Pastry Casing

First Method

Use two sheets of chilled brioche dough. Place one sheet of dough on a baking sheet. Remove the plastic

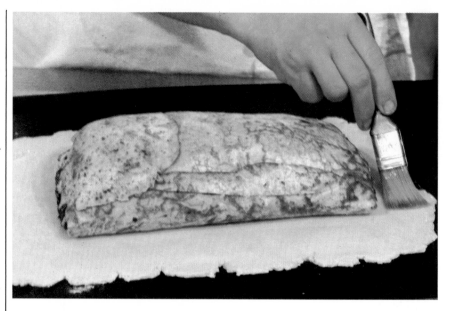

wrap from the prepared filling and place it in the center of the brioche.

Brush egg glaze on the border of dough around the filling.

Place the second sheet of dough, slightly larger than the first, on top of the filling. Press down around the border to stick the two layers of dough together.

Trim the edges of the dough then make a decorative fluted edge by crimping the pastry with the tips of your fingers which also serves to stick the two layers together. Brush the top of the koulibiac with egg glaze.

Carefully place the puff pastry lattice on top and press lightly to stick it to the brioche. Trim the edges and press them into the base of the brioche.

Very carefully, brush a light coat of egg glaze on the lattice without dripping which would keep the puff pastry decoration from rising correctly.

Make six tiny air vents by pricking the pastry evenly with the tip of a paring knife or a skewer, taking care not to cut into the lattice.

Second Method

Use a single sheet of brioche dough and wrap it around the filling as shown in the recipe for sausage in brioche.

Brush the dough with egg glaze. Cut decorative shapes from a sheet of puff pastry and arrange them in an attractive pattern on the brioche. Brush the decorations with egg glaze. Score the puff pastry shapes with a paring knife. Make a few air vents by pricking the pastry evenly with the point of paring knife or a skewer.

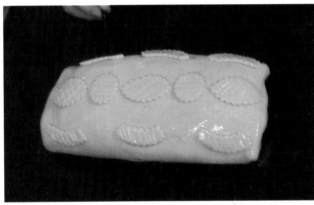

Cooking
Place the completed koulibiac in a high oven (210 C (400 F)). After a few minutes, lower the heat to 180 C (350 F) to bake the filling and pastry evenly. The baking time will depend on the size of the koulibiac. The pastry should be evenly browned and crisp. A skewer inserted into the center should be hot and clean when withdrawn after a few seconds, with an even temperature along the surface that was inserted.

When it is baked, remove the koulibiac immediately to a cooling rack. After it has completely cooled, wrap it in plastic wrap or a hand towel to keep the pastry from drying out.

Storage
The baked koulibiac will keep for up to 3 days at 4 C (40 F).

Presentation
The koulibiac is served warm and should be reheated just before being served.

A whole koulibiac should be warmed slowly in a low oven to heat it throughout without drying it out. If the koulibiac is sliced for sale in a specialty food shop, each slice should be wrapped in aluminum foil to protect the slices from drying out while being reheated.

Whether presented whole on a platter or sliced on a plate, the classic sauce to serve is a beurre blanc.

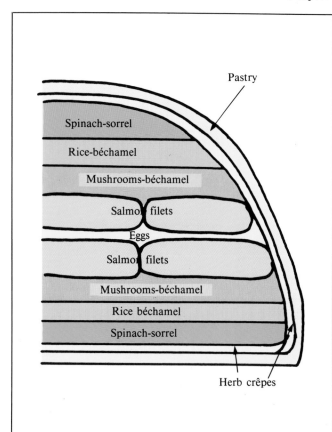

Beurre Blanc

Beurre blanc is a very delicate sauce that is often served with elaborate dishes because it complements the flavors without being overpowering.

This sauce is relatively easy to prepare but once prepared is somewhat fragile and should be reheated with great care.

Equipment

Cutting board, paring knife, pan with lid, conical sieve, ladle, tablespoon, wooden spoon, whisk, plates, water bath

Ingredients

30 g (1 oz) clarified butter, 100 g (3 1/2 oz) shallots, 5 cl (1/4 cup) wine vinegar, 5 cl 1/4 (cup) dry white wine, 3 cl (2 tbsp) heavy cream, 400 g (14 oz) good quality butter, salt and pepper

Procedure

Peel the shallots and cut them

into very fine dice. Heat a little clarified butter in a pan and cook the shallots until soft but not brown.

Add the vinegar and wine and reduce over medium high heat until the liquid is completely evaporated.

Add the heavy cream and bring the mixture to a boil.

Cut the butter into small pieces and whisk them one at a time into the boiling shallot mixture, whisking constantly with a wooden spoon or a whisk.

Remove from the heat and season to taste with salt and pepper. Pass the sauce through a fine-meshed conical sieve to remove the shallots and to achieve a smooth sauce.

Serve the beurre blanc immediately or transfer the sauce to a stainless steel container and store at 4C (40F). Like the koulibiac, the beurre blanc can be stored refrigerated for up to 3 days.

Service

The beurre blanc is served warm and should be reheated just before it is served.

This is a delicate sauce that must be reheated carefully in a water bath as too high a temperture will cause the sauce to separate.

In a specialty food shop the beurre blanc is sold separately in small plastic containers to be reheated by the customer at home.

Count on about 30-40g (1-1 1/2 oz) of sauce per person.

Salmon Koulibiac

Procedure Diagram

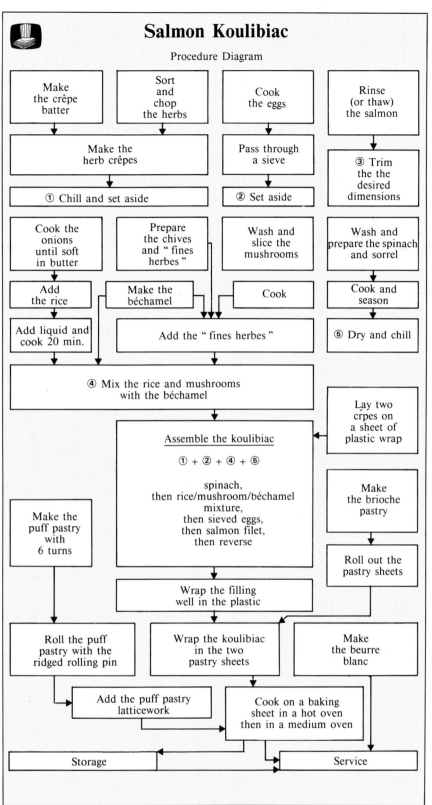

- Make the crêpe batter
- Sort and chop the herbs
- Cook the eggs
- Rinse (or thaw) the salmon
- Make the herb crêpes
- Pass through a sieve
- ① Chill and set aside
- ② Set aside
- ③ Trim the the desired dimensions
- Cook the onions until soft in butter
- Prepare the chives and "fines herbes"
- Wash and slice the mushrooms
- Wash and prepare the spinach and sorrel
- Add the rice
- Make the béchamel
- Cook
- Cook and season
- Add liquid and cook 20 min.
- Add the "fines herbes"
- ⑤ Dry and chill
- ④ Mix the rice and mushrooms with the béchamel
- Lay two crpes on a sheet of plastic wrap
- Assemble the koulibiac
- ① + ② + ④ + ⑤
- spinach, then rice/mushroom/béchamel mixture, then sieved eggs, then salmon filet, then reverse
- Make the brioche pastry
- Make the puff pastry with 6 turns
- Roll out the pastry sheets
- Wrap the filling well in the plastic
- Roll the puff pastry with the ridged rolling pin
- Wrap the koulibiac in the two pastry sheets
- Make the beurre blanc
- Add the puff pastry latticework
- Cook on a baking sheet in a hot oven then in a medium oven
- Storage
- Service

Chapter 3

Terrines

Terrines take their name from the earthenware molds in which they were traditionally baked (" terre " means " earth " in French). Porcelain or heat-resistant glass molds can also be used.

In specialty food shops the terrines are often sold in their molds. A deposit charge is added to the price of the terrine which is reimbursed when the customer returns the mold.

Many well-known caterers have their insignia embossed on the molds which are then sold to the customer with the terrine and are a very good publicity for the caterer.

Introduction to Terrines

Terrines are usually baked in rectangular or oval molds. In some cases, the mold is used to simply form the terrine using ingredients that are cooked separately then assembled in the mold.

Generally, terrines are always cooked slowly in a water bath in a low oven. Depending on the ingredients, the temperature is 155-170C (310-340F).

The cooking time will depend on the size of the terrine.

The size and shape of the mold can vary to suit any occasion.

The meat-based terrines are weighted after they are cooked. After they have cooled a little, but are still warm, they are covered with a board or piece of cardboard, cut to fit the top of the terrine, then topped with weights which make the terrine more compact. The denser terrines will be less perishable and will slice more neatly.

Saltpeter is called for in many of these recipes. This is an optional ingredient which helps to keep a rosy color in the terrine. It does not affect the taste or the shelf life.

Storage

The shelf life of each terrine will vary according to the ingredients and the method of cooking. For example, the vegetable and fish terrines are more perishable and will remain fresh for a maximum 3-7 days. The meat terrines are less perishable and can be further preserved by sealing the top with aspic or fat. The aspic layer is more attractive, but the method using fat is more effective for keeping the terrine fresh.

The Essential Role of the Marinades

For the meat terrines, the forcemeat ingredients and the garnishes are marinated with wines and seasonings that are chosen specifically to enhance the flavors of each type of terrine. The choice of marinade personalizes the terrines and gives them a complex flavor. The marinade also tenderizes the meats.

The forcemeat ingredients are then passed through a meat grinder and bound with eggs and sometimes foie gras.

Some terrines are enriched with the addition of a reduced stock made from the bones of the meats used in the terrine, which makes these terrines moist and delicious.

Adding a Layer of Aspic

As with the pâtés that were topped with aspic, cool liquid aspic is poured over the cooled terrine, filling any gaps in the top to seal in freshness. An attractive decoration can be arranged on the terrine which will show through the aspic. The taste of the aspic, which is eaten with the terrine, can be flavored to enhance the ingredients of the terrine.

Adding a Layer of Fat

Even though the kind of fat can vary in accordance with the terrine (rendered duck fat for example), the choice is often lard since the fat is usually not eaten with the terrine.

The procedure is similar to using aspic. The fat is melted, then left to cool. When cool but still liquid, it is poured onto the cooled terrine so that it fills any gaps and covers the top completely. Once the layer of fat has set, cover the terrine with aluminum foil and store in the refrigerator at 4C (40F). Under these conditions, terrines will stay fresh for a few weeks.

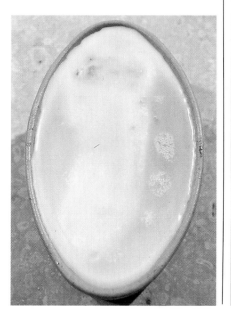

A Variety of Ingredients

This selection provides the caterer with a variety of flavors for his customers as well as an overview of the different techniques in making terrines.

Whether baked in the mold or assembled after cooking the ingredients separately, the selection and arrangement of the components is of the utmost importance so that each slice of terrine is attractive and delicious.

The terrines in this chapter are classified in 3 categories:

1. Meat
Terrines made with rabbit, hare, duck, goose, chicken livers and foie gras.

2. Fish
Terrines made with pike, red mullet, bream.

3. Vegetables
Terrines of assorted vegetables made with aspic, vegetable mousse or sweetbread mousse.

Denis Ruffel's Selection of Terrines

Meat Terrines

A 1 - Rabbit Terrine with Hazelnuts

Forcemeat: rabbit meat, rabbit liver, pork jowl
Garnish: rabbit filets, barding fat, kidneys, hazelnuts
Marinade: Cognac, white wine

Seasoning: Salt, saltpeter, pepper, thyme, bay leaf, allspice, shallots, mushrooms

Binding: liver purée, eggs
Stock: rabbit
Sealing: aspic or lard

A 2 - Duck Terrine with Green Peppercorns

Forcemeat: duck meat, duck liver, pork jowl
Garnish: duck breast, fat back, green peppercorns
Marinade: cognac, port, white wine

Seasoning: Salt, saltpeter, pepper, thyme, bay leaf, allspice, shallots, garlic

Binding: liver purée, eggs
Stock: duck
Sealing: aspic or lard

A 3 - Terrine of Chicken Livers

Forcemeat: chicken livers, pork jowl, fresh bacon
Garnish: caul fat, chicken livers
Marinade: cognac, port

Seasoning: Salt, saltpeter, sugar, pepper, thyme, bayleaf, allspice, shallots, garlic, onion

Binding: eggs, cream
Sealing: aspic or lard

A 4 - Terrine of Hare

Forcemeat: hare meat, pork jowl
Garnish: hare filets, fat back, pistachios
Marinade: cognac, white wine

Seasoning: Salt, saltpeter, pepper, thyme bay leaf, allspice, shallots, garlic

Binding: liver purée, eggs
Stock: hare
Sealing: aspic or lard

A 5 - Goose Rillettes

Forcemeat: goose meat, goose fat, pork filet

Seasoning: salt, pepper, thyme, bay leaf, parsley, shallots, garlic, onion, clove

Stock: water, white wine, chicken stock
Sealing: goose fat

A 6 - Terrine of Foie Gras

Forcemeat: fresh goose or duck foie gras
Marinade: sherry, cognac

Seasoning: Salt, saltpeter, pepper, mace, allspice

Sealing: aspic or goose fat

B - Fish Terrines

B 1 - Terrine of Pike with Asparagus Tips

Mousse: pike filets, whole eggs, egg whites, heavy cream, butter
Garnish: chervil, tarragon, chives, sole filets, anise, lemon, asparagus tips

Seasoning: salt, cayenne pepper

Assembly: butter, egg whites, powdered gelatin
Accompaniment: "Andalouse" sauce

B 2 - Tricolor Terrine of Red Mullet

Mousse: red mullet filets, whole eggs, egg whites, heavy cream, butter
Garnish: truffles, pistachios, " Américaine " sauce

Seasoning: salt, cayenne pepper

Assembly: butter, egg whites, powdered gelatin
Accompaniment: zucchini mousse

B 3 - Bream Terrine Royale

Mousse: bream filets, egg whites, heavy cream
Garnish: scallop coral, prawns, spinach

Seasoning: Salt, cayenne pepper

Assembly: butter, herb crêpes
Accompaniment: cocktail sauce

C - Vegetable Terrines

C 1 - Vegetable and Aspic Terrine

Vegetables: shallots, spring onions, chervil, tarragon, chives, green beans, zucchini, carrots, turnips, chanterelles, avocado

Base: chicken or meat aspic

C 2 - "Rainbow" Terrine

Vegetables: carrots, spinach and sorrel, celeriac

Base: leaf gelatin, powdered gelatin

Sauce: cream, salt, pepper, paprika

C 3 - Terrine of Sweetbread Mousse with Vegetables

Vegetables: carrots, turnips, peas, green beans, artichokes

Base: sweetbread mousse (sweetbreads, sirloin tip of veal, egg whites, heavy cream, light stock, armagnac, shallots, chanterelles, thyme, bay leaf, salt, pepper, allspice)

Rabbit Terrine with Hazelnuts

Introduction

The delicate flavor of rabbit makes this terrine delicious. Mushroom duxelles round out the special additions to the forcemeat. A garnish of toasted hazelnuts enhances the taste perfectly and adds texture to each slice.

Rabbit meat, however, is somewhat lean, therefore the amount of pork jowl is higher than in other terrines. A purée of goose liver and reduced rabbit stock add richness to the filling as well.

Equipment

Cutting board, paring knife, sharpening steel, cleaver, meat grinder, mixing bowls, hotel pans, terrine molds, bain-marie, ladle, skimmer, spoon, large saucepan, colander, conical sieve, roasting pan, measuring cups, spatulas, round baking sheet and pastry ring, sauté pan with lid

Ingredients

A rabbit weighing 1.6kg (3 1/2lb) yield:

500g (1lb) carcass

45g (1 1/2oz) tendons and trimmings

800g (1lb 12oz) meat for the forcemeat

250g (1/2lb) filets and kidneys for the garnish

1.6kg (3 1/2lb) skinned pork jowl,

400g (14oz) goose liver purée

250g (1/2lb) barding fat
3 eggs

First Day's Work

Seasoning

Salt, pepper, saltpeter
Mace or nutmeg
Thyme, bay leaf
Allspice

For the Mushroom Duxelles

100g (3 1/2oz) mushrooms
30g (1oz) clarified butter
1/2 lemon

For the Marinade

Forcemeat Marinade

2 shallots
2 cloves garlic
30g (1oz) clarified butter
5cl (1/4 cup) white wine (for deglazing the shallots)
2dl (3/4 cup) white wine (for pouring over the meats)
5cl (1/4 cup) cognac

Garnish Marinade

1dl (1/2 cup) white wine
3cl (2tbsp) cognac

For the Rabbit Stock

Carcass

30g (1oz) clarified butter or oil
45g (1 1/2oz) onions
30g (1oz) shallots
30g (1oz) garlic

1 carrot
Bouquet garni (leek green, parsley stems, thyme, bay leaf, celery branch)
1 medium tomato

Salt, peppercorns
Coriander seed
1/4L (1 cup) white wine
1.5L (6 cups) reduced stock

Preparing the Meats

Boning the Rabbit

Lay the rabbit, back side up, on a cutting board with its four legs spread flat.

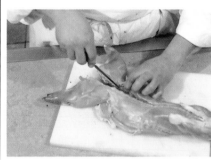

Using a very sharp paring knife, make an incision the length of the back bone, which is located by feeling with your fingers.

Starting just below the head at the shoulder, angle the knife blade toward the bone. Cut away the meat from the backbone, then from the rib cage. Continue cutting down to the joint of the hind leg and cut the filet free at each end. Turn the rabbit over and cut away the triangular flank section of meat that runs from under the rib cage to the hind leg.

Twist the thigh at the joint and detach it. This yields the front leg, the filet, the flank and the hind leg.

Repeat the procedure for the other side. Turn the carcass with the back to the board to remove the

two "filets mignons" on either side of the backbone. Remove the kidneys, which will be used for the garnish.

Scrape the carcass to remove any bits of meat clinging to the bones.

Trimming the Meats

Each piece of meat is trimmed to remove tendons and skin. The legs are carefully boned and the tendons removed.

Take care not to cut into the filets, which will be used as the garnish.

Cut the other sections of meat into pieces to be used in the forcemeat.

The tendons are kept along with the bones, cartilage and the rest of the carcass to make the stock.

Weigh the meat to be used for the forcemeat--use twice the weight in pork jowl.

Skinning the Pork Jowl

When calculating how much pork jowl to use, estimate about 5-8% weight loss from skinning. Because the rabbit meat is dry, more pork jowl is used in this recipe than in the other terrine recipes.

As the pork is very tender and the fat rich and melting, this rabbit terrine will have more richness and flavor than many similar rabbit dishes.

The skinned pork jowl is cut into 2cm (3/4in) pieces, then combined with the rabbit meat in a bowl to be marinated together.

Preparing the Kidneys

Peel the skin from the kidneys and cut them in half. Place the kidneys with the trimmed filets in a glass or stainless steel receptacle to be marinated.

Preparing the Marinade

The Marinade for the Forcemeat

Peel the shallots and garlic and remove the green sprout from the garlic, which is bitter. Cut the shallots into very fine dice and crush the garlic with the side of a chef's knife, then chop it finely.

Cook the prepared shallots and garlic in the clarified butter until very soft but not brown. Add the white wine and reduce until the liquid is evaporated.

Set aside to cool. Season the prepared meats for the forcemeat with salt, pepper, nutmeg or mace and allspice. Add bay leaf, fresh thyme, the white wine and the cognac.

Stir the marinade with the meats to mix thoroughly. Cover and leave to marinate overnight in the refrigerator.

The Marinade for the Garnish

The rabbit filets and kidneys are marinated together. Season them with salt, pepper, nutmeg or mace, thyme, bay leaf and allspice.

Sprinkle the white wine and cognac over the garnishes and set aside in the refrigerator to marinate.

Making the Rabbit Stock

With the cleaver, chop the carcass into small pieces.

Cut the vegetables into small pieces. In the roasting pan, brown the bones along with the trimmings.

Since the rabbit is lean, it is necessary to add a little clarified butter.

When the bones and trimmings have browned a little, add the vegetables and continue to cook until the bones and vegetables are a deep golden color.

(Rabbit stock continued)

Drain the browned bones and vegetables in a colander.

Deglaze the roasting pan with a little white wine, scraping up the delicious browned meat juices stuck to the bottom of the pan.

In a large pot, put the drained bones and vegetables and the deglazing juices.

Add a bouquet garni and the tomato cut in half, which will add color and a touch of acidity. Add also whole peppercorns and coriander seeds that have been tied securely in a piece of cheesecloth. This "bundle" will be easy to remove at the end and the separate grains will not be skimmed away during cooking.

Add reduced rabbit stock to

cover and a pinch of coarse salt and simmer 1-2 hours, skimming

away all impurities that rise to the surface.

When the stock has absorbed the flavor of the bones, remove the bouquet garni and cheesecloth and pass the stock through a conical sieve into another pot.

With a ladle, press on the bones and vegetables to extract the flavorful juices.

Skim away any fat that rises to the surface then reduce the stock over a medium heat, skimming if necessary.

When the stock has reduced to a syrupy glaze, set aside in the refrigerator until ready to finish the forcemeat.

This robust stock adds a very rich rabbit flavor as well moisture to this terrine.

Second Day's Work

Making the Mushroom Duxelles

Using a paring knife, trim the stems of the mushrooms which are often very sandy. Wash the mushrooms in a large basin of cold water, changing the water several times until there is no sand or dirt left.

Rub the mushrooms with lemon to keep them from darkening. Chop them finely with a stainless steel chef's knife and sprinkle the chopped mushrooms with a little

lemon juice. Do not chop them in a food processor which would draw out moisture and make them watery.

Heat some clarified butter in a heavy pan, add the chopped mushrooms and season with a little salt and pepper. Cover the pan and cook over a high heat to draw out moisture then remove the cover and cook until the liquid is evaporated. Remove to a plate or hotel pan to cool completely.

Preparing the Hazelnuts

Put the hazelnuts in a pastry ring on a baking sheet and cook in a moderate oven until the skins start to split from the nuts. Remove them and rub off the skins. Return the skinned hazelnuts to the oven to thoroughly toast them until they are golden brown. Do not overcook, as they will be bitter.

Preparing the Garnish

Remove the filets of rabbit from the marinade and drain them in a strainer.

Heat a little clarified butter in a pan and sear the filets on all sides.

This process will keep the filets from shrinking when they are cooking in the terrine.

As soon as the searing is completed, drain the filets on a paper towel and leave to cool.

The kidneys are not seared. While the filets are cooling, unroll the sheets of barding fat and cut pieces large enough to wrap 1 1/2 times around each filet.

Roll the cooled filets tightly in the sheets of barding fat.

Making the Forcemeat

Take the forcemeat ingredients from the refrigerator and remove the thyme and bay leaf.

These seasonings should never be ground with the other ingredients as the taste is too overpowering.

Pass the pieces of marinated rabbit and pork jowl through the meat grinder fitted with a medium disk.

In a bowl large enough to hold all the filling ingredients, stir the purée of goose liver to a smooth

consistency that will blend easily into the meat. Stir in the cooled duxelles.

Stir in the eggs until they are completely incorporated. Melt the reduced rabbit stock until it is liquid but still cool and mix this into the forcemeat mixture.

Finally stir in the toasted hazel-

nuts and stir all of the ingredients together to achieve a smooth even mixture. Poach or pan-fry a spoonful of the forcemeat; cool, taste and adjust seasoning if necessary.

Note: All of the ingredients must be cool before mixing with the meat, because warm ingredients would cause the meat to spoil quickly.

Preparing the Terrine Mold

Choose the size and shape of mold needed and line it with a sheet of barding fat large enough to wrap around the top of the filling.

This step is optional.

Filling the Terrine Mold

Fill the mold halfway with forcemeat.

Place a prepared filet in the center and arrange the kidneys which have been cut in half on either side of the filet as shown.

Fill the mold to the top with filling. Wrap the barding fat over the top of the filling, overlapping a little.

Protect the top with a double sheet of aluminum foil and prick three holes to let steam escape during cooking.

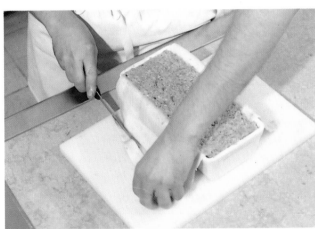

137

Cooking

Set the terrines in a water bath that is high enough to fill with water halfway up the mold.

Cook in a low oven--170C (340F). The cooking time will vary according to the size of the terrine.

A skewer inserted into the center should be hot to the touch and the cooking juices should be clear.

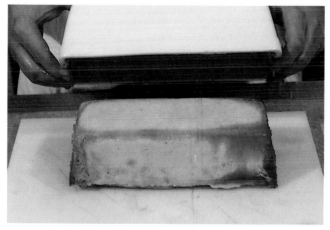

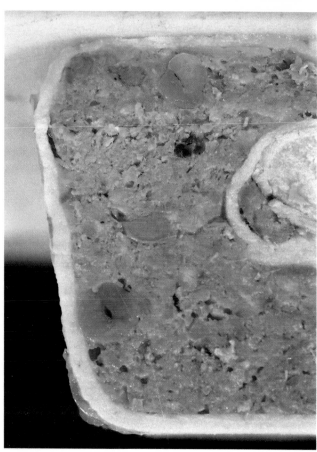

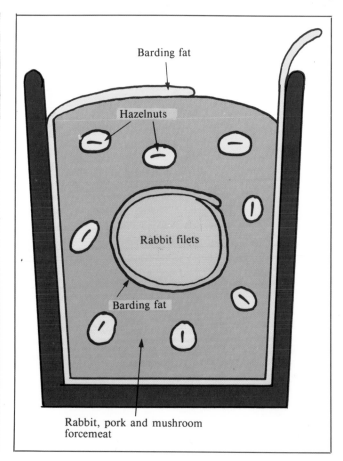

Barding fat

Hazelnuts

Rabbit filets

Barding fat

Rabbit, pork and mushroom forcemeat

Rabbit Terrine with Hazelnuts

Procedure Diagram

— — — — — — First Day's Work/First Day — — — — — —

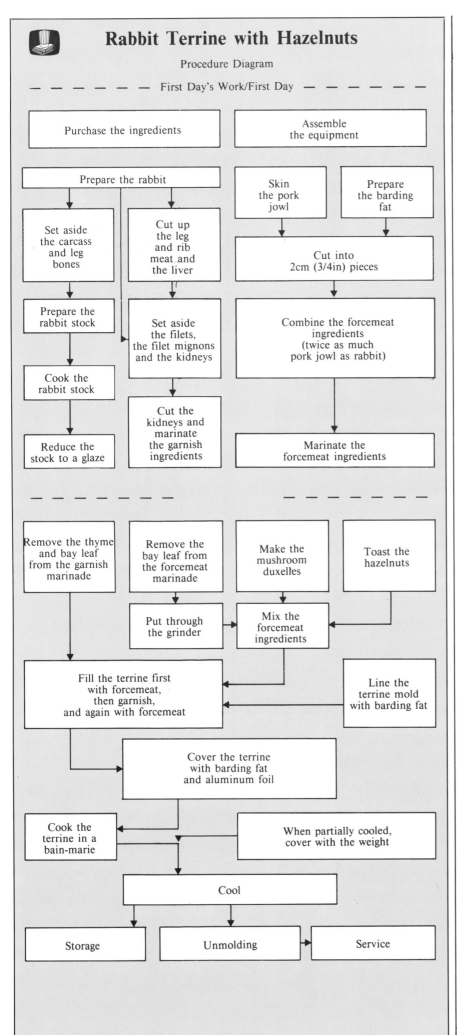

| Purchase the ingredients | | Assemble the equipment |

Prepare the rabbit

Skin the pork jowl — Prepare the barding fat

Set aside the carcass and leg bones

Cut up the leg and rib meat and the liver

Cut into 2cm (3/4in) pieces

Prepare the rabbit stock

Set aside the filets, the filet mignons and the kidneys

Combine the forcemeat ingredients (twice as much pork jowl as rabbit)

Cook the rabbit stock

Cut the kidneys and marinate the garnish ingredients

Reduce the stock to a glaze

Marinate the forcemeat ingredients

— — — — — — — — — — — — — — — — —

Remove the thyme and bay leaf from the garnish marinade

Remove the bay leaf from the forcemeat marinade

Make the mushroom duxelles

Toast the hazelnuts

Put through the grinder

Mix the forcemeat ingredients

Fill the terrine first with forcemeat, then garnish, and again with forcemeat

Line the terrine mold with barding fat

Cover the terrine with barding fat and aluminum foil

Cook the terrine in a bain-marie

When partially cooled, cover with the weight

Cool

Storage — Unmolding — Service

Cooling

Remove the terrine from the water bath and place it on a cooling rack to cool quickly and evenly.

When the terrine is still warm, place a piece of wood or cardboard cut to fit the top of the terrine. This helps to distribute the weight evenly. Top this board with weights--about 1kg (2lb) for the terrine shown here.

Storage

After the terrine has cooled completely, it can be stored, covered with aluminum foil, for 8-15 days in the refrigerator (4C (40F)).

Presentation

Small terrines are usually sold whole then unmolded and sliced just before being served. Large terrines are often sliced in advance and sold by the portion.

Appropriate garnishes to serve with the sliced terrine are pickled onions, " cornichons " (small sour gherkins) or pickled sour cherries.

The flavor of this terrine goes very well with specialty breads made with nuts or olives.

Duck Terrine with Green Peppercorns

Introduction

Terrines made with duck are particularly refined and are always among the most popular with customers. Ducks are available year-round so this terrine is a good choice in any season.

Equipment

Cutting board, paring knife, sharpening steel, cleaver, meat grinder, mixing bowls, hotel pans, terrine molds, bain-marie, ladle, skimmer, spoon, saucepan, colander, conical sieve, roasting pan, measuring cups, spatula

Ingredients

1 large duck
Pork jowl
Fat back, barding fat
Purée of duck liver
2 eggs
Cognac, port, white wine
Salt, pepper, allspice
Saltpeter, green peppercorns
Thyme, bay leaf, garlic, shallots

For the Duck Stock

Garlic, leeks, celery, bouquet garni (parsley, leek green, thyme, bay leaf), coriander, peppercorns, salt, white wine, reduced stock

First Day's Work

Preparing the Meats

Boning the Duck

This is a time-consuming task requiring close attention in order to get the best results.

Preliminary Preparations

If you are able to obtain a fresh duck, it may still contain its innards, head, feet and a few feathers.

In this case, stretch the duck out by holding its neck and feet and pass it over a flame, such as a gas burner, to singe off any remaining feathers and down. Because the skin will be discarded eventually, this step does not need to be performed too thoroughly.

Chop off the feet at the lower joint of the legs; chop off the head.

Place the bird breast-down on the work surface, hold the neck in your left hand, pulling the skin taut. With a sharp paring knife, slit the skin the length of the neck.

Chop off the neck as close to the body as possible. Pull away the windpipe and other tubes from the neck skin and chop them off. Pull out the grain sack from just inside the neck opening and discard it, taking care not to spill the contents.

Insert your index finger and, holding it close to the bone, slide it all around the cavity. This will loosen the lungs, which are relatively flat, bright pink organs attached closely to the back of the rib cage.

At the other end of the bird, make a slit to enlarge the rear opening. Insert your finger and slide it around to loosen the other organs, then carefully pull them out all in one piece. Take care not the break the small green bile sack attached to the liver. Remove the liver and trim away any green or yellow parts.

Remove the gizzard, split it down the middle and cut away any hard whitish skin. Wash it thoroughly. Locate the oiling glands just above the "parson's nose" and cut them out; they will ruin the taste of the duck if left in.

Boning

With a paring knife, cut along the v-shaped wishbone located just under the breast bone. Scrape the meat away and pull out the bone. This will make it easier to remove the breast meat without damaging it.

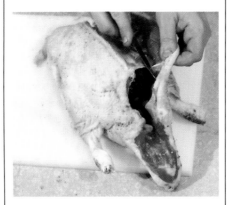

Place the duck with its back down on the work surface. Locate the breast bone with your fingers, then slice all along the length of the bone. Keeping the blade of the knife angled toward the bone, cut the

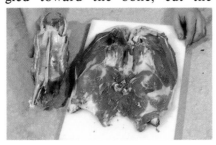

breast meat away.

Follow the contour of the carcass and continue cutting the meat away under the wings and thighs. To separate the wings and thighs from the body, open them out flat to expose the connecting joint and cut through it.

Repeat the procedure on the other side of the duck. This yields the carcass and the two halves of the duck, each comprised of a filet, a wing and a thigh.

Scrape off any bits of meat remaining on the carcass and remove as much neck meat as possible.

Separate the filets from the wings and thighs by pulling them away from the skin, cutting with a knife if necessary. Trim off fat and tendons carefully without gouging the filets, using the point of the paring knife. Remove the small filet from the large breast filet and cut away the bit of silver skin. Remove the small tendon from the small filet and the larger one from the large filet.

Set the prepared filets aside until ready to marinate.

To remove the skin, slide the knife between the meat and skin to loosen it, then pull the skin off completely. Check the skin to make sure no bits of meat are still attached; if so, cut them off with a knife.

Bone the wings and thighs; make

a cut along the length of the bone and scrape the meat away trying not to cut into it too much, which would make it difficult to remove the tendons.

Add the bones to the carcass for use in the stock. Cut the tendons out of each piece of meat; the wing meat, thigh meat and other meat cut from the carcass. With the paring knife, remove all the tendons, cartilage and large veins, which would mar the texture of the forcemeat.

Note: The skin may be discarded; the trimmings (veins, tendons and cartilage) are used in the stock.

The prepared duck yields three different products: the carcass, the cut up meat and the filets.

Preparing the Fat Back

Weigh the trimmed breast filets and take an equal weight of skinned fat back; trim the fat back into strips 6mm (1/4in) wide and 8-10cm (3 1/4-4in) long.

Preparing the Pork Jowl

The pork jowl is used in terrines because it provides the right proportion of lean to fat, with lean

meat that is tender and fat that melts easily.

For this terrine, weigh the duck meat then use the same weight of pork jowl, counting on about 5-8% loss from removing the skin.

Remove the skin and cut the pork jowl into 2.5cm (1in) chunks.

Preparing the Meats for the Marinade

Ingredients for the Forcemeat: cut up duck meat (wings, thighs, liver) with an equal weight of pork jowl cut in chunks.

Ingredients for the Garnish: whole filets with strips of fat back.

Preparing the Duck Stock

Chop the duck carcass into pieces with a cleaver. Place all the bones and trimmings in a lightly oiled roasting pan and place in a hot oven. The high heat will melt the fat which is heavy tasting and would ruin the taste of the stock.

After about 10 minutes, the fat will be melted and the bones will be browned. Remove the pan from the oven and put the bones in a colander to drain thoroughly. Pour off all the fat from the roasting pan.

Deglaze the roasting pan with white wine and scrape the bottom with a wooden spoon to loosen all the flavorful meat juices that have stuck to the pan.

Put the drained bones and the deglazing liquid into a large pot. Add a little white wine and reduce by half. Cover the bones with full-flavored veal or chicken stock.

Add a bouquet garni made of thyme, bay leaf and parsley tied up in a leek green with a piece of celery.

Add as well a small tomato cut in half which will add color and a touch of acidity.

Finally add whole peppercorns and coriander seeds that have been tied securely in a piece of cheesecloth. This "bundle" will be easy to remove at the end and the separate grains will not be skimmed away during cooking.

Season with a pinch of coarse salt and simmer the stock, uncovered for 2-3 hours.

It is important to skim all impurities and fat that rise to the surface with a ladle or skimmer. It is also advised to taste the stock from time to time to make sure the flavor of one ingredient, the celery for example, is not too overpowering, in which case the strong ingredient can be removed during cooking.

When the stock has developed a full flavor, remove the bouquet garni and the spice "bundle", drain the stock through a conical sieve, pressing on the bones with a ladle to extract the maximum amount of flavor.

Skim away any fat that floats to the surface of the strained stock.

Simmer the stock over medium heat until it is reduced to a thick syrupy glaze.

It is kept refrigerated until incorporated into the forcemeat. The unctuous and intensely flavored glaze adds a pronounced duck flavor and moistness, making it an essential ingredient in this delicious terrine. Just before adding it to the terrine, heat the glaze over very low heat until it is liquid, but still cool.

Marinating the Meats

While the stock is cooking, the marinade ingredients can be added to the prepared meats.

The Marinade for the Forcemeat

Cut the shallot into fine dice, chop the garlic finely and cook them in clarified butter until soft but not brown. Add the white wine and cook to evaporate the liquid. Thoroughly cool before adding to the prepared meats.

Season the forcemeat ingredients with salt, pepper, saltpeter, a pinch of allspice, thyme and a bay leaf. If using fresh thyme, it can be tied up

with the bay leaf.

Sprinkle the wine and cognac over the meat then stir gently to

coat the meat evenly with the seasonings.

Marinade for the Garnish

Season the garnish ingredients with salt, pepper, saltpeter, thyme, bay leaf and allspice. Sprinkle the port and cognac over the meats and stir gently to coat evenly.

Cover with plastic wrap and marinate overnight in the refrigerator.

Second Day's Work

Remove the bay leaf and fresh thyme (if used) from the marinade.

Preparing the Forcemeat

Pass the meats through a meat grinder fitted with a medium disk. Place the ground meats in a large

bowl and stir in the purée of duck liver, eggs, reduced duck stock and green peppercorns. Blend well to incorporate the ingredients thoroughly. Poach or pan-fry a spoonful of the forcemeat; cool, taste and adjust seasoning if necessary.

143

Preparing the Garnish

Remove the duck breasts from the marinade and drain thoroughly.

Sear them on all sides over a high heat in clarified butter, much like pan-frying a steak. The searing process keeps the meat from shrinking as it cooks in the terrine.

Drain the meat on paper towels to absorb the excess fat.

The duck breasts are then cut into strips the same size as the fat back.

Preparing the Molds

The molds may be lined with barding fat which keeps the outside of the terrines moist.

If barding fat is used, cut the pieces so they are large enough to wrap over the top of the terrine as well.

Note: The barding fat is optional, notably for small terrines that do not cook as long.

If the fat is not used, you do not need to butter the mold as there is enough fat in the forcemeat to ensure easy unmolding.

Assembling the Terrine

This terrine is made of alternating layers of forcemeat and strips of duck breast and fat back.

The number of layers will depend on the size of the terrine.

In the terrine pictured here, forcemeat is added to fill the bottom 1/3 of the mold and smoothed out with a spoon.

The strips of fat back and duck are placed in rows as shown to make a pretty checkered pattern when the terrine is sliced.

A second layer of forcemeat is spread over the garnish then another layer of the strips.

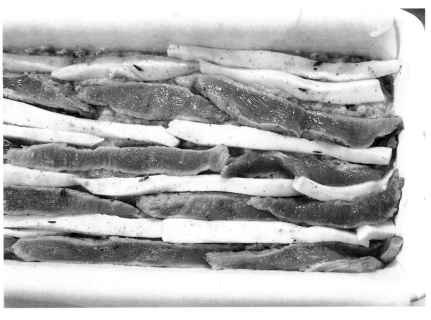

The mold is then filled to the top with forcemeat. The barding fat is wrapped around the top of the forcemeat.

The top is further protected with a sheet of aluminum foil that is pressed around the rim of the mold to hold it in place.

Pierce three holes through the foil to let steam escape during cooking. If the terrine you are using has a lid it should be secured into place with luting paste, a gluey mixture of water and flour that is applied around the rim.

Cooking

Place the terrines in a water bath high enough to bring the water halfway up the side of the mold.

Cook the terrines in a low oven- 170C (340F). The cooking time will depend on the size of the terrine. For the terrine pictured here for example, the cooking time is approximately 1 1/2 hours.

Checking the Cooking

To determine whether the terrine is cooked, a metal skewer can be inserted into the center of the terrine for a few seconds. The skewer should come out clean and feel hot to the touch.

The juices should be clear and not pink. The cooked terrine should also be firm to the touch.

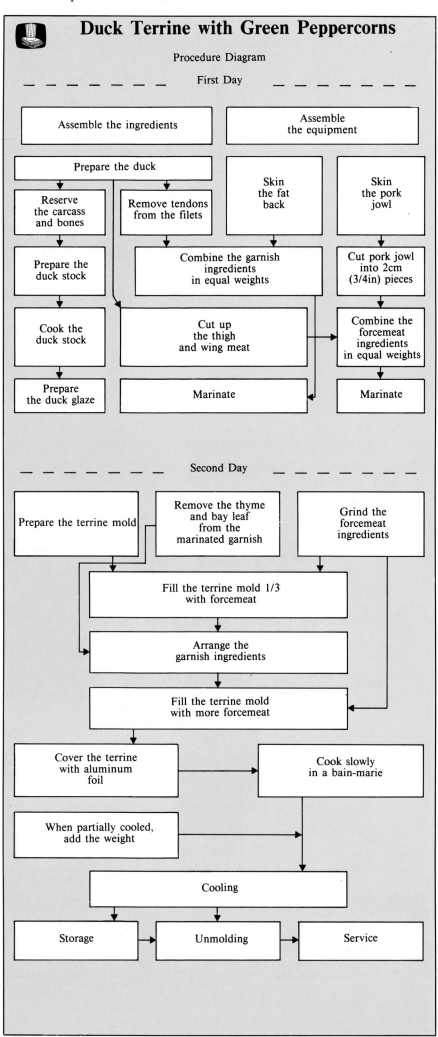

Duck Terrine with Green Peppercorns

Procedure Diagram

First Day

- Assemble the ingredients
- Assemble the equipment
- Prepare the duck
- Reserve the carcass and bones
- Remove tendons from the filets
- Skin the fat back
- Skin the pork jowl
- Combine the garnish ingredients in equal weights
- Cut pork jowl into 2cm (3/4in) pieces
- Prepare the duck stock
- Cook the duck stock
- Cut up the thigh and wing meat
- Combine the forcemeat ingredients in equal weights
- Prepare the duck glaze
- Marinate
- Marinate

Second Day

- Prepare the terrine mold
- Remove the thyme and bay leaf from the marinated garnish
- Grind the forcemeat ingredients
- Fill the terrine mold 1/3 with forcemeat
- Arrange the garnish ingredients
- Fill the terrine mold with more forcemeat
- Cover the terrine with aluminum foil
- Cook slowly in a bain-marie
- When partially cooled, add the weight
- Cooling
- Storage
- Unmolding
- Service

Cooling

Remove the cooked terrine from the water bath and place it on a cooling rack so that it cools quickly and evenly on all sides.

When it is no longer hot, but still warm, place a piece of cardboard or wood, cut to fit, on the terrine and place a weight on top. A weight of about 1kg (2lb) is used for the terrine pictured here.

Storage

After the terrine has completely cooled, it can be kept refrigerated at 4C (40F) for 8-15 days, covered with aluminum foil.

To keep the terrine longer, pour a thin layer of lard over the top to seal it completely. Cover with plastic wrap or foil and store at 4C (40F) for up to 2-3 months.

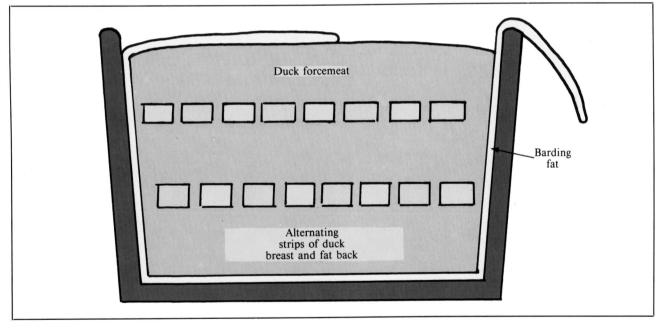

Duck forcemeat

Barding fat

Alternating
strips of duck
breast and fat back

Presentation

Small terrines are usually sold whole, then unmolded and sliced just before being served. Large terrines are often sliced in advance and sold by the portion.

Appropriate garnishes to serve with the sliced terrine are pickled onions, " cornichons " (small sour gherkins), or pickled sour cherries.

The flavor of this terrine goes very well with specialty breads made with nuts or olives.

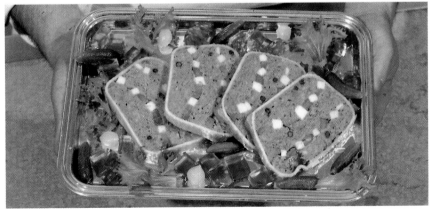

Terrine of Chicken Livers

Introduction

This is a delicious terrine that is not expensive to make and is as popular with customers as terrines that are more complex and expensive.

Made with ingredients that are available all year round, this classic terrine can be part of a menu in any season.

Pork caulfat is used to line the mold, which protects the terrine during cooking and keeps it moist. The caulfat also contributes a rustic note to the presentation.

The chicken livers that garnish this terrine are moist and add a lovely rosy color to each slice. The chicken livers should be very fresh, preferably purchased from a purveyor who specializes in poultry. The bacon is fresh, that is to say, not salted or smoked. Smoked bacon would be too strong and would overpower the delicate taste of the chicken livers. The combination of ingredients in this recipe is more perishable than many of the other terrines in this chapter.

Equipment

Cutting board, meat grinder, sauté pan, spatula, mixing bowls, hotel pans, terrine molds, paring knife, flexible thin-bladed knife, bain-marie, pastry scrapers, colander, platter, plate, tablespoon, scissors, skewer, palette knife

Ingredients

1.5kg (3lb 5oz) chicken livers
800g (1lb 14oz) pork jowl
300g (10oz) fresh bacon
3 eggs
1dl (1/2 cup) heavy cream
45g (1 1/2oz) onions
45g (1 1/2oz) shallots

20g (2/3oz) garlic
Thyme, bay leaf
Salt, saltpeter, sugar, pepper
Allspice
1dl (1/2 cup) cognac
1.5dl (2/3 cup) port
Pork caul fat

First Day's Work

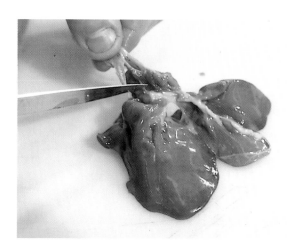

Preparing the Chicken Livers

Degorge the chicken livers by putting them in a bowl of cold water which will draw blood from the livers. Soak the livers about 1 hour, changing the water 2 or 3 times.

Drain the degorged livers in a strainer then dry them thoroughly on a hand towel.

Trim each liver, removing any yellow or green parts left from the bile sack, which will be bitter. With the tip of a paring knife, cut away all connective tissue as shown as well as the fine skin which may cover part of the liver.

Preparing the Pork Jowl

While the livers are soaking in cold water, trim the tough outer skin from the pork jowl. Cut the trimmed pork jowl in slices, then in small cubes (about 2cm (3/4in)). Set aside until ready to use.

Preparing the Fresh Bacon

Trim the tough outer skin from the fresh bacon. Cut in slices, then in small cubes about 1cm (3/8in).

Peel and cut the onion and shallot in very fine dice. Peel the garlic and cut in half to remove the green sprout which is bitter. Crush the garlic with the broad side of a chef's knife and chop it finely.

Cook the cubes of bacon in a pan over medium heat. The fat contained in the bacon will be enough to keep the cubes from sticking to the pan.

Preparing the Bacon, continued

When the bacon has browned a little, add the onion, shallot and garlic and continue cooking to

brown these vegetables and to cook the bacon thoroughly without drying it out.

Drain the excess fat from the bacon in the sieve and cool completely on a plate or in a hotel pan.

Marinating the Meats

The chicken livers are marinated in one bowl and the cubes of pork jowl and the cooked and cooled bacon in another.

The separate meats are seasoned with the same ingredients: salt, pepper, saltpeter, thyme (fresh or dried), bay leaf and allspice.

Sprinkle the port and cognac over each batch of meat and stir to incorporate evenly.

Cover each bowl with plastic wrap and leave to marinate in the

refrigerator for 6-8 hours.

Preparing the Forcemeat

Remove the branch of thyme (if used) and bay leaf from each marinade before grinding the meat.

Set aside about 1/5 of the chicken livers to use as a garnish in the terrine, choosing the best looking ones.

The remaining livers are passed through a meat grinder fitted with a fine disk.

The cubes of pork jowl and bacon are also ground finely. To do this, first pass the meat through a medium disk, then through the fine disk. (This will prevent it from

a smooth consistency.

Lastly, add the cream and stir until it is just incorporated. Poach

or pan-fry a spoonful of the forcemeat. Cool, taste and adjust seasoning if necessary.

overheating and melting when passed through the fine disk.)

The ground livers and pork are combined in a large bowl.

To bind the meat mixture, stir in the eggs one at a time, blending thoroughly after each egg to assure

Assembling the Terrines

The terrine molds should be perfectly clean and dry. Line the molds with a piece of caul fat large enough to eventually cover the top of the terrine as well. (If caul fat is not available, barding fat or strips of bacon could be substituted.)

The terrine is then filled with layers of forcemeat and chicken livers. For small terrines, you may choose to have just one layer of chicken livers in the center. For larger terrines like the one pictured here, it is recommended to use two

Trim the caul fat if necessary and fold it over the top to cover completely.

Sealing the Molds

There are two methods for sealing the molds.

If the mold does not have a cover, use a double thickness of

layers of chicken livers always finishing with forcemeat that is smoothed on the top with the back of a spoon.

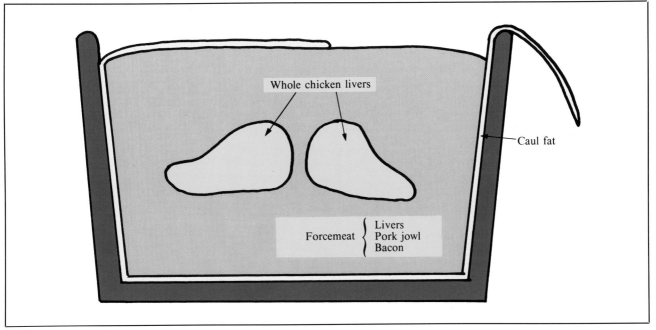

Whole chicken livers

Caul fat

Forcemeat { Livers
Pork jowl
Bacon

aluminum foil and press it firmly around the lip of the mold to hold it in place. Pierce the foil with the tip of a skewer to make air vents so that steam created by the terrine can escape during cooking.

To secure a lid on the mold, make a luting paste from flour and water and apply the mixture around the rim of the lid. The hole in the lid will serve as an air vent.

Cooking

Place the terrines in a water bath high enough to bring the water halfway up the side of the molds.

Cook the terrine in a low oven- 170C (340F). The cooking time

will depend on the size of the terrine. For the terrine pictured here for example, estimate 1 1/4 - 1 1/2 hours. For smaller terrines weighing about 400g (14oz), estimate 35 minutes.

Cooling

Remove the cooked terrine from the water bath and place it on a cooling rack so that it cools quickly and evenly on all sides.

When partially cooled, place cardboard or wood pieces, cut to fit, and then weights on top of the terrines--700-800g (about 1 1/2lb) for the large terrine pictured here.

Storage

After the terrine has completely cooled, the terrine can be kept refrigerated at 4C (40F) for 8-10 days.

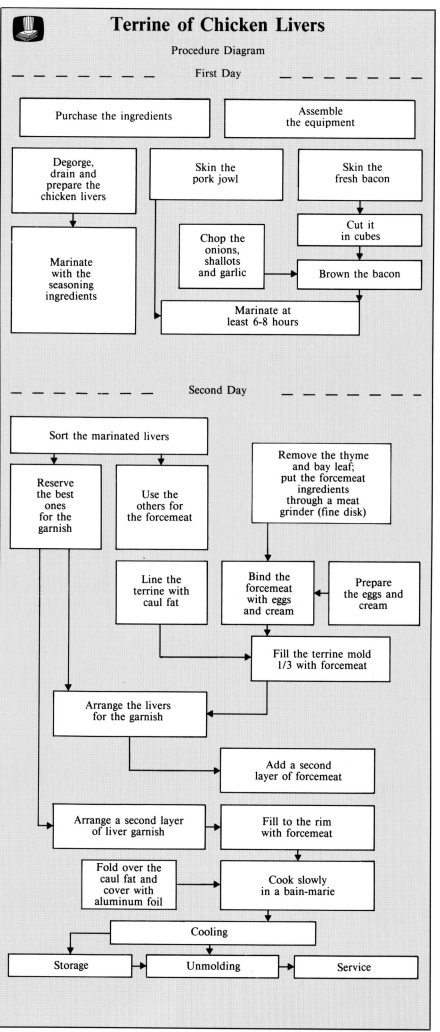

Terrine of Chicken Livers

Procedure Diagram

— — — First Day — — —

Purchase the ingredients

Assemble the equipment

Degorge, drain and prepare the chicken livers

Skin the pork jowl

Skin the fresh bacon

Cut it in cubes

Marinate with the seasoning ingredients

Chop the onions, shallots and garlic

Brown the bacon

Marinate at least 6-8 hours

— — — Second Day — — —

Sort the marinated livers

Reserve the best ones for the garnish

Use the others for the forcemeat

Remove the thyme and bay leaf; put the forcemeat ingredients through a meat grinder (fine disk)

Line the terrine with caul fat

Bind the forcemeat with eggs and cream

Prepare the eggs and cream

Fill the terrine mold 1/3 with forcemeat

Arrange the livers for the garnish

Add a second layer of forcemeat

Arrange a second layer of liver garnish

Fill to the rim with forcemeat

Fold over the caul fat and cover with aluminum foil

Cook slowly in a bain-marie

Cooling

Storage

Unmolding

Service

To keep the terrine longer, pour a thin layer of melted lard over the top to seal it completely.

Cover with plastic wrap or aluminum foil and store at 4C (40F) for up to one month.

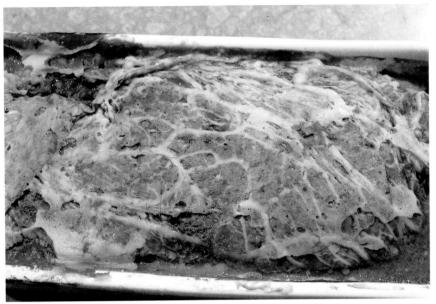

Presentation

Small terrines are usually sold whole, then unmolded and sliced just before being served. Large terrines are often sliced in advance and sold by the portion.

Appropriate garnishes to serve with the sliced terrine are pickled onions, " cornichons " (small sour gherkins), or pickled sour cherries.

The flavor of this terrine goes very well with specialty breads made with nuts or olives.

Terrine of Hare

Introduction

This distinctive terrine can be made only during hunting season when fresh hare is available. Choose a medium-sized meaty hare that has not been damaged by the hunt. The pronounced flavor of this terrine is appreciated by those customers who enjoy the taste of wild game.

Like other terrines in this chapter, the preparation takes two days. First the hare is boned and marinated along with the other forcemeat ingredients. The second day, the meat is ground and mixed with eggs, then the terrine is assembled and cooked.

Equipment

Cutting board, knife, cleaver, sharpening steel, meat grinder, mixing bowls, saucepans, terrine molds, bain-marie, ladle, skimmer, spoon, colander, conical sieve, roasting pan, measuring cup, spatula

Ingredients

1 medium hare--this recipe uses a cleaned hare weighing 2.25kg (5lb), which yields: 750g (1 1/2lb) carcass, 100g (3 1/2oz) tendons, 1.4kg (3lb) meat, 1.4kg (3lb) pork jowl, 400g (14oz) goose liver purée, 3 eggs, 2dl (3/4 cup) white wine, 1.5dl (1/2 cup) cognac.

Seasoning for the Marinades

Salt, pepper, saltpeter, allspice, thyme, bay leaf, 7cl (1/4 cup) cognac, 1.5dl (1/2 cup) and 2dl (3/4 cup) dry white wine, 2 shallots, 2 cloves garlic

For the Stock

1 carrot, 2 shallots, 2 garlic cloves, 2 leeks, 1 bouquet garni (thyme, bay leaf, parsley, leek green), 5cl (1/4 cup) oil or 30g (1oz) clarified butter, 1/4L (1 cup) red wine, 1.5L (6 cups) reduced stock, few coriander seeds, few black peppercorns, pinch of salt, 45g (1 1/2 oz) butter, 5cl (1/4 cup) white wine

First Day's Work

Preparing the Meats

Boning the Hare

Lay the hare back side up on a cutting board with its four legs spread flat.

Using a very sharp paring knife, make an incision the length of the

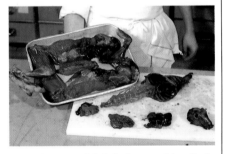

back bone, which is located by feeling with your fingers.

Scrape the meat away from the back bone and from around the rib cage, taking care not to cut into the filet too much.

At the top of the back bone, locate the shoulder joint and twist then cut through the tendons to detach the front leg. Detach the hind leg in the same way.

Repeat the process for the other side of the hare. This will yield the

carcass and two halves, each containing a front leg, the filet and the hind leg.

With a paring knife, cut the filets away from the hare, taking care not to damage them.

Using a well-sharpened paring knife, carefully remove any tendons from the filets, as well as any silver skin and damaged flesh.

Weigh the filets and set them aside in a shallow dish until ready to marinate.

With the blade angled against the bone, scrape away the meat, trying not to cut it too much, which would make it difficult to extract the tendons.

Remove the tendons from each piece; remove any large veins, damaged flesh and/or buck shot.

Cut the trimmed meats into chunks that will fit easily into the meat grinder.

Preparing the Pork Jowl

Remove the tough skin from the pork jowl. Weigh the meat from the hare that will be used for the forcemeat, and weigh out the same amount of pork jowl.

The pork jowl is selected because the proportion of lean to fat is just right for forcemeat.

Cut the pork jowl into cubes the same size as the meat from the hare and mix all of this meat together in a bowl to be marinated.

Marinating the Forcemeat Ingredients

Peel the shallots and garlic. Cut the shallots into very fine dice. Remove the green sprout from the garlic and chop the garlic finely. Cook them in clarified butter until soft but not brown. Deglaze with the white wine and set aside to cool completely.

Season the meats with salt, pepper, saltpeter, allspice, thyme (fresh or dried) and bay leaf. Add white wine and stir all of the ingredients together.

Cover the bowl with plastic wrap and marinate in the refrigerator for about 12 hours.

Marinating the Garnish Ingredients

Weigh the filets of hare and weigh out the same weight of fat

back. Cut the filets and fat back into thin strips (about 1cm (3/8in) on each side) and place the strips in a non-reactive dish.

Season the strips with salt, pepper, allspice, saltpeter, thyme (fresh or dried) and bay leaf. Stir in the

cognac and the white wine. Cover the dish with plastic wrap and marinate in the refrigerator for about 12 hours.

Making the Hare Stock

Begin by preparing the aromatic vegetables.

Peel the carrot and onion and cut them into medium dice.

Peel the garlic and cut in half to remove the green sprout.

Remove the green leaves of the leek and use one of them to make a bouquet garni with a branch of fresh thyme, 2 bay leaves and some

parsley stems all tied together in kitchen twine.

Rinse the white part of the leek to remove the sand between the leaves and cut into pieces.

To make the stock, cut the hare carcass into pieces with a cleaver and put the bones with the clarified butter and oil in a large pot. Brown the bones over high heat, stirring with a wooden spatula to brown them evenly.

When the bones are browned, add the prepared vegetables and the full-bodied red wine. Reduce until the liquid is thick and syrupy. Add 1.5L (6 cups) of veal stock and the bouquet garni, a few peppercorns and few coriander seeds.

Simmer the stock for 1 1/2-2 hours.

Remove the bouquet garni and pass the stock through a conical sieve, pressing on the bones with a ladle to extract the flavor from them.

Reduce the stock by 3/4 to make

a thick glaze. Set aside to cool completely.

Second Day's Work

Making the Forcemeat

Remove the fresh thyme (if used) and bay leaf from the marinade.

Pass the cubes of hare and pork jowl through a meat grinder fitted with a medium disk and put the ground meat in a large bowl.

Add the eggs and goose liver purée, white wine and cognac. Melt the meat glaze so it is liquid but still cool and blend this into the forcemeat mixture. Stir the ingredients thoroughly with a wooden spatula to achieve a smooth texture. Poach or pan-fry a spoonful of the forcement; cool, taste and adjust seasoning if necessary.

Preparing the Garnish

Remove the strips of filet and fat back from the marinade and drain them in a strainer; set aside.

Assembling the Terrines

It is recommended to use earthenware molds in whatever shape and size to suit the occasion. The number of layers will differ depending on the size of the mold. For the large mold pictured here, there are four layers of forcemeat alternated with three layers of garnish.

Begin the assembly by filling the bottom of the mold with forcemeat and smoothing out the layer with the back of a spoon. Arrange alternating strips of filet and fat back down the length of the forcemeat, leaving a little space between them, as shown.

Spread another layer of forcemeat over the strips. Place the next layer of strips reversing the arrangement of filet and fat back so that each slice of terrine has an attractive checkerboard design.

Continue layering the forcemeat and garnish, finishing with forcemeat on the top. The large terrine pictured here (23cm x 13cm x 8cm (9in x 5in x 3in)) holds about 1.5kg (3lb 5oz) forcemeat arranged in 4 layers with 3 layers of garnish.

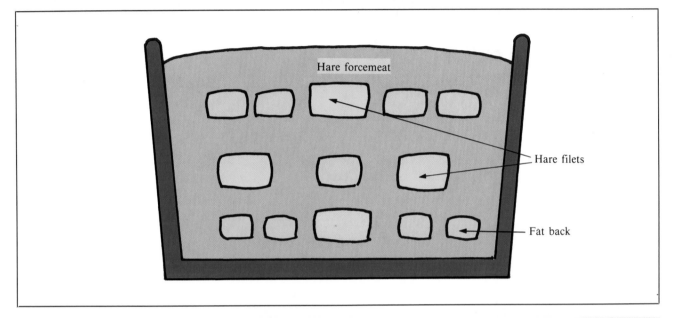

Hare forcemeat

Hare filets

Fat back

Sealing the Molds

Place a double layer of aluminum foil on top of the mold and press it firmly around the lip to keep it in place. Pierce the foil with a skewer to make air vents so that the steam created by the terrine during cooking can escape.

Cooking

Place the sealed terrines in a water bath high enough to cover the molds halfway.

Cook the terrines in a low oven 170C (340F). The cooking time will vary depending on the size of the terrine. For the large mold which holds 1.5kg (3lb 5oz) forcemeat, count on about 1 1/2 hours. For smaller molds holding 400g (14oz), count on about 30 minutes.

Checking the Cooking

The doneness of the terrine can be verified by checking the temperature in the center of the terrine.

Insert a metal skewer into the center and leave it for 10-20 seconds. The skewer should come out clean and hot to the touch along the full length of the skewer (about 70C (170F)). To judge this, touch the skewer to your lip or check on the top of your hand.

The fat and juices around the edge of the terrine should be clear and the texture should be firm and "spongy".

Cooling

Remove the cooked terrine from the water bath and place it on a cooling rack so that it cools quickly and evenly on all sides.

When it is no longer hot, but still warm, place a piece of cardboard or wood, cut to fit, on the terrine and place a weight on top. A weight of about 1kg (2lb) is used for the terrine pictured here.

Storage

After the terrine has completely cooled, it can be kept refrigerated at 4C (40F) for 8-15 days, covered with aluminum foil.

To keep the terrine longer, pour a thin layer of lard over the top to seal it completely. Cover with plastic wrap or foil and store at 4C (40F) for 2-3 months.

Presentation

Small terrines are usually sold whole, then unmolded and sliced just before being served. Large terrines are often sliced in advance and sold by the portion.

Appropriate garnishes to serve with the sliced terrine are pickled onions, "cornichons" (small sour gherkins), or pickled sour cherries.

The flavor of this terrine goes very well with specialty breads made with nuts or olives.

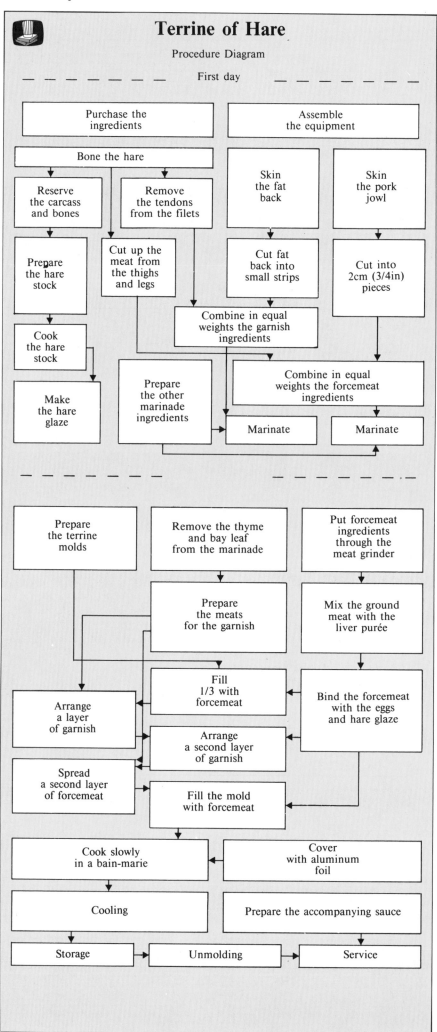

Terrine of Hare

Procedure Diagram

First day

Goose Rillettes

Introduction

Rillettes are generally made from pork, using a mixture of fat and lean. A combination of pork with rabbit, duck or goose also makes delicious rillettes.

The meat is cut into small pieces and cooked slowly in lard or goose fat with white wine and a little stock. They are cooked in the oven for 3-4 hours, then cooled slightly before the meat is flaked apart and mixed with the fat to create a spreadable mixture.

The rillettes will keep quite a long time due to the long slow cooking process. They are not difficult to make and only one day is needed to complete the preparation. In addition, the food cost is relatively low.

In France, it is becoming more difficult to find properly made rillettes with the rich flavor that comes from good quality ingredients and proper cooking.

Mass produced rillettes are found everywhere. Some of these products are quite good, such as the rillettes from the cities of Tours and Le Mans, which are well known for their high quality.

Ingredients

A goose weighing 4.1 kg (9lb) yields:
1.75 kg (3 3/4 lb) boneless, skinless meat
1.1 kg (2 1/2lb) carcass
450g (1lb) fat
550g (about 1lb) skin
300g (10oz) organ meats

Set aside the organ meats for another use and the carcass for use in making the stock.

400g (14oz) canned goose fat
1kg (2lb) pork filet
3 shallots (100g (3 1/2oz))
1 onion (100g (3 1/2oz))
3 garlic cloves (30g (1oz))
Thyme, bay leaf, 2 cloves
Salt, pepper, allspice
3dl (1 1/4 cup) dry white wine
3dl (1 1/4 cup) chicken stock
2dl (3/4 cup) water

Equipment

Cutting board, roasting pan, cheesecloth, kitchen twine, pastry scraper, large heavy pot, lid, sharpening steel, chef's knife, paring knife, thin-bladed flexible knife, cleaver, spoon, fork, measuring cup, mixing bowls, conical sieve, spatulas, skimmer, small ladle, plates, terrine molds

Preparing the Pork Filet

The filet of pork is a good choice for rillettes because it is a tender cut of meat with very few tendons and it flakes apart easily when cooked for a long time. The slightly chewy texture of the filet is appropriate for rillettes, which should maintain some body when cooked.

Trim the skin and tendons from the filet with a paring knife.

The trimmed filet is then easily cut into slices which are then cut into strips. Finally, cut these strips into small cubes (about 1cm

(3/8in)) and set aside in the refrigerator until ready to use.

Preparing the Seasoning

The herbs, spices and aromatic vegetables used to season the rillettes are prepared then tied in

cheesecloth. This cheesecloth "bundle" is easy to remove at the end of cooking and can be squeezed to release all the juices that were absorbed during cooking.

Peel the onions, shallots and garlic. Cut the onions and shallot in medium dice. Cut the garlic in half and remove the green sprout which

tends to be bitter and hard to digest. Crush the garlic with the side of a chef's knife.

Put these prepared vegetables in a piece of cheesecloth with thyme, bay leaf and cloves and tie up the bundle securely with kitchen twine.

Measure the salt, pepper and allspice which is added directly to the rillettes.

White wine and chicken stock are also added for flavor and can be measured out at this time.

Preparing the Goose

Cut off the feet and discard.
Make an incision on the underside of the neck, pull the skin away from the neck. Cut off the head

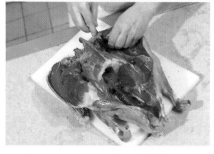

and discard; cut off the neck and reserve.
Make an incision beneath the

parson's nose. Spread open the skin and remove the lump of fat (the goose is a very fatty animal).

Reach inside the body and pull out the innards (heart, gizzard and liver).

Remove the fat that surrounds these organs and set aside for use in the rillettes.

Sort the organs, carefully remove and discard the bile sack, cut open the gizzard and empty it. Set the

heart and liver aside for another use.

Boning the Goose

With a paring knife, cut along the v-shaped wishbone. Scrape the meat and pull out the bone. This will make it easier to remove the breast meat without damaging it.

Follow the techniques outlined in the recipe for Duck Terrine with Green Peppercorns in this chapter.

With a ladle, press on the skin to extract the maximum amount of fat. The cooked pieces of skin that remain can be reserved for use in salads.

Locate the breastbone with your fingers, then cut along the length of the bone.

Keeping the blade of the knife angled toward the bone, cut the breast meat away. Trim tendons and silver skin.

Remove the legs and wings and bone them, trimming all tendons as you proceed.

Scrape as much meat as possible off the carcass. Reserve the bones and tendons to make stock.

Separate the skin from the breast meat then cut into 1cm (3/8in) pieces.

Rendering the Goose Fat

Cut the skin in small pieces. Use a pot that will fit in the oven and is heavy enough to ensure even cooking.

Put the pieces of skin in this heavy pot and cook over low heat for 6-8 minutes, stirring frequently, to melt the fat in the skin.

Be careful to maintain a low heat as the fat may become bitter if it gets too hot.

Add the water to the pot and cover. Continue to cook the skin over a low heat or in a low oven for about 5-10 minutes. The water will evaporate during this stage.

Remove the bits of skin that remain with a slotted spoon, put them in a conical sieve and drain the fat into the pot.

Into this rendered fat, put the pieces of fat that were trimmed from the goose during the boning process.

Melt the fat over low heat, stirring occasionally. Using a slotted spoon, strain out any bits of meat that may have been attached to the fat and drain them in a conical sieve held over the pot.

Add the canned goose fat to the rendered fat and heat to gently melt it.

Cooking

Into the pot containing the fat, put the small cubes of pork and goose and cook them over low heat for about 10 minutes. (Note: if the fat is too hot, it will dry out the meat).

Add the cheesecloth bundle of seasoning, pushing it down into the meat so that the vegetables cook and release their flavor.

Next, pour in the white wine and slowly bring the ingredients to a simmer for 1-2 minutes to evaporate some of the acidity of the wine.

Add the chicken stock and bring back to a simmer so that the mixture is hot when it goes into the oven to finish cooking.

Season with a little salt, pepper and allspice, taking into account that the cooking will concentrate the flavors.

It is preferable to underseason slightly at this stage and adjust the seasonings during cooking.

Cooking the Rillettes in the Oven

Put a tight fitting lid on the pot and continue to cook the rillettes in a low oven (160 (325F)) for about 3 hours so that they cook slowly and evenly.

Check the rillettes from time to time, stirring them about every half hour. If the liquid is evaporating too quickly, which is rarely the case, add a little more stock.

Cooling the Rillettes

Put the pot of cooked rillettes on a cooling rack to cool quickly and evenly.

Taste the rillettes and adjust the seasonings if necessary.

Flake apart the pork and goose using two forks, as shown.

You can also use your fingers to break up the meat into strands.

Taste the flaked meat and season if necessary.

Remove the cheesecloth bundle of seasoning and press on it to extract the maximum amount of flavor and fat.

Molding the Rillettes

Spoon the rillettes into ramequins or larger molds, taking care to pack them firmly so that there are no air pockets. Smooth the top with the back of a fork or spoon.

Chilling the Rillettes

It is recommended to chill the rillettes for at least one day before serving.

Before placing them in the refrigerator, cover them with plastic wrap or wax paper to protect the surface from drying out and becoming discolored.

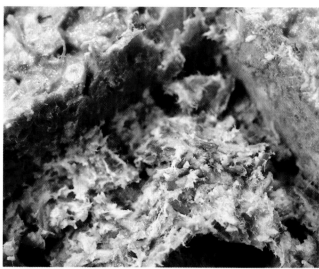

Storage

For a maximum shelf-life of 15-30 days, pour melted lard or rendered goose fat over the top, making sure it completely covers the surface to create an airtight seal when it chills and hardens.

Presentation

The rillettes can be unmolded onto a plate or platter or served directly from the mold.

In a specialty food store they can be sold in slices cut from a large "terrine" of rillettes. In this case, it is important to keep the cut surface covered with plastic wrap.

In a restaurant, the rillettes can be spread on slices of crusty bread and served "open face" or served in a ramequin with toasted bread on the side. For a buffet, rillettes can be used to make canapés or molded into a decorative shape (a pig or goose would be appropriate) and served with small toasts.

Rillettes are traditionally served with "cornichons", small sour gherkins.

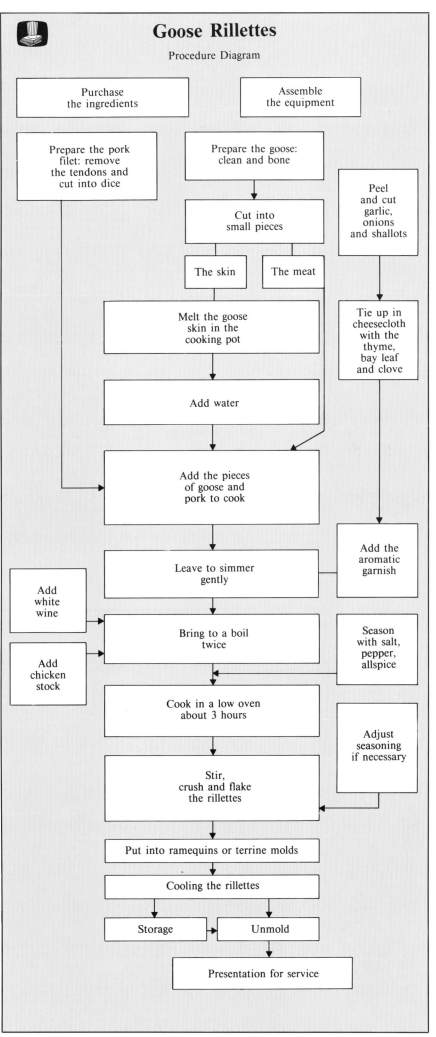

Goose Rillettes
Procedure Diagram

Purchase the ingredients

Assemble the equipment

Prepare the pork filet: remove the tendons and cut into dice

Prepare the goose: clean and bone

Peel and cut garlic, onions and shallots

Cut into small pieces

The skin

The meat

Melt the goose skin in the cooking pot

Tie up in cheesecloth with the thyme, bay leaf and clove

Add water

Add the pieces of goose and pork to cook

Leave to simmer gently

Add the aromatic garnish

Add white wine

Bring to a boil twice

Season with salt, pepper, allspice

Add chicken stock

Cook in a low oven about 3 hours

Adjust seasoning if necessary

Stir, crush and flake the rillettes

Put into ramequins or terrine molds

Cooling the rillettes

Storage

Unmold

Presentation for service

Terrine of Foie Gras

Introduction

This terrine is considered to be one of the most delicate in flavor and texture.

Foie gras refers to the fattened liver of a force-fed duck or goose. The velvety texture of the enlarged liver is highlighted in simple terrines like the one here and also enters into the preparation of many other luxurious dishes. The legs of the force-fed duck or goose are most often used to make "confit", while the meaty breast is sold separately and can be cooked much like beef and is delicious when eaten medium rare.

Different Preparations

Preparing foie gras intimidates many people. However, if you work methodically and take the proper precautions with this perishable ingredient, the techniques are not difficult.

Top quality livers should be left whole if possible as the liver retains more of its fat if not cut into pieces or puréed and therefore the texture is superior.

There are several ways to prepare the whole foie gras. Marinated, seasoned and baked in an earthenware mold is the method shown here. It is important to choose an appropriate wine for the marinade (madeira, port, armagnac, cognac or sauternes or sherry) and to use just enough to augment the dish without adding too much alcohol, which can ruin the taste of the foie gras. The whole liver can also be wrapped snugly in cheesecloth and poached in wine.

Choosing a Top Quality Foie Gras

Foie gras of lesser quality can be cut in pieces and used in other meat terrines where it adds richness and makes a design in each slice.

In France, top quality foie gras is produced in the regions of Gers, Landes, Perigord and Alsace. France also imports fattened livers from Poland, Czechoslovakia, Hungary and Israel to meet the large demand for this luxury.

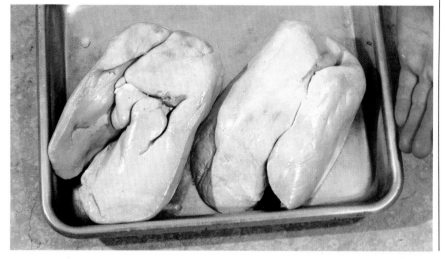

In France, the average weight of a fattened duck liver is between 600-800g (1lb 3oz-1lb 10oz), while goose livers are larger, usually between 800g-1kg (1lb 10oz-2lb) or more.

Raw foie gras has recently become available in the United States. The livers, from ducks only, are produced in New York and California at present and although usually smaller than the foie gras pictured here, are certainly appropriate for this terrine. It is recommended to choose the best grade that is available.

Choosing a foie gras is difficult as they are often kept in ice to keep them fresh. When they are very cold, they are always very firm to the touch due to the amount of fat in them that hardens at low temperatures. Foie gras that are slightly soft to the touch when cold but not icy will usually render less fat when cooked. A good liver should appear supple and perfectly smooth. Livers that are very large are often too "fatty".

The color can range from very creamy white to rosy pink and does not always indicate the quality. Lighter colored livers are usually a better choice. In any case, the liver should not be discolored in any way.

Which is better, duck or goose liver? This is a difficult choice because there are advantages and disadvantages to both. Duck liver is considered to be more flavorful but tends to be harder to work with and renders more of its fat during cooking. Goose liver has a smoother, creamier texture as well as a lighter more delicate color.

Equipment

Hotel pan, mixing bowls, cutting board, hand towels, paring knife, thin-bladed knife, palette knife, plate, non-reactive platter, drum sieve, pastry scraper, plastic wrap, aluminum foil, water bath, weight, terrine mold

Ingredients

For seasoning 1kg foie gras:

12g (about 2tsp) salt
3-4g sugar (about 3/4tsp), to counter the bitterness of some livers
1 pinch mace
1 pinch saltpeter
1 pinch allspice
Ground pepper

For the Marinade

The amount of wine used for the marinade will vary between 2-5cl (4tsp-4 tbsp) per kilogram (2lb) of foie gras according to the strength of the wine.

For example, 2-3cl (4tsp-6tsp) of cognac would be appropriate and if using sauternes or light port, add 3-4cl (6-8tsp).

First Day's Work

Preparing the Foie Gras

Degorge the livers in room-temperature water for about 2 hours, changing the water from time to time.

The degorging process in this case is done with water at room temperature to soften the livers

which are difficult to work with if they are too cold and stiff.

Drain the degorged livers on a hand towel.

Trimming the Foie Gras

It is important to work on a very clean surface. A clean hand towel is

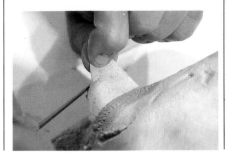

recommended as the livers tend to be slippery.

If the hand towel becomes soiled from fat melting out of the foie gras, replace it with a clean one.

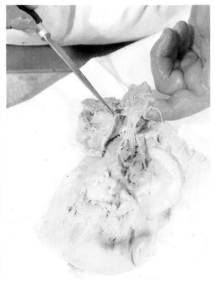

Separate the two lobes of the liver. With the help of a paring knife, delicately remove the thin skin that envelops each lobe.

Remove any bits of fat and connective tissue on the outside of the lobes. Cut away any part of the liver that is stained yellow or green from being in contact with the bile sack and discard, as this part tends to have a bitter taste.

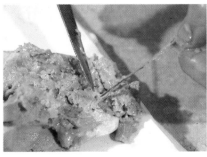

Make an incision in the center of the flat side of the lobe. Open this incision with your finger to expose the blood vessels that run through the middle of each lobe.

Using the point of the paring knife and your finger, dislodge these veins and remove them. Reserve the trimmings.

Work as carefully as possible because if the liver is too broken up at this stage, it will lose more of its fat during cooking.

Take the reserved trimmings and put them in a drum sieve.

With a plastic scraper, push the foie gras that is adhered to the veins through the sieve.

This sieved purée of foie gras can be used to augment the flavor of a filet of beef baked in pastry or to bind a sauce " Perigueux ".

The purée can also be used in place of the canned liver purée called for in other terrine recipes in this chapter.

The lobes of foie gras that are now thoroughly trimmed of blood vessels and skin are put in a dish to marinate.

Marinating the Foie Gras

Choose a glass, earthenware or other non-reactive dish that is large enough to accommodate all of the lobes in a single layer.

Sprinkle the bottom of this dish with half of the seasonings and half of the wine you are using for the marinade.

With the lobes of foie gras still opened from trimming them, lay them cut side up in the dish.

Sprinkle the rest of the seasonings and wine evenly over the interior of the lobes.

Gently close up the lobes and cover the dish with plastic wrap.

Put the seasoned livers into the refrigerator to marinate for 18-24 hours, turning them over every 4 hours or so to distribute the marinade evenly.

During this time, the livers will absorb the marinating liquid.

Second Day's Work

Note: It is recommended to take the marinated livers out of the refrigerator 1-2 hours before assembling the terrines so the livers will have a chance to soften slightly, which will keep them from cracking when pressing them into the mold.

Assembling the Terrines

As was stated earlier, the lobes that are more intact after trimming lose less of their fat during cooking. Therefore place the nicest looking lobes on the bottom of the mold which is usually hotter during cooking, so this step minimizes the loss of fat.

Press gently on this first layer of livers to fill the corners. Place the remaining livers in the terrine, matching the shapes of the lobes like puzzle pieces to fill the terrine evenly. Press gently to compact the foie gras.

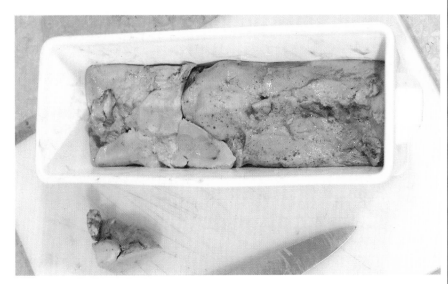

To protect the terrine during cooking, pierce three holes in a sheet of aluminum foil and cover

the mold with it, or replace the lid of the mold.

Cooking

The cooking of the terrine of foie gras is very delicate and demands attention. The terrine can be baked in a steamer or a low oven. In either case, it is very important that the mold is set in a bain-marie to ensure even cooking. The water in the bain-marie should be hot but not boiling.

The terrine here, weighing about 1.5kg (3lb 5oz), is cooked for 25 minutes in a convection oven that has been preheated to 200C (375F) and then turned off. If the terrine is cooked in a regular oven or steamer set the temperature at 70C (158F) and cook for 40-45 minutes.

Checking the Cooking

The " doneness " of the terrine is a matter of choice. If it cooks a little longer, it will lose more of its fat which collects on the top, leaving less "meaty" portions to sell. It is, however, less perishable. If it is slightly "underdone", it is more rosy and creamy but does not keep as long.

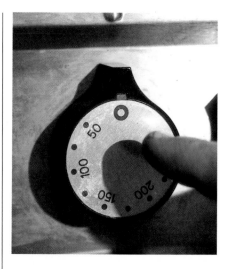

Cooling

Remove the terrine from the bain-marie and set on a cooling rack to cool quickly and evenly.

When the terrine is still warm, weigh it down to compact it. Do this by placing a board on top to distribute the weight evenly and use about a 500g (1lb) weight for a terrine like the one shown here.

When the fat begins to harden slightly, remove the weights, cover the terrine with plastic wrap or aluminum foil and refrigerate for 2-3 days so the flavors mellow.

Storage

For best results, keep the terrine in the mold covered with aluminum foil until ready to serve.

Protected from the air like this, it will keep in the refrigerator for 8-10 days.

To prolong shelf life, pour cool liquid goose or duck fat over the top, filling all the gaps around the sides and covering the entire surface to seal the terrine completely.

Sealed with fat and covered with plastic wrap or aluminum foil, the foie gras terrine will keep for 2-3 weeks in the refrigerator at 4C (40F).

Unmolding and Slicing

To unmold the terrine, set the mold in a basin of warm water for a few seconds, run a knife carefully around the edge, then turn the terrine out onto a cutting board.

To achieve smooth neat slices, use a thin-bladed knife and dip it in hot water before cutting each slice.

Presentation

For sale in a specialty food shop, keep the terrine in the mold. Keep the cut end covered with plastic wrap.

175

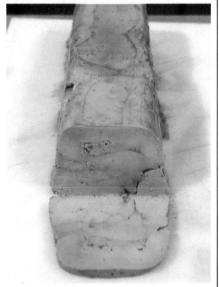

Terrine of Foie Gras

Procedure Diagram

— — — — — First day — — — — —

Degorge the livers in room temperature water (2 hrs)

Prepare the marinade ingredients

Drain the livers → Remove the nerves

Prepare the mold for marinade

Put the trimmings through a drum sieve and reserve the resulting liver purée ← Remove the skin and veins → Combine and reshape the lobes

Add half the wines

Place the lobes in the marinade dish

Season the top of the lobes

Add the rest of the wines

Leave to marinate for 24 hours, turning 3 or 4 times

— — — — — Second day — — — — —

Take the livers from the refrigerator 1-2 hours before assembling the terrine

Prepare the terrine molds

Fill the terrine molds with the livers

Cover the terrines with aluminum foil

Cook in a bain-marie ← Check the cooking

When partially cool, set a weight on top → After cooling, put in refrigerator to chill → Unmolding / Presentation

Carefully slice portions to order using a thin-bladed knife dipped in hot water.

In a restaurant, it is most appropriate to serve a single slice adorned with just a little chopped aspic with toasted brioche on the side.

As well, the terrine can be used to make elegant canapés for a stand-up buffet.

General Advice on Fish Terrines

Introduction

These elegant terrines fit right in to the new style of eating "light". They are all made with a delicate fish mousse layered with an interesting assortment of garnishes that add color and taste to each slice.

A different fish is used for the mousse in each recipe for a subtle variety of textures and flavors.

Each terrine is assembled differently as well. The mousse is used to "frame" the garnishes by applying it on the bottom and sides of the mold first. Crêpes line the mold in another original presentation.

Even though the terrines in this chapter are made in the classic rectangular mold, other shapes can be used, most notably a ring mold, often used to make a "turban" of sole.

Cooking

These terrines must be cooked in a bain-marie in a low oven (160-180C (325-350F)) sealed with aluminum foil, brushed with butter to keep them from drying out.

The cooking of the terrine must be monitored carefully. A thermometer inserted into the center of the cooked terrine should read 70-75C (158-167F).

In most cases, it is recommended to apply a light weight to the top of the terrines while they are cooling in the refrigerator to compact the mixture a little and to assure easy slicing and an attractive presentation.

To unmold the terrine, set the mold in warm water for a few seconds, run a knife carefully around the edge, then turn out onto a cutting board or platter.

Storage

These terrines will keep for about a week if stored in the refrigerator at 4C (40F) in their mold and covered securely with plastic wrap.

Once unmolded, the terrine will stay fresh for only two days or so in the refrigerator, and individual slices will keep just one day.

Presentation

For a buffet, these terrines are simply sliced and arranged neatly on platters, dressed perhaps with chopped aspic or a few greens.

A slice of any of these terrines makes a lovely first course or light main course in a restaurant.

They are equally successful in specialty food shops where they can be sold by the slice or by weight. To further enhance the taste and presentation, serve these terrines with an appropriate sauce.

Terrine of Pike with Asparagus Tips

Introduction

This delicate terrine is made with a very light mousse of pike, some of which is flavored with a puree of spinach and herbs to add color and taste.

A subtle garnish of asparagus and filet of sole complete the composition.

An " Andalouse " sauce makes a perfect accompaniment to this terrine.

Molds of different sizes and shapes can be used. For this recipe, a medium-size rectangular mold is used which will yield 18-20 slices.

Equipment

Food processor, pastry scraper,

terrine mold, cutting board, aluminum foil, spatula, knives, palette knife, bain-marie, measuring cup, pastry brush, mixing bowls, drum sieve, fish shears

Ingredients

600g (1lb 3oz) pike filet (about 1.5kg (3lb 5oz) whole pike)
6 egg whites and 4 whole eggs
250g (8oz) heavy cream
250g (8oz) softened, creamed butter
10g (1/3oz) clarified butter
100g (3 1/2oz) spinach
1 tsp each chopped chives and chervil
1/2 tsp chopped tarragon
6 filets of sole (from soles weighing about 600g (1lb 3oz))
1/2 lemon
10cl (1/2 cup) Ricard or other anise-flavored liqueur
Approximately 24 asparagus tips
Salt, cayenne pepper, sprig of thyme, bay leaf
For assembly:
3 egg whites, powdered gelatin

Preparing the Garnish

The Sole

Season the filets of sole with salt and pepper, place them in a dish or hotel pan with lemon, thyme and bay leaf to marinate for 30 minutes in the refrigerator, turning them after 15 minutes.

The Spinach

Preparing the Pike

If using whole pike, remove the filets and skin them as shown. Dry them on a hand towel. The filets should be very cold before making the mousse.

Fifteen to thirty minutes in the freezer is recommended to chill them thoroughly.

The bowl of the food processor, which will be used to make the mousse, should be very cold as well.

Remove the stems of the spinach, wash thoroughly, then sauté the leaves in the clarified butter. Squeeze the cooked spinach to remove excess liquid, chop finely and chill.

The Herbs

Sort and trim the herbs. Chop the chervil and tarragon finely. Cut the chives neatly in very fine dice. Set aside in the refrigerator.

Making the Pike Mousse

Cut the filets of chilled pike into large pieces, put them in the bowl of the food processor and grind them into a purée.

Whisk the egg whites and whole eggs together and add them through the feed tube in a steady stream and process until blended and the mixture is a bit elastic. Add the heavy cream and process just enough to incorporate.

Remove the mousse from the processor and pass it through a drum sieve, using a plastic scraper, to remove any bones, scales or connective tissue.

Scoop the sieved purée into a bowl set in a larger bowl filled with ice. Stir the mousse gently to lighten and make it smooth and firm.

Poach or pan-fry a spoonful of the mousse; cool, taste and adjust seasoning if necessary.

Mix one third of the mousse with the prepared spinach and herbs. Set aside the remaining 2/3 to line the inside of the mold.

Assembling the Terrine

Butter the mold evenly with a pastry brush and put in the freezer for a few minutes. Line the chilled mold with a thin layer of mousse as shown, reserving enough to cover the top. Smooth the surface with a brush or palette knife dipped in egg white. Sprinkle a little powdered gelatin over the surface. Add half of the flavored mousse in an even layer on the bottom of the mold. Smooth the surface with egg white and sprinkle with a little gelatin. Arrange half of the sole filets, brush with egg white and sprinkle with a little gelatin.

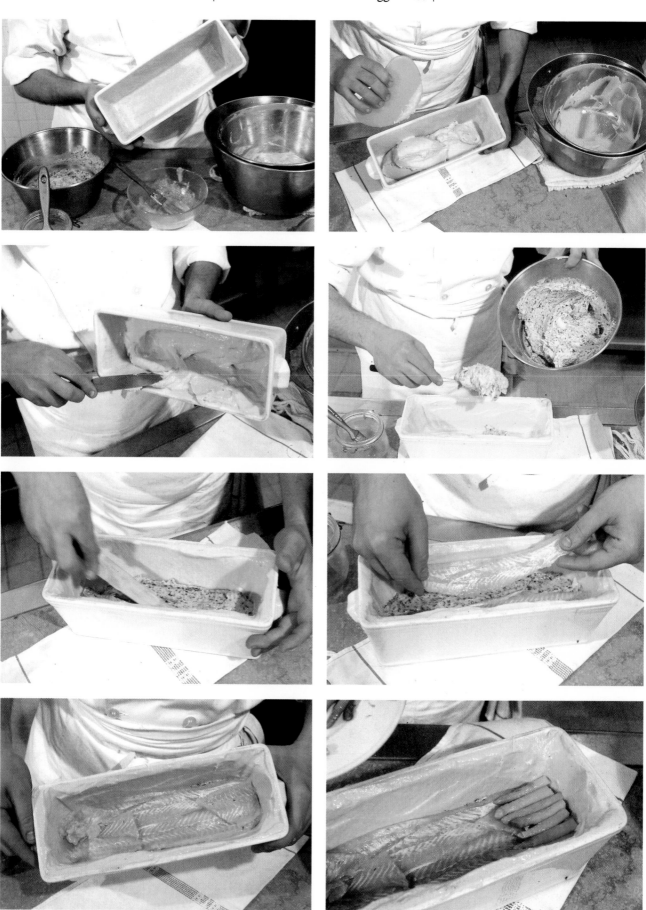

Arrange a neat layer of asparagus tips, brush with egg white and sprinkle with gelatin, then arrange the rest of the sole filets on top. Once again brush with egg white and sprinkle with a little gelatin.

Fill the mold almost to the top with the rest of the flavored mousse. Smooth the surface by brushing with egg whites and sprinkle with gelatin.

Finish the terrine with an even layer of the plain mousse on the top.

The egg white and gelatin between each layer help to hold the terrine together to ensure easy slicing and a neat presentation.

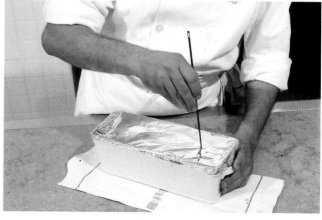

Cooking

Cover the assembled terrine with buttered aluminum foil, attaching it firmly around the rim. Pierce three holes in the top so steam can escape during cooking.

Place the terrine in a water bath and bring to a simmer on top of the stove. Cook the terrine in the oven at 160C (325F).

The one pictured here requires about 1 hour and 15 minutes to cook. The temperature at the center of the cooked terrine should read 70C (158F).

Remove the cooked terrine from the bain-marie and place it on a cooling rack. While still warm, but no longer hot, place a weight on the terrine as shown.

Storage

Left in the mold and covered with plastic wrap, the terrine will keep about a week in the refrigerator at 4C (40F).

If unmolded for sale in the refrigerator case of a specialty food shop, the terrine will stay fresh about two days.

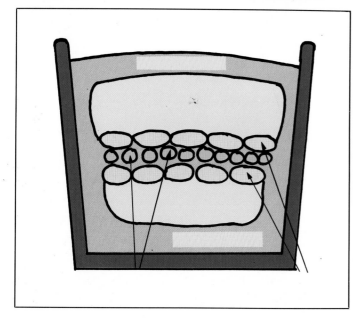

"Andalouse" Sauce

Procedure

Whisk together the mayonnaise, ketchup and vodka, then fold in the whipped cream. Season with salt and cayenne pepper and gently fold in the diced red pepper and salmon eggs.

Ingredients

1/2L (2 cups) mayonnaise
8cl (1/3 cup) ketchup
3cl (2 tbsp) vodka
2dl (3/4 cup) whipped heavy cream
10g (1/3 oz) cooked red pepper, cut in small dice
45g (1 1/2oz) salmon eggs
Salt, cayenne pepper

185

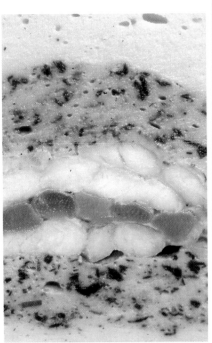

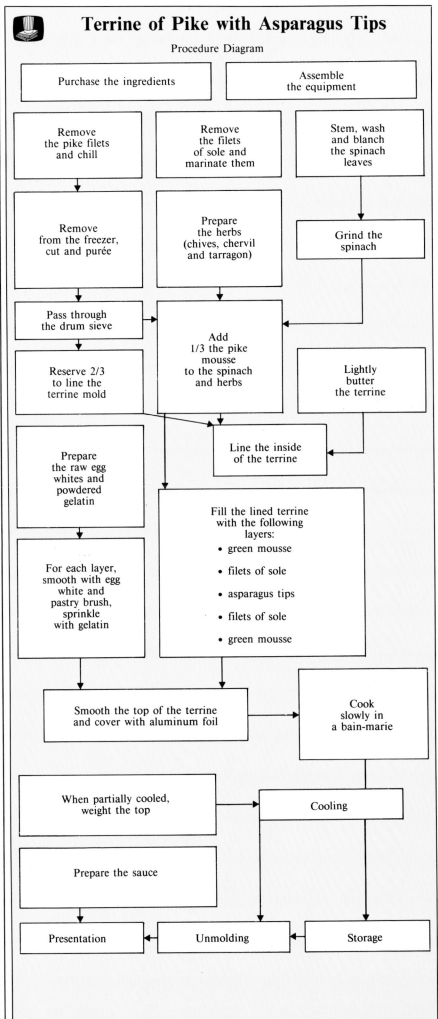

Terrine of Pike with Asparagus Tips

Procedure Diagram

Purchase the ingredients

Assemble the equipment

Remove the pike filets and chill

Remove the filets of sole and marinate them

Stem, wash and blanch the spinach leaves

Remove from the freezer, cut and purée

Prepare the herbs (chives, chervil and tarragon)

Grind the spinach

Pass through the drum sieve

Add 1/3 the pike mousse to the spinach and herbs

Lightly butter the terrine

Reserve 2/3 to line the terrine mold

Line the inside of the terrine

Prepare the raw egg whites and powdered gelatin

Fill the lined terrine with the following layers:
- green mousse
- filets of sole
- asparagus tips
- filets of sole
- green mousse

For each layer, smooth with egg white and pastry brush, sprinkle with gelatin

Smooth the top of the terrine and cover with aluminum foil

Cook slowly in a bain-marie

When partially cooled, weight the top

Cooling

Prepare the sauce

Presentation

Unmolding

Storage

Bream Terrine Royale

Introduction

This is an extremely light and digestible terrine, as the bream mousse is made without eggs or butter. As a result, this mousse is a little more fragile than the others, so that the mold should be lined to give the terrine stability. Herbed crêpes are used here; blanched spinach leaves could be used as well.

The color of this delicate mousse is rather pale, so colorful garnishes have been chosen to make the slices attractive as well as delicious.

If bream is not available, substitute another firm-fleshed white fish such as bass.

Ingredients

Basic Mousse
700g (1 1/2lb) bream filets
4 egg whites
700g (1 1/2lb) heavy cream
Salt, cayenne pepper

Crêpe Batter

1/4L (1 cup) milk
115g (about 1 cup) flour
2 eggs
45g (1 1/2oz) melted butter
Salt, pepper, nutmeg
1/2 tsp each chopped chives, chervil, tarragon

Garnish

15 salt-water crayfish
15 spinach leaves
25 large pieces scallop coral

187

Equipment

Food processor, terrine mold, aluminum foil, knives, bain-marie, pastry brush, drum sieve, heavy pot, skimmer, skewer, pastry scraper, cutting board, spatula, palette knife, measuring cup, mixing bowls, fish shears, cooling rack, hand towels

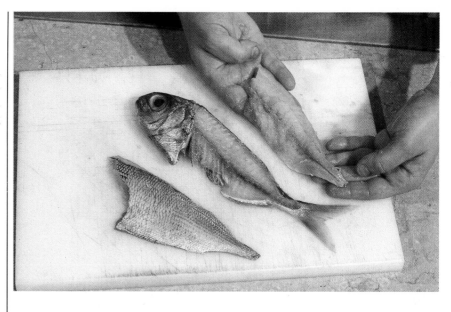

General Advice

Since this terrine involves the extra step of lining the mold, allow the time necessary to prepare the crêpes.

The crêpe batter is a standard recipe with the addition of chives, which are cut, and chervil and tarragon, which are chopped.

As with all fish terrines, it is necessary to keep the ingredients and equipment chilled.

Cayenne pepper is used in these light colored terrines because ground black pepper would mar the appearance.

Procedure

Preparing the Bream

Remove the scales of the bream and rinse thoroughly. Using a flexible thin-bladed knife, remove the filets.

It is recommended to chill the fish filets in the freezer until they are slightly firm but not frozen.

Preparing the Crayfish

Remove the shells from the crayfish, taking care not to damage the tail meat.

The shells can be reserved to make a stock or flavored butter. Carefully remove the dark vein that runs along the length of the tail, which would mar the appearance of the terrine.

To remove this vein, it is sometimes necessary to make a small cut with a paring knife.

Lay the trimmed tail meat out flat on a hand towel to dry and reserve in the refrigerator until ready to roll in the blanched spinach.

Preparing the Spinach

Choose spinach leaves that are unbroken and bright green. Medium-sized leaves are about right to wrap around the crayfish.

Remove the stem and wash the spinach in cold water to remove all sand and dirt. Change the water several times to make sure all of the sand is rinsed away.

The leaves are then blanched to soften them so they can be rolled around the crayfish.

Use a heavy pot that will maintain the lightly salted water at a rolling boil.

To blanch the spinach leaves, plunge them one at a time using a skimmer, removing them immediately, taking care not to break them.

The blanched leaves are then plunged into ice water to stop the cooking quickly.

Lay the refreshed leaves carefully on a handtowel to dry thoroughly.

Follow this procedure with each leaf.

Preparing the Crayfish "Roulades"

Each prepared crayfish tail is rolled in a blanched, cooled spin-

ach leaf. Roll them tightly so that each "roulade" will keep its shape.

Preparing the Scallop Coral

The vibrant color of the scallop coral looks particularly attractive

with the bright green of the spinach.

In France, the coral can be purchased frozen and then defrosted and set on a hand towel to dry. If using fresh scallops, wash thoroughly to remove all sand and impurities and dry on a hand-towel before assembling the terrine.

Making the Herb Crêpes

Mix the crêpe ingredients and let the batter rest. Make crêpes that are large enough to cover half of the mold you are using. They should be slightly thicker than usual and should not be overcooked. Keep the crêpes on a plate with a second plate on top to keep them from dryng out until ready to use.

189

Making the Bream Mousse

All of the ingredients for the mousse as well as the bowl of the processor should be very cold.

Measure out the egg whites (4 whites = approx. 1dl (1/2 cup)) and measure the cream.

Remove the bream from the freezer and cut the chilled fish into pieces so that long fibers in the flesh do not get caught in the blade of the processor.

Process the fish until it is puréed and comes together in a ball.

Add about 1 1/2 tsp salt and a pinch of cayenne.

Add the egg whites in a steady stream which will make the purée smooth.

Add the cold cream in a steady stream, taking care not to overprocess which would warm the mixture and cause it to separate.

Pass the completed mousse through a fine-meshed drum sieve

using a plastic scraper. This procedure will remove any bones, scales, sinews and make the mousse perfectly smooth and homogeneous. Use the plastic scraper to recover

all of the mousse that adheres to the underside of the sieve.

Place the mousse in a bowl.

Poach or pan-fry a spoonful of the mousse; cool, taste and adjust seasonings if necessary.

Stirring the Mousse Over Ice

Place the bowl of mousse in a larger bowl filled with crushed ice and stir with a large spoon.

Chilling the mixture makes it firmer and easier to work with. Stirring the mousse incorporates air and lightens it.

Assembling the Terrine

Butter the inside of the mold lightly with a pastry brush.

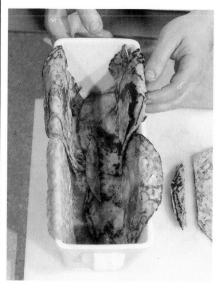

Line the mold with the crêpes, as shown, overlapping the edges a little in the bottom of the mold and letting the other edge hang over the edge of the mold.

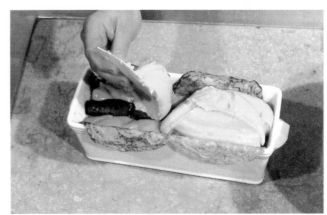

For this mold, two crêpes are placed overlapping on each side so that there are no gaps. The ends of the mold do not need to be lined as they are trimmed before the terrine is served.

Fill the bottom of the mold with 1/3 of the fish mousse and smooth this layer so that it is even.

Place two rows of the crayfish roulades on either side of the mold. Place one row of coral down the middle as shown.

Add another 1/3 of the fish mousse and smooth out this layer as well.

Arrange a second layer of garnishes, this time placing two rows of coral on either side with one row of crayfish roulades down the middle.

This makes each slice look balanced and attractive.

Fill the mold with the remaining mousse and smooth the top.

Fold over the edges of the crêpes. If they do not completely cover the top of the mousse, cut pieces from another crêpe to cover.

Place a sheet of buttered aluminum foil over the top of the terrine and secure it around the edges.

Pierce three holes through the aluminum foil down the middle of the terrine with a skewer or trussing needle. These " air vents " will allow steam to escape during cooking.

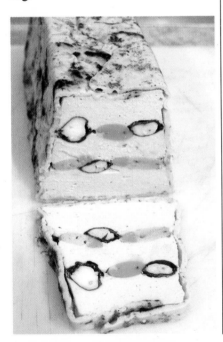

Cooking

Place the terrine in a bain-marie with the water coming halfway up the sides of the mold. Cook the terrine in a low oven, about 160-180C (325-350F). The terrine pictured here cooks for about 1 hour and 15 minutes.

Checking the Cooking

When cooked, the terrine will be firm to the touch and "spongy". To be certain that the terrine is cooked throughout, insert a metal skewer and test the heat at the center of the terrine or insert a thermometer into the center which should read 70C (158F).

The Curry Sauce

Introduction

This is a delicious cold sauce that marries very well with fish, especially the delicate taste of bream. The curry makes it slightly spicy and the lemon adds a refreshing note.

Ingredients

Mayonnaise

1/2L (2 cups) corn or peanut oil
2 tsp mustard
2 egg yolks
Salt and pepper
Few drops vinegar or lemon juice

Remove the cooked terrine from the bain-marie and set it on a rack to cool.

Storage

This terrine will keep 8-10 days in the mold covered with plastic

wrap and stored at 4C (40F) in the refrigerator.

Curry Sauce with Lemon and Anchovy

3cl (2 tbsp) olive oil
8 anchovy filets, drained
4 slices of lemon
2 tsp curry powder (more or less to taste)

Procedure

This sauce is made by combining a classic mayonnaise with a flavorful curry sauce made with anchovies.

Make the mayonnaise and set aside. To make the curry sauce, pour the olive oil into the saucepan and heat it over low heat. Add the drained anchovies and the lemon slices, pressing on the anchovies with a fork to mash them.

Stir in the curry powder, cover the pan and cook over very low heat for 5-8 minutes. The lemon slices will be very soft. Note: If using a strong curry powder, use a little less.

No other seasoning is added as the curry is spicy and the anchovies are salty.

Pass this mixture through a fine-meshed sieve using a plastic scraper to extract all of the flavor of the lemon and remove the lemon peel and small bones of the anchovies.

Scrape the underside of the sieve to remove all of the mixture that adheres to the sieve. Put the sauce on a plate to cool in the refrigerator.

Whisk the cooled curry mixture into the mayonnaise.

Taste the sauce and add seasoning if necessary.

This curry sauce will keep for 2-3 days in the refrigerator in a covered container.

Bream Terrine Royale

Procedure Diagram

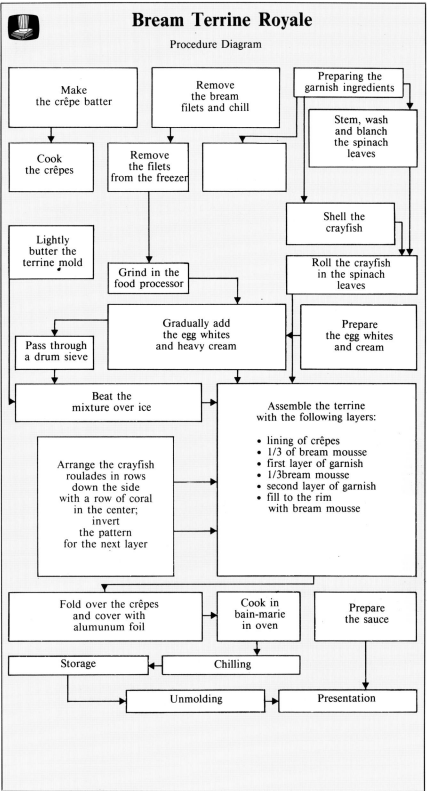

- Make the crêpe batter
- Remove the bream filets and chill
- Preparing the garnish ingredients
- Cook the crêpes
- Remove the filets from the freezer
- Stem, wash and blanch the spinach leaves
- Lightly butter the terrine mold
- Grind in the food processor
- Shell the crayfish
- Roll the crayfish in the spinach leaves
- Gradually add the egg whites and heavy cream
- Prepare the egg whites and cream
- Pass through a drum sieve
- Beat the mixture over ice
- Arrange the crayfish roulades in rows down the side with a row of coral in the center; invert the pattern for the next layer
- Assemble the terrine with the following layers:
  - lining of crêpes
  - 1/3 of bream mousse
  - first layer of garnish
  - 1/3 bream mousse
  - second layer of garnish
  - fill to the rim with bream mousse
- Fold over the crêpes and cover with alumunum foil
- Cook in bain-marie in oven
- Prepare the sauce
- Storage
- Chilling
- Unmolding
- Presentation

Tri-color Terrine of Red Mullet

Introduction

This attractive terrine is made from three layers of delectable red mullet mousse. Each layer is flavored with a different colorful ingredient. You can use other flavorings to personalize this terrine, but it is important to keep a nice balance of colors.

The pastel zucchini sauce accompanies this terrine perfectly.

Ingredients

For the basic mousse: 750g (1 1/2lb) red mullet filets (about 2kg (4 1/2lbs) whole fish), 7 egg whites, 3 whole eggs, 300g (10oz) heavy cream, 300g (10oz) butter

For the garnish ingredients: 30g (1oz) truffle, 45g (1 1/2oz) pistachios, 3cl (2 tbsp) reduced " Américaine " sauce (reduced to a glaze)

The size terrine pictured here would yield about 18-20 slices. The zucchini mousse may be replaced by other sauces that are quicker to make.

Equipment

Food processor, pastry scraper, terrine mold, cutting board, aluminum foil, spatula, knives, palette knife, bain-marie, measuring cup, pastry brush, mixing bowls, drum sieve, fish shears, sauté pan

Procedure

Like the other fish terrines in this chapter, it is necessary to chill the ingredients as well as the bowl of the processor to ensure satisfactory results.

Trim, clean and bone the fish as shown. Rinse the filets, dry them on a hand towel, then chill them thoroughly.

Preparing the Garnishes

The "Américaine" Sauce

This classic fish-based sauce, often served with lobster, enhances the flavor of the red mullet.

The sauce is reduced until it is very concentrated before adding it to the mousse.

Reduce the sauce over a low heat, stirring from time to time and scraping the sides of the pan until very thick and rich.

Chill until ready to use.

Adding the Garnish Ingredients to the Mousse

The Truffles

Chop the truffles very finely with a chef's knife and cover tightly until ready to use.

The Pistachios

Plunge the shelled pistachios into boiling water to loosen the skins. Remove the skins and chop finely with a chef's knife and set aside until ready to use.

Preparing the Mousse

Measure the cream and gelatin, prepare the eggs, and cream the butter.

Cut the chilled fish filets into pieces and place them in the chilled bowl of the food processor.

Process the pieces of fish until they are puréed.

Add the eggs in a steady stream, scraping down the sides of the bowl to make sure the ingredients mix evenly.

Add the cream and the butter and blend just enough to incorporate.

Pass the mousse through a fine-meshed drum sieve as shown to remove any scales, bones or sinews and to give the mousse a smooth homogeneous texture.

Scrape the underside of the sieve to remove any mousse that adheres to the sieve.

Stir the mousse over ice, as in the previous fish terrine recipes, to lighten it and make it firm.

Divide the mousse into three equal parts in three separate bowls.

Add the cooled reduced "Américaine" sauce to one portion of mousse and blend just until it is incorporated.

Sprinkle the chopped truffles over the second portion of mousse and fold them gently into the mixture.

Fold the chopped pistachios into the third portion of mousse.

It is important not to overmix the ingredients at this stage. Poach or pan-fry a spoonful of each mousse mixture.

Cool, taste and adjust seasonings if necessary.

Assembling the Terrine

Butter the mold using a pastry brush. Set the buttered mold in the refrigerator to harden the coating of butter.

The assembly of this terrine is very easy. The different mousses are simply layered evenly in the mold.

Start with the pistachio mousse and fill the bottom third of the terrine. Smooth out the mousse with the back of a spoon.

To help hold the layers together, egg whites and powdered gelatin are used in between each portion of mousse.

Dip a pastry brush in egg whites and brush a thin coating over the surface of the mousse. Sprinkle a little powdered gelatin over the egg white.

Proceed with the rose-colored mousse which has been flavored with reduced Américaine sauce, adding just enough to fill the mold to 2/3.

Smooth the surface, brush with egg white and sprinkle with gelatin.

Fill the top third of the mold with the truffle flavored mousse and smooth the top of the terrine.

Cover the top of the terrine with a sheet of buttered aluminum foil. Secure the foil tightly around the edges.

Pierce three holes through the aluminum foil down the middle of the terrine with a skewer or trussing needle. These " air vents " will

allow steam to escape during cooking.

Cooking

Like the other terrines that we have seen in this chapter, this one is cooked in a deep bain-marie, so the water comes at least halfway up the sides of the mold.

Cook the terrine in a low oven, 160C (325F). The terrine pictured here requires about 1 hour and 15 minutes to cook.

Checking the Cooking

The doneness of the terrine can be determined by touch. It should feel firm and slightly "spongy".

To ensure that the terrine is cooked throughout, a thermometer inserted into the center should read 70C (158F).

Cooling the Terrine

Remove the cooked terrine from the bain-marie and place it on a rack to cool evenly and quickly.

While the terrine is still warm, place a rectangle of wood or cardboard on top of the terrine and place a weight of about 300-400g (about 3/4lb) on top.

This will compact the terrine a little, which will facilitate slicing.

Storage

This terrine will keep 8-10 days in the mold covered with plastic wrap and stored at 4C (40F) in the refrigerator.

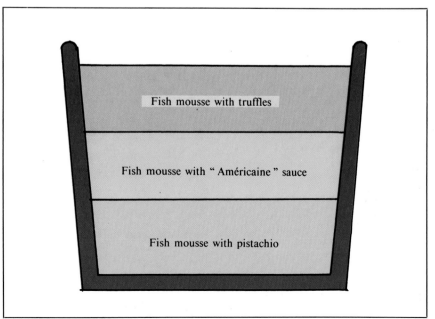

Fish mousse with truffles

Fish mousse with " Américaine " sauce

Fish mousse with pistachio

Zucchini Mousse

Introduction

This light and creamy sauce is an elegant accompaniment to this terrine. Its color and taste are the ideal complement to the finesse of the ingredients used to make this dish.

Serve the sauce cold, presented in a sauceboat or alongside a slice of the terrine.

This sauce is quite perishable, so it cannot be made a long time in advance.

Ingredients

30g (1oz) clarified butter
45g (1 1/2oz) chilled butter, cut in cubes
100g (3 1/2oz) onions
3 cloves garlic
450g (1lb) zucchini
150g (5oz) spinach
Bouquet garni (1 bay leaf, thyme, 4 parsley stems, leek green)
1/2L (2 cups) light stock
45g (1 1/2oz) flour
2dl (3/4 cup) heavy cream
Salt, pepper
5 leaves (10g (1/3oz)) of gelatin per liter

Equipment

Sauté pan, mixing bowls, drum sieve, plates, food processor, spatulas, whisks, pastry scraper, paring knife, chef's knife, measuring cup, lid, fork, spoon, sauceboat

Procedure

The Spinach

Remove the stem from each leaf of spinach and rinse the spinach in a large basin of cold water, changing the water several times until there is no dirt left.

Drain the clean leaves in a colander and set aside.

The Zucchini

Choose medium-size zucchini. Large ones tend to be less flavorful. For this recipe, the green skin will add color to the sauce so the zucchini are not peeled. Rinse the zucchini and cut into large dice.

The Onions and Garlic

Peel the onion and garlic. Cut the onion into small dice. Cut the garlic in half, remove the green sprout which tends to be bitter and crush the garlic with the side of a chef's knife.

The Bouquet Garni

Wrap the bay leaf, thyme and parsley stems in leek green and tie up securely with kitchen twine.

Cooking the Ingredients

Heat the clarified butter in the pan, add the onions and cook them over low heat until they are soft and lightly browned.

Add the zucchini and just a little salt and pepper. Turn the heat up and sauté for a few minutes.

Add the crushed garlic, the bouquet garni and the spinach. Cover the pan with a tight fitting lid and cook over medium heat to draw the moisture out of the spinach. Steaming the spinach like this ensures a deep green color and lots of flavor.

Stir the ingredients often to make sure that they are not sticking to the pan. If they are allowed to burn even a little, the mousse will have a bitter flavor.

When the liquid from the vegetables has evaporated, add the butter and stir until it melts. Sprinkle the flour over the vegetables, stir, and return to the heat to cook the flour. (The mixture can cook in the oven at this stage, which lowers the risk that the ingredients will stick to the bottom.)

When the flour has cooked, pour in stock and bring the mixture to a boil, then lower to a simmer and cook the sauce gently.

Puréeing the Sauce Ingredients

Remove the bouquet garni and place the other ingredients into the bowl of the processor and process into a purée.

Pass the purée through a fine-meshed drum sieve or conical sieve to achieve a smooth, homogeneous mixture.

This purée should still be hot enough to melt the softened gelatin, which is whisked into the purée to be incorporated evenly. If the purée has cooled, heat it very gently and whisk in the softened gelatin.

The purée is now cooled over a bowl of ice and stirred from time to time so that it cools evenly.

While the purée is cooling, beat the heavy cream until it forms soft peaks. When the purée is cold and has just begun to set, fold in the whipped cream a little at a time, using a whisk to gently blend the purée and the cream.

Taste and add salt and pepper if necessary.

Storage

The finished sauce can be put directly into sauceboats or stored in a

larger bowl, covered in the refrigerator.

This light mousse will keep refrigerated at 4C (40F) for about 48 hours.

It is always served cold.

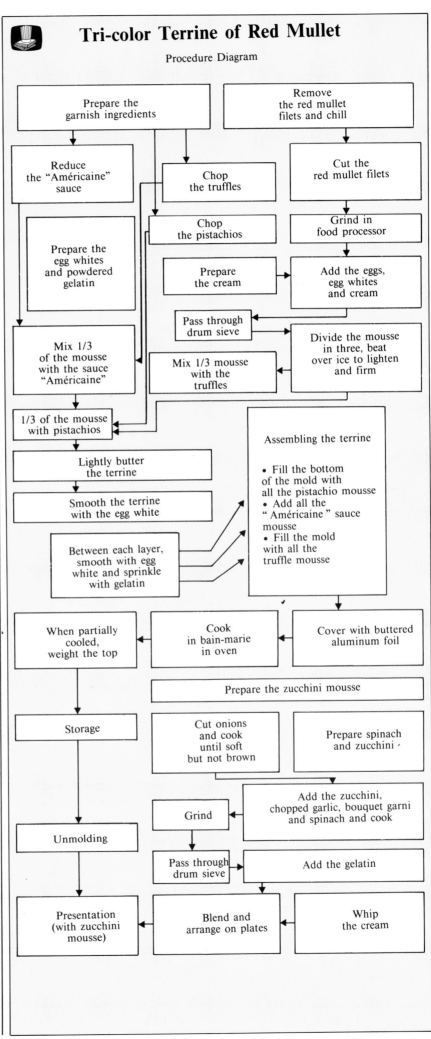

Tri-color Terrine of Red Mullet

Procedure Diagram

```
Prepare the                                    Remove
garnish ingredients                            the red mullet
                                               filets and chill

Reduce                  Chop                   Cut the
the "Américaine"        the truffles           red mullet filets
sauce

                        Chop                   Grind in
                        the pistachios          food processor

Prepare the             Prepare               Add the eggs,
egg whites              the cream              egg whites
and powdered                                   and cream
gelatin
                        Pass through           Divide the mousse
                        drum sieve             in three, beat
Mix 1/3                                        over ice to lighten
of the mousse           Mix 1/3 mousse         and firm
with the sauce          with the
"Américaine"            truffles

1/3 of the mousse                              Assembling the terrine
with pistachios
                                               • Fill the bottom
Lightly butter                                 of the mold with
the terrine                                    all the pistachio mousse
                                               • Add all the
Smooth the terrine                             "Américaine" sauce
with the egg white                             mousse
                                               • Fill the mold
Between each layer,                            with all the
smooth with egg                                truffle mousse
white and sprinkle
with gelatin

When partially          Cook                   Cover with buttered
cooled,                 in bain-marie          aluminum foil
weight the top          in oven

                        Prepare the zucchini mousse

Storage                 Cut onions             Prepare spinach
                        and cook               and zucchini
                        until soft
                        but not brown

                        Add the zucchini,
                        chopped garlic, bouquet garni
                Grind   and spinach and cook

Unmolding       Pass through   Add the gelatin
                drum sieve

Presentation    Blend and      Whip
(with zucchini  arrange on plates   the cream
mousse)
```

Vegetable Terrines

Introduction

These terrines make a light and refreshing first course. They are sometimes accompanied by a light sauce, such as the Paprika Cream which enhances the Rainbow Terrine.

Special breads made with nuts, whole grains or herbs, make nice partners for vegetable terrines.

Choosing the Vegetables

These terrines can be made year-round, choosing vegetables that are best in each season.

It is imperative to choose top quality vegetables that are unblemished, vibrant and not too large. Choose a variety of vegetables for each terrine that provide a contrast of lovely colors.

Food Cost

The vegetable terrines made with aspic or a purée of vegetables are relatively inexpensive to make, which allows the caterer to offer the customer a wide range of terrines at different prices.

The vegetable terrine that is made with a mousse of sweetbreads is more expensive.

Methods of Assembly

Three methods of assembly are presented in this chapter to show the variety of terrines that can be made using vegetables. Their taste as well as presentation are all very different.

The first two methods involve simply molding the prepared ingredients; no further cooking is required.

a) Aspic

To assemble a terrine using aspic, the vegetables are shaped and cooked in advance. The aspic is poured into the mold in layers with different vegetables in each layer.

b) Vegetable Purée

The vegetables for this terrine are cooked thoroughly and puréed. Gelatin is added to each purée to add stability. Different colors are used to make an attractive terrine.

c) Mousse

Terrines in this category can be made with a mousse of chicken, fish, veal or, as in this example, sweetbreads. The vegetables are cooked in advance, layered in the mousse, which is then cooked in a bain-marie like the other meat and fish terrines in this chapter.

Vegetable and Aspic Terrine

Introduction

This refreshing terrine is an attractive combination of colorful vegetables and crystal clear aspic.

Choose seasonal vegetables that are vibrant and full of flavor. It is also important to have a balanced variety of colors and flavors which will make the terrine beautiful when served and exciting to taste.

The aspic is a major ingredient in this terrine and therefore must be of very high quality.

Begin with a full-flavored chicken or veal stock, clarify it carefully to achieve a clear aspic. The flavor of the aspic should be pronounced, but not too strong so that it does not overpower the flavor of the vegetables.

You need to add enough gelatin to the aspic so that the terrine will slice neatly. However, too much gelatin will give the terrine an unpleasant texture and taste.

Presentation

This aspic terrine is quite fragile and must be kept cold until it is served. If the customer will be transporting the terrine to serve at home, advise the customer to keep the terrine cold and handle it gently.

A slice of this terrine is an excellent first course or light main course, arranged on a plate and served with bread. It can also be arranged on platters and served on a buffet.

Equipment

Saucepans, mixing bowls, colanders, skimmers, ladles, chef's knife, paring knife, vegetable peeler, cutting board, fine-meshed conical sieve, cheesecloth, pastry scraper, terrine molds, heavy pot

Ingredients

For 2 terrines 29cm long by 10cm wide by 9cm high (11 1/2in x 4in x 3 1/2in)

Vegetables

300g (10oz) carrots
200g (7oz) turnips
250g (8oz) green beans
250g (8oz) green peas
400g (14oz) zucchini
2 avocados
200g (7oz) spring onions
150g (5oz) chanterelles
1 lemon

Flavoring

3 shallots
Small bunch chives
Small bunch chervil
2 sprigs tarragon

Aspic

2L (2 qts) aspic made from meat or poultry

Procedure

The Aspic

The aspic should be made in advance because its preparation, which involves making a full-flavored stock then clarifying it, takes several days.

Preparing the Vegetables

Rinse the vegetables, then prepare each one: peel the carrots and turnips, shell the peas, remove the strings and ends of the green beans, sort and trim the chanterelles, peel the spring onions and shallots.

Rinse the vegetables again if necessary.

The carrots, turnips are cut into slices then into "batonnets" (long rectangular pieces) so that they will cook more quickly.

Cut the zucchini in half, remove the soft portion in the middle which holds the seeds and cut into "batonnets".

The root vegetables (carrots, turnips and onions) are cooked separately, starting them in cold salted water and bringing the water to a boil.

The green beans and zucchini are plunged into rapidly boiling water to keep their bright green color.

The mushrooms are sautéed in clarified butter with salt and pepper. Start over high heat to draw out the moisture, lower the heat and continue cooking to evaporate the liquid.

Checking the Cooking

It is very important that the vegetables are cooked just right:
• overcooked, the vegetables lose color, flavor and texture;
• undercooked, the vegetables are too firm to cut easily when slicing the terrine.

Check the vegetables as they are cooking by piercing them with the point of a knife. They should be firm but not crunchy.

As soon as they are cooked, stop the cooking process by plunging them into ice water. The vegetables should not sit too long in the ice water, or they will become soggy and flavorless. As soon as they are cooled, drain them in a colander, then dry them thoroughly on hand towels.

Shaping the Vegetables

The pieces of the vegetables in the terrine should all be about the same size. Cut the batonnets of zucchini, carrots and turnips into small cubes, about 6mm (1/4in) on each side.

Cut the onions in half if necessary, so that they are about the same size as the other vegetables.

The avocados are peeled and scooped out. They require no cooking, however, it is important to choose avocados that are just right:

• underripe - the taste is bitter and the flesh is too hard;

• overripe - the flesh is too soft to cut into dice and often discolored and will therefore not be attractive.

Remove the skin and the pit of the avocado, and sprinkle with lemon juice. Using a stainless steel knife that will not darken the avocado, cut it into dice the same size as the other vegetables. Sprinkle the dice with lemon juice.

Finally the herbs are prepared. Cut the chives neatly into very fine pieces. Chop the chervil and tarragon with a chef's knife. Cut the shallots into very fine dice.

Each element is placed on separate plates which will facilitate the assembly of the terrine.

Assembling the Terrine

The aspic is chilled over ice until it thickens slightly, which speeds up the assembly of the terrine as

each layer must set before the next one is added.

Begin by pouring a layer of aspic about 6mm (1/4in) thick in the bottom of the mold.

Sprinkle some of the herbs and chopped shallots evenly over the surface and chill to set.

Pour a little more aspic over the herbs and shallots and chill to set.

Place a row of green beans down the center of the terrine with diced carrot and turnip on either side, as shown. Pour aspic to cover the vegetables and chill to set.

Place a row of onions down the center of the terrine (over the green beans) and place peas and diced zucchini on either side, as shown.

Pour aspic to cover the vegetables and chill to set.

205

When the aspic has set, arrange a row of mushrooms down the center of the terrine with dice of

avocadoes on either side, as shown.

Cover the vegetables with aspic and chill to set.

Add another row of green beans down the center with diced carrots and turnip on either side. Cover with aspic and chill to set.

Finish the terrine with a final layer of herbs and chopped shallots.

Pour aspic to completely cover and chill to set.

The assembled terrine should have time to chill thoroughly in the refrigerator before being sliced. It is therefore advisable to prepare it the day before it will be served.

Storage

Cover the terrine securely with plastic wrap and refrigerate. Left in the mold, it will keep for about one week.

It is quite fragile once it is unmolded, so keep it refrigerated until you are ready to unmold, slice and arrange the terrine on plates.

Unmolding the Terrine

Prepare a basin of hot water (50C (125F)). Remove the terrine from the refrigerator and place the mold up to the rim in the hot water. As soon as the water has heated the mold enough to melt the aspic around the edge, turn the mold over onto a platter or cutting board.

Rock the mold from side to side, to allow air to penetrate between the aspic and the mold. Lift the mold and knock it gently on the board and let the terrine slip out.

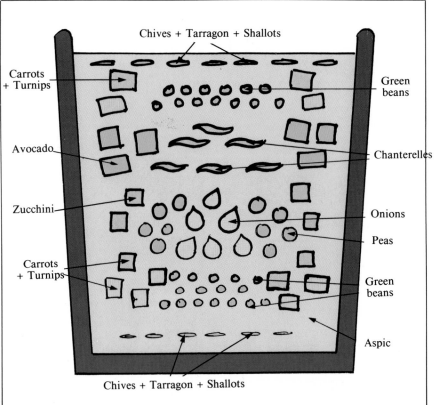

Slicing the Terrines

Slice the terrine just before serving. To ensure a clean, neat slice, dip a thin-bladed knife into hot water before cutting each slice.

Using a wide spatula as shown will facilitate the transfer of the slices to the plates.

The thickness of the slice is important: a slice that is too thin is difficult to handle; a slice that is too thick is unattractive and unpleasant to eat.

A slice about 1cm (3/8in) thick is just right.

Storage

Unmolded and covered in the refrigerator, the terrine will keep about 1 week. Once unmolded and sliced, the terrine should be served immediately.

If it is necessary to slice the terrine in advance, it can be left on the cutting board, sliced, covered with plastic wrap and stored in the refrigerator.

If arranged on plates in advance, cover each slice with plastic wrap and refrigerate until ready to serve.

Presentation

This terrine is always served cold. The decoration on the platter or plate should be kept simple; a few leaves of lettuce and tomato wedges perhaps.

Bread made with olives or other flavorful breads make a nice accompaniment.

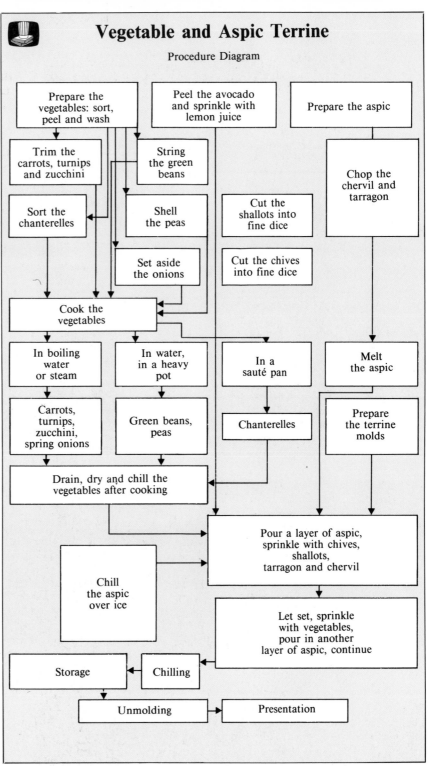

Vegetable and Aspic Terrine

Procedure Diagram

Prepare the vegetables: sort, peel and wash

Peel the avocado and sprinkle with lemon juice

Prepare the aspic

Trim the carrots, turnips and zucchini

String the green beans

Chop the chervil and tarragon

Sort the chanterelles

Shell the peas

Cut the shallots into fine dice

Set aside the onions

Cut the chives into fine dice

Cook the vegetables

In boiling water or steam

In water, in a heavy pot

In a sauté pan

Melt the aspic

Carrots, turnips, zucchini, spring onions

Green beans, peas

Chanterelles

Prepare the terrine molds

Drain, dry and chill the vegetables after cooking

Pour a layer of aspic, sprinkle with chives, shallots, tarragon and chervil

Chill the aspic over ice

Let set, sprinkle with vegetables, pour in another layer of aspic, continue

Storage

Chilling

Unmolding

Presentation

" Rainbow " Terrine

Introduction

This is the easiest to make of the vegetable terrines. Only three vegetables are used and the preparation is not difficult.

The three colors make each slice very pretty. Different vegetables can be used according to the season, however, the choice of vegetables should always have colors and tastes that go well together.

The " Rainbow " terrine is made with no cream, butter or eggs, therefore it is a perfect choice for those on a low-fat diet.

The ingredients are cooked and puréed and simply layered in the mold. The terrine does not cook in the oven.

You may choose to serve a light creamy sauce with this terrine to enhance the flavor.

Ingredients

(For two rectangular terrines)
5kg (11lb) spinach
2 bunches sorrel
3kg (6 1/2lb) celeriac
1 lemon
3.5kg (7 3/4lb) carrots
4-6g (1/5oz) leaf or powdered gelatin per 1kg (2lbs) mousse of cooked and reduced vegetables
Salt
Nutmeg (optional)

Sauce

1L (4 cups) heavy cream
Salt, pepper, paprika

Equipment

Saucepans, mixing bowls, colanders, skimmer, chef's knife, paring knife, 2-pronged fork, vegetable peeler, cutting board, drum sieve, whisks, pastry scrapers, spoons, spatulas, terrine molds

Procedure

Preparing the Vegetables

Peel the carrots, then rinse them. Cut them into medium-size chunks.

Peel the celeriac with a stainless steel knife, rinse it.

Rub the celeriac with lemon to keep it from darkening. Cut into medium-size chunks and sprinkle with lemon juice.

Remove the stems from the spinach and sorrel and rinse the leaves in a large basin of cold water, changing the water several times until all the sand and dirt is rinsed away.

Cooking the Vegetables

Cook the carrots and celeriac separately in salted water.

These vegetables should be cooked until they are very soft so they can be puréed easily. Drain the vegetables in a colander.

The spinach and sorrel are cooked together in a pot with a little clarified butter. Cover the pot with a tight-fitting lid and start the cooking over high heat to draw out the moisture from the vegetables.

Remove the cover, lower the heat, and stir the spinach and sor-

rel with a long-tined fork. Continue to cook until the moisture is evaporated.

Season with salt, pepper and nutmeg and drain the vegetables in a colander.

Drying Out the Vegetables

So that the purées are not watery, it is necessary to dry out the vegetables a little.

The cooked carrots and celeriac are spread on a baking sheet and placed in a low oven to dry them slightly.

The drained spinach and sorrel is squeezed dry in a hand towel.

Puréeing the Vegetables

Pass the carrots and celeriac separately through a fine-meshed drum sieve. Be sure to scrape the underside of the sieve to recover the purée that adheres to the sieve.

Chop the spinach and sorrel very finely with a chef's knife.

Adding the Gelatin

Weigh each purée to determine how much gelatin is needed. The purées should be warm or room temperature, not chilled.

Soften the gelatin for each purée in cold water, then melt it gently in a water bath.

To facilitate the blending of the gelatin, stir a little purée into the melted gelatin, then stir this mixture back into the purée and blend thoroughly.

Taste each purée and season with salt and pepper if necessary.

Assembling the Terrine

Line the mold with plastic wrap which will make it easier to unmold the terrine. The sheet of plastic should be large enough so that there is enough to cover the top of the mold.

Fill the bottom 1/3 of the mold with spinach purée. Smooth this layer with the back of a spoon to make it even.

Add a layer of celeriac purée to fill the middle 1/3 of the mold. Smooth this layer with the back of a spoon to make it even.

Fill the top 1/3 of the mold with carrot purée and smooth this layer with the back of a spoon to make it even. Fold the edges of the plastic wrap over the top to cover it completely.

Put the terrine in the refrigerator at 4C (40F) to chill and set throughout. This will take several hours depending on the size of the terrine.

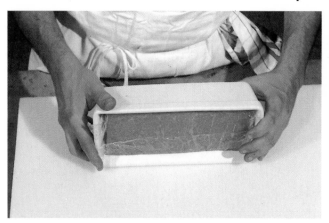

Unmolding the Terrine

Remove the terrine from the refrigerator. Fold back the plastic wrap covering the top of the terrine and turn the mold over onto a platter or cutting board. Remove the plastic wrap.

Making the Sauce

To enhance the flavor of this terrine, serve it with a little whipped cream seasoned with some paprika.

Slicing the Terrine

To slice this terrine neatly, dip a thin-bladed knife in hot water before cutting each slice.

It is recommended to cut the slices about 1cm (3/8in) thick. Thin slices are too fragile and if the slices are too thick, their appearance and flavor are not at their best.

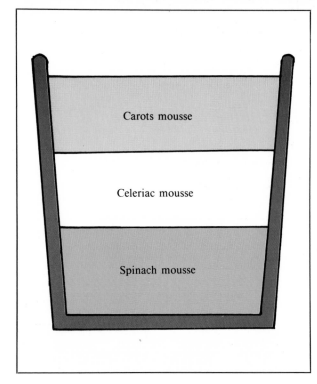

Carots mousse

Celeriac mousse

Spinach mousse

Unmolded and covered in the refrigerator, the terrine will keep about 1 week at 4C (40F). Once unmolded and sliced, the terrine should be served immediately.

If it is necessary to slice the terrine in advance, it can be left on

the cutting board, sliced, covered with plastic wrap and stored in the refrigerator.

If arranged on plates in advance, cover each slice with plastic wrap and refrigerate until ready to serve.

Presentation

Serve this terrine arranged on a platter or sliced on a plate with a simple garnish of lettuce leaves.

The whipped cream sauce can be served in a bowl or piped decoratively on the plate.

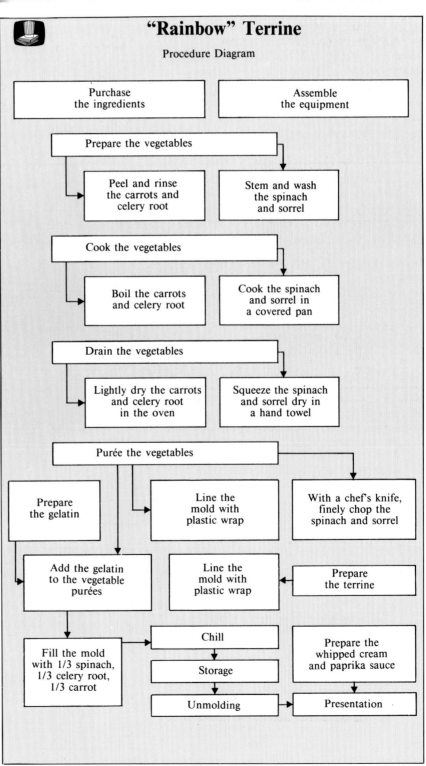

"Rainbow" Terrine

Procedure Diagram

Purchase the ingredients → Assemble the equipment

Prepare the vegetables →
- Peel and rinse the carrots and celery root
- Stem and wash the spinach and sorrel

Cook the vegetables →
- Boil the carrots and celery root
- Cook the spinach and sorrel in a covered pan

Drain the vegetables →
- Lightly dry the carrots and celery root in the oven
- Squeeze the spinach and sorrel dry in a hand towel

Purée the vegetables →
- Prepare the gelatin
- Line the mold with plastic wrap
- With a chef's knife, finely chop the spinach and sorrel

Add the gelatin to the vegetable purées → Line the mold with plastic wrap ← Prepare the terrine

Fill the mold with 1/3 spinach, 1/3 celery root, 1/3 carrot → Chill → Storage → Unmolding → Presentation ← Prepare the whipped cream and paprika sauce

Terrine of Vegetables with Mousse of Sweetbreads

Introduction

This is a very refined dish which marries the subtle flavor of a sweetbread mousse with an assortment of colorful vegetables.

Since sweetbreads are expensive, the food cost of this terrine is relatively high. The preparation is lengthy, but not particularly difficult.

This vegetable terrine is assembled, then cooked in a water bath like the meat and fish terrines in this chapter. It is therefore necessary to allow enough time for the terrine to cool thoroughly before it is sliced.

Left in the mold and covered securely with plastic wrap, it will keep one week in the refrigerator.

Equipment Cutting board, mixing bowls, shallow platters, colanders, saucepans, fine-meshed conical sieve, spatulas, pastry scrapers, whisks, paring knife, chef's knife, vegetable peeler, thin-bladed flexible knife, meat grinder, terrine molds, measuring cups, skimmer, sauté pan, heavy pot, spoon, fork, pastry brush, 2-pronged fork, plates, aluminum foil

Ingredients (For two terrines)

For the Forcemeat

1kg (2lb) sweetbreads
600g (1lb 3oz) sirloin tip of veal
300g (10oz) fat back
45g (1 1/2oz) clarified butter
1/4L (1 cup) light stock
3 shallots, 1 thyme sprig, 1 bay leaf
12-15g (approx. 1 tbsp) salt per kg
  (per 2lb)
2g (approx. 1/2tsp) pepper per kg
  (per 2lb)
1 clove
Pinch allspice
7cl (approx. 1/3 cup) armagnac
3dl (1 1/4 cup) heavy cream
3 egg whites

For the Vegetable Garnish

100g (3 1/2oz) carrots
100g (3 1/2oz) turnips
100g (3 1/2oz) green beans
100g (3 1/2oz) peas
3 artichokes

For the Artichoke Cooking Liquid ("Blanc")

1L (4 cups) water
1 tbsp flour
2 tbsp olive oil
Juice of 1/2 lemon
10g (2 tsp) salt
Few peppercorns
Few coriander seeds

Degorging the Sweetbreads

Before the actual preparation of the terrine begins, the sweetbreads must be degorged to draw out blood and impurities.

Trim the sweetbreads, removing the thin skin that covers them and any little bits of fat or connective tissue.

To degorge them, soak them in cold water for 3-4 hours, changing the water several times, or leave them under cold running water.

Drain and dry them on a hand towel.

Procedure

Marinating the Sweetbreads

The first step is to prepare the ingredients for the marinade. Peel the shallots and cut them into fine dice. Measure the stock and the armagnac.

Assemble the seasonings: salt, pepper, allspice, bay leaf, thyme and cloves.

Searing the Sweetbreads

Cut the degorged sweetbreads into large slices and season with salt and pepper.

Heat clarified butter in the pan and sear the pieces of sweetbread on both sides. Immediately remove them and drain to remove all excess fat.

The sweetbreads must not cook at this stage. Reserve the pan to make the marinade.

Preparing the Marinade

Pour off all excess fat from the pan used to sear the sweetbreads.

Add a little clarified butter and the shallots to the pan and cook until soft but not brown. Deglaze with stock.

Add the seasonings and reduce the stock by half. Set aside to cool.

Marinating the Sweetbreads

Sprinkle the seared sweetbreads with armagnac. Pour the cooled marinade over the sweetbreads and stir to blend the ingredients.

Marinate the sweetbreads for about 2 hours, turning them over from time to time.

Preparing the Forcemeat Ingredients

Trim the tendons and fat from the sirloin tip of veal, cut it into small pieces and set aside.

Remove the skin from the fat back, cut the fat back into small pieces and refrigerate until ready to use.

217

Preparing the Vegetables

Peel the carrots and turnips, rinse them and cut them into pieces, as shown.

Remove the strings from the green beans, rinse them.

Remove the peas from the shells.

Cut away the leaves of the artichoke using a stiff-bladed stainless steel knife.

Trim around the base so that only the ends of the tough leaves remain attached to the base.

Rub with lemon to keep them from darkening.

Cooking the Vegetables

Cook the carrots and turnips separately in salted water.

Cook the green beans and peas in salted water as well, being sure to plunge them into rapidly boiling water to keep their bright color.

The vegetables should remain firm because they will be cooked a second time in the terrine.

Cook the artichokes in the

"blanc" and let them cool in the cooking liquid.

To stop the cooking and to ensure a bright color, plunge the vegetables into ice water. As soon as they are cooled, drain them in a colander so they do not become watery.

Shaping the Vegetables

Remove the choke of the artichokes and cut them into slices about 6mm (1/4in) thick.

Cut the carrots and turnips the same size as the slices of artichokes.

Making the Mousse

Pass the fat back through the medium disk of the meat grinder (this will prevent it from overheating and melting when passed through the fine disk with the other meats). Pass the ground fat back, the veal and the sweetbreads through the fine disk of the meat grinder. Place the ground meats in a bowl set in a larger bowl with crushed ice.

Stir the meats together so the mixture is smooth.

Add the egg whites a little at a time and stir to blend completely without overworking the mixture. Stir in the cream until it is just incorporated.

Poach or pan fry a little of the mousse; cool, taste and adjust the seasonings if necessary.

Assembling the Terrine

Butter the inside of the mold using a pastry brush.

Fill the bottom third of the mold with mousse and smooth out this layer with the back of a spoon.

Arrange rows of the vegetable garnish as shown, being sure to alternate the colors.

Add another layer of mousse to fill the middle third of the terrine.

Arrange a second layer of vegetables, reversing the order of vegetables to make each slice more attractive.

Fill the mold to the top with mousse and cover with a sheet of buttered aluminum foil.

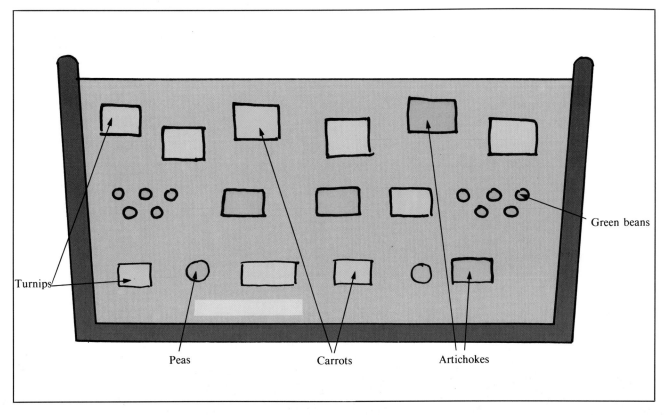

With a skewer or trussing needle, pierce three holes in the foil down the center of the terrine. These air vents will allow steam to escape during cooking.

Cooking the Terrine

Cook the terrine in a water bath in a low oven (160C (325F)). The terrine shown here takes about 1 hour and 15 minutes to cook.

When it is cooked, a thermometer inserted into the center will read 75-80C (167-175F).

When the terrine is cooked, remove it from the bain marie and place on a rack to cool evenly and quickly.

While it is still warm, apply a weight of about 500g (1lb) to the top.

Unmolding and Slicing

To unmold, dip the mold into a basin of hot water and turn it over onto a platter or cutting board.

Cut the mousse into slices about 1cm (3/8in) thick using a thin-bladed knife.

Storage

Left in the mold and covered securely with plastic wrap, this terrine will keep refrigerated at 4C (40F) for about 1 week.

Ideally, the terrine should be served as soon as it is sliced. If it is necessary to arrange the slices on plates in advance, cover each one individually with plastic wrap.

Presentation

This refreshing terrine needs no accompaniment. It is best served plain with toasted slices of good crusty french bread.

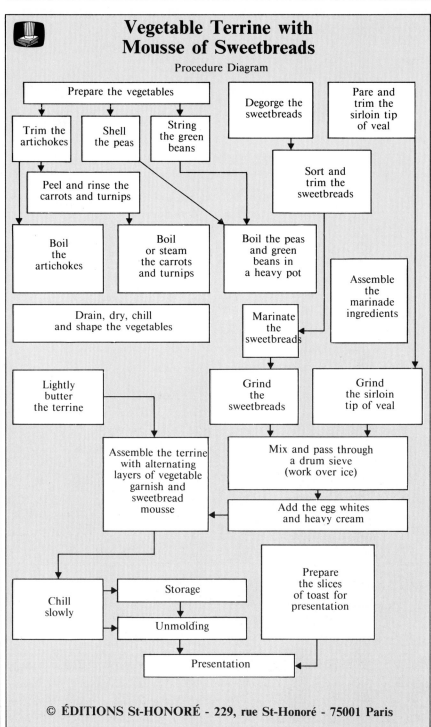

Vegetable Terrine with Mousse of Sweetbreads
Procedure Diagram

© ÉDITIONS St-HONORÉ - 229, rue St-Honoré - 75001 Paris

222

Chapter 4

Galantines and Ballotines

Unlike terrines, which are cooked in earthenware, cast-iron or ceramic molds, and pâtés, which are wrapped in pastry, galantines and ballotines are cooked by poaching them in a liquid that complements the taste of the filling ingredients. For example, meat galantines or ballotines are poached in chicken or meat stock, while fish galantines or ballotines are poached in fish stock or a court bouillon.

The term "ballotine" is generally applied to preparations made in small or individual portions (using small

birds such as squabs, quails, or "drumsticks" from larger birds). The ingredients used in the fillings are the same as those used in the larger galantines.

The term "galantine", on the other hand, designates a large preparation, most often decorated and presented on a platter. They may be based on meat, poultry or fish.

Galantines and ballotines are usually coated with aspic once they are cool. Part of the appeal of these dishes is visual, therefore they are always beautifully decorated.

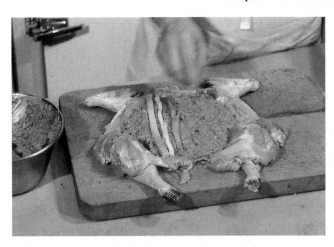
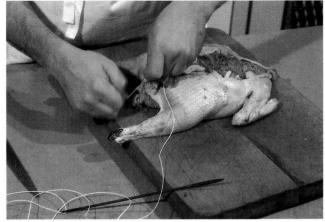

Introduction to Galantines and Ballotines

These preparations are considered as a luxurious product, whose ingredients are costly and therefore whose price is relatively high.

Imbued with the flavors of the stock in which they were poached, the subtle taste of the galantine and ballotine is the secret to their success.

The decoration of the platter is an important element which is constantly being developed and refined, as these dishes are often included in culinary contests.

Any size platter can be coated with aspic or chaud-froid sauce to use as a base for these dishes. Mixtures based on colored milk and gelatin provide numerous possibilities for making checkerboard or mosaic patterns. All kinds of designs can be made between two layers of clear aspic on a bed of chaud-froid, including floral designs, exotic birds and geometric patterns.

The decorations are made from entirely edible ingredients. The decoration on the base of the platter may include three dimensional designs as well, such as radish flowers, carrots, tomato roses, parsley, chervil, tarragon, lemons cut into baskets or slices, hard boiled eggs cut to look like mushrooms, snowmen and swans (whose necks are made from strips of carrot coated in white aspic).

Shrimp, prawns and mussels coated with chaud-froid sauce may also be used in the decoration, as well as " fleurons " (pastry crescents), " timbales " (hollowed cylinders of vegetables such as cucumbers) or " barquettes " (boat-shaped pastry shells) filled with diced vegetables.

It goes without saying, there are no limits to the decorative possibilities for galantines and ballotines which are a showcase for the artistic talents of the caterer.

Galantines and ballotines may be sold whole or by the slice; they are appropriate for many types of sale: in a specialty food store, as part of a buffet, or as part of a restaurant menu.

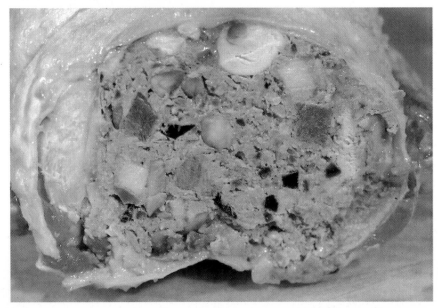

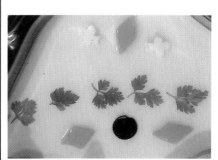

Guinea Hen Ballotines

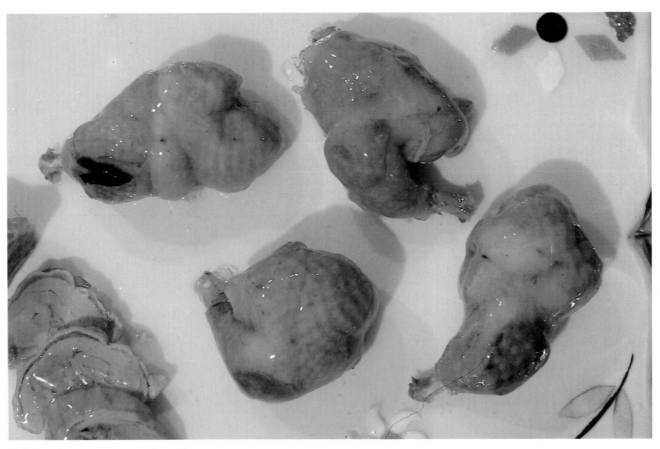

Introduction

This example of a ballotine is delicate and delicious, and its appearance is as refined as the taste. A slice of truffle slipped under the skin adds an elegant touch to the simple decoration.

It is part of the classic catering repertory because it is easy to make, adapts well to small quantities, and can be made in any season.

The guinea hen drumsticks, which have a delicate texture and delicious taste, are boned and stuffed, then poached in a chicken stock, which helps enhance the flavors.

They may be served as a first course, as part of the restaurant menu, or on a buffet. They may be presented on a decorated platter, or on a plate with a small salad or other vegetable accompaniment.

Ingredients

2 guinea hens
4 slices of truffle

Forcemeat

45g (1 1/2oz) guinea hen breast meat
2 guinea hen livers
45g (1 1/2oz) pork jowl
10g (1/3oz) clarified butter
10g (1/3oz) shallots
30g (1oz) mushrooms
Few drops lemon juice
20g (2/3oz) pistachios
1/2 egg
1cl (2tsp) cognac
1cl (2tsp) sherry
Salt, pepper, allspice

Poaching Liquid

3L (3qts) chicken stock
Aromatic vegetables (optional)

Aspic Glaze

Chicken or meat aspic

Equipment

Cutting board, flexible fine-bladed knife, paring knife, chef's knife, spatula, scissors, plates, mixing bowls, measuring cup, small sauté pan with lid, saucepan, colander, skimmer, fine-mesh conical sieve, meat grinder, trussing needle, kitchen twine, pastry bag and medium plain tip, pastry scraper, thermometer, pastry brush, hand towel

Preparing the Guinea Hens

Choose plump young birds. If there is any down or feathers left on the skin, pass the bird through a flame to singe them off and leave the skin clean and smooth.

With a cleaver or chef's knife,

cut off the neck, wing tips and feet at the lower leg joint.

If the bird still has its innards, remove them by following the technique outlined in the recipe for Terrine of Duck with Green Peppercorns, Chapter 3. Reserve the liver for use in the forcemeat. Be sure to discard the dark green bile sack.

Boning the Guinea Hen

Bone the guinea hen following the techniques for duck in the Terrine of Duck with Green Peppercorns recipe, Chapter 3. Reserve the bones to make the stock. Remove the breast filet to use in the forcemeat.

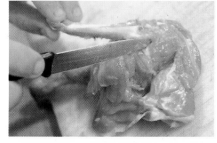

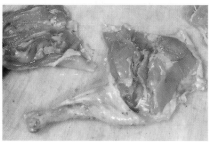

Detach the leg and thigh together and bone it carefully, without cutting into the meat. Remove the upper thigh bone, and loosen the leg bone by scraping the meat away from it. Cut the bone off in the middle, leaving the skin and meat intact and the lower half of the bone still attached. Chill until ready to stuff.

Preparing the Forcemeat Ingredients

Remove the skin from the jowl and cut it into 2 cm (3/4 in) cubes.

Cut the breast meat and the liver into chunks also. Combine these ingredients and put them through a meat grinder fitted with a fine disk. Mix the ground meats and set aside in a small bowl in the refrigerator.

Preparing the Pistachios

Shell the pistachios, then plunge them into boiling water for a few seconds to loosen the skin. Peel off the skin, dry the pistachios and chop them with a chef's knife. Set aside.

Making the Mushroom Duxelles

Peel the shallots, cut them in half, then cut into very fine dice.

Sort, trim and wash the mushrooms, then chop them finely. Melt the clarified butter in a small saucepan, add the chopped shallots and cook over low heat until soft but not brown.

Add the mushrooms. Season with salt and pepper. Cover the pan and let them cook a few minutes so the moisture is drawn out. Remove the lid and continue cooking until all the liquid has evaporated.

When the duxelles are very dry, transfer to a plate and leave to cool.

Preparing the Forcemeat

Mix the forcemeat ingredients: ground meats seasoned with salt, pepper, allspice, to which the cognac, sherry and beaten egg are added. Poach or pan-fry a spoonful

of forcemeat, taste and adjust seasoning if necessary.

Add the chopped pistachios and

the mushroom duxelles.

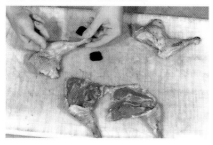

Filling the Ballotines

To add the truffle decoration, carefully insert your finger between the skin and meat of the upper thigh and loosen it slightly, then slide a slice of truffle underneath and position it on the fleshy part of the top of the drumstick.

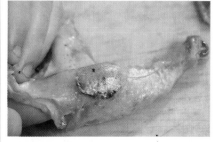

Turn the pieces over so they are truffle-side down on the work surface.

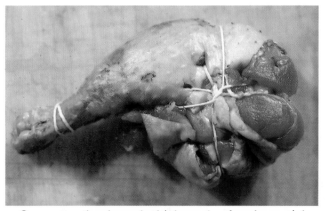

Open up the boned thigh and season the inside lightly with salt and pepper.

Using the pastry bag and tip, fill the drumstick with the forcemeat, making sure to fill the entire cavity.

Trussing and Shaping the Ballotines

Pull the skin over the top of the thigh to cover completely and secure it in place with a few stiches made with the trussing needle and kitchen twine.

Wrap some more twine around

the drumsticks as shown to help them keep the proper shape during cooking.

Cooking

Place the ballotines in a large saucepan. Add chicken stock to cover. Heat until the stock reaches 85 °C (185F), then keep the temperature steady. This is best achieved with a thermometer.

For average size drumsticks, estimate 15-20 minutes poaching at 85 °C (185F).

Remove from the heat and leave

to cool in the poaching liquid. This step needs to be done several hours before serving to allow enough

time to cook and cool. The ballotines may even be cooked several days ahead and kept refrigerated in their poaching liquid until ready to use.

Glazing the Ballotines

When the drumsticks are completely cool, remove them from their liquid, lay them on a rack to drain, then place them on a hand towel to dry completely.

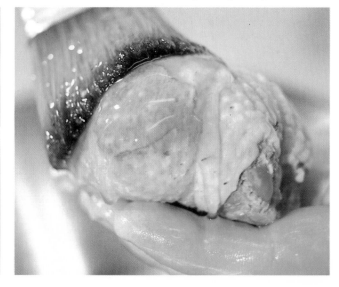

To glaze them, stir the aspic over ice to thicken slightly.

Apply a first coat of aspic, chill until it is set, then apply a second coat for a perfect finish.

If the ballotines are made far in advance of service, they should be reglazed daily in order to keep their attractive shine.

Storage
The drumsticks may be kept 3-4 days at 4 ^{0}C (40F). Wrap them, un-

glazed in plastic wrap and apply the aspic to order or leave them in the poaching liquid.
Presentation
The ballotines may be served on decorated platters or on plates garnished with a salad or on a base of other decorative ingredients.

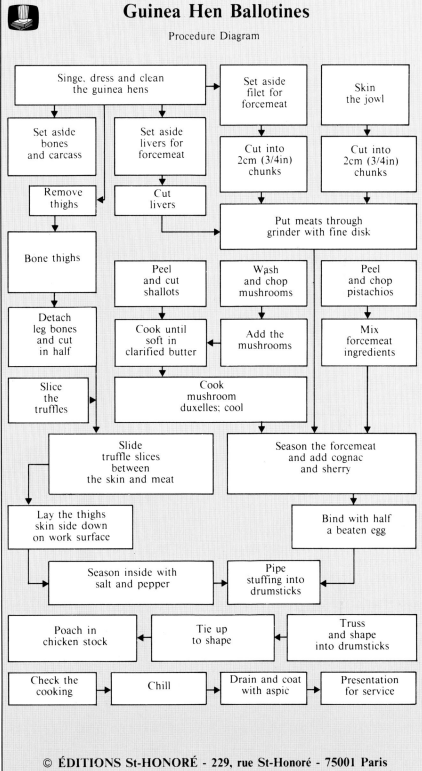

Guinea Hen Ballotines
Procedure Diagram

Singe, dress and clean the guinea hens → Set aside filet for forcemeat → Skin the jowl

Set aside bones and carcass

Set aside livers for forcemeat

Cut into 2cm (3/4in) chunks

Cut into 2cm (3/4in) chunks

Remove thighs

Cut livers

Bone thighs

Put meats through grinder with fine disk

Peel and cut shallots

Wash and chop mushrooms

Peel and chop pistachios

Detach leg bones and cut in half

Cook until soft in clarified butter

Add the mushrooms

Mix forcemeat ingredients

Slice the truffles

Cook mushroom duxelles; cool

Slide truffle slices between the skin and meat

Season the forcemeat and add cognac and sherry

Lay the thighs skin side down on work surface

Bind with half a beaten egg

Season inside with salt and pepper

Pipe stuffing into drumsticks

Poach in chicken stock

Tie up to shape

Truss and shape into drumsticks

Check the cooking

Chill

Drain and coat with aspic

Presentation for service

Galantine of Duck

Introduction

The ingredients in this dish give it great finesse. The garnish of foie gras, tongue, pistachios and truffles marries perfectly with the forcemeat for delicious results.

The decoration and aspic glaze give this dish visual appeal, especially when presented on a decorated platter.

The galantine can be served whole or sliced and arranged on plates, and is appropriate for many occasions--as a first course for a special lunch or dinner, as part of a buffet selection, or as part of a restaurant menu.

Ingredients

For a galantine that is 35cm (14in) long and 9cm (3 1/2in) in diameter, yielding 30 1-cm (3/8-in) slices (estimate a loss of 5cm (2in) when the ends are trimmed):

1 large duck (2.8kg (approx. 6lb))

Forcemeat

750g (1 1/2lb) duck meat, 750g (1 1/2lb) boned blade end of pork, 250g (1/2lb) pork jowl, 45g (1 1/2oz) shallots, 10g (1/3oz) garlic, 1 egg, salt, saltpeter, pepper, allspice, 4cl (3tbsp) cognac, 5cl (1/4 cup) port

Garnish

400g duck breast
200g duck foie gras
150g (5oz) cooked tongue
45g (1 1/2oz) pistachios
20g (2/3oz) truffles
2cl (4tsp) cognac
Salt, saltpeter, pepper, allspice

Cooking Liquid

5-6L (5-6qts) chicken stock or light duck stock

Aspic Glaze

1L (1qt) chicken or duck aspic flavored with port

Decoration

Truffle, cooked egg white, blanched leek green

Equipment

Cutting board, cleaver, chef's knife, paring knife, flexible thin-bladed knife, boning knife, slicing knife, palette knife, spatula, pastry brush, plates, mixing bowls, fish poacher, sheet pan, cooling rack, thermometer, cheesecloth, plastic wrap, galantine " bandage ", kitchen twine, meat grinder, truffle cutter

Preparing the Duck

Pass the duck over a flame to singe off any down and feathers. This step must be done carefully and thoroughly because the skin will be used to wrap the galantine. It will show through the aspic glaze and therefore must be unblemished and intact.

With a chef's knife or cleaver, cut off the neck, wing tips and feet at the lower leg joint.

Boning the Duck

This must be performed carefully so as not to pierce the skin, which will enclose the galantine. For a full explanation of the boning technique, see the recipe for Terrine of Duck and Green Peppercorns, Chapter 3.

Cut the skin around the point where the wings and thighs are attached to the body, then separate the skin completely from the meat.

Cut off the wings and thighs and bone them.

Remove the duck breasts, carefully remove the tendons, then cut

into thin strips before marinating with salt, saltpeter, pepper and allspice and sprinkling with cognac. Two to three hours marination is long enough.

Preparing the Forcemeat

Remove the tendons from the meat taken from the wings and thighs and any other pieces of meat trimmed from the carcass, and cut the meat into chunks.

Skin the jowl and cut it, as well as the blade end, into chunks.

Pass the pork and duck through a meat grinder fitted with a fine disk. Peel the shallots, cut them in half, then cut into fine dice. Peel the garlic, crush it, remove the green

sprout and chop it finely.

Season the ground meat with salt, saltpeter, pepper and allspice.

Mix all the ingredients well with the spatula. Cover and set aside to marinate for 3-5 hours.

The bones and carcass should be reserved for the stock to use in poaching or for the aspic.

Preparing the Garnish Ingredients

Slice the foie gras into strips.

Remove the skin from the

tongue then cut the tongue into strips. Dip the pistachios in boiling water for a few seconds, dry them and then rub off the skin. Slice the truffles into little matchsticks. Set each ingredient aside separately.

Assembling the Galantine

Preparing the Skin

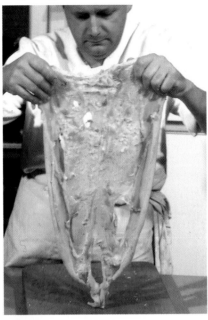

Lay the skin flat on a piece of cheesecloth covered with a piece of plastic wrap. Spread the inside with a layer of forcemeat. Arrange rows of garnish ingredients--duck strips, tongue, foie gras and truffles--over the surface of the forcemeat. Sprinkle with pistachios.

Spread another layer of forcemeat over the rows of garnish.

Arrange a second layer of garnish ingredients (truffles, foie gras, tongue, duck strips).

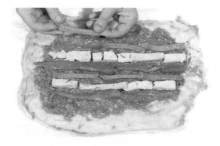

Sprinkle with pistachios and spread a final layer of forcemeat on top.

To make it easier to spread even amounts of forcemeat, divide the mixture in thirds before beginning the assembly.

Rolling the Galantine

Using the skin, roll up the galantine into a neat roll, overlapping the skin at the seam by about 3-4 cm (1 1/4-1 3/4 in). Squeeze the roll tightly with the plastic wrap. Twist the two ends to close them and tie up tightly with twine.

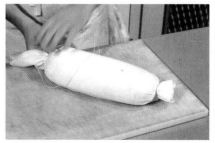

Roll the cheesecloth tightly around the galantine and tie the ends with twine.

Wrap the galantine in a galantine bandage (a long cloth strip specially made for wrapping galantines; if not available, cut a hand

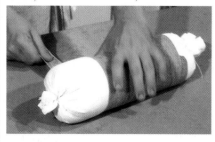

towel into strips or use a whole towel) from one end to the other. Tie the roll securely as if it were a roast, as shown.

Cooking

Place the prepared galantine into a fish poacher with light duck stock or chicken stock. If you wish, add a

bouquet garni or some aromatic vegetables.

Place over a medium heat and bring the temperature of the stock to 85 °C (185F). Check the temperature with a thermometer. For a galantine the size of the one in this recipe, estimate 50-60 minutes of poaching.

Checking the Cooking

The galantine may be tested for

doneness by the time and temperature, but also by touch or with a meat skewer. Insert a skewer or trussing needle into the center of the galantine; leave it in for a few seconds, then remove it and feel it- it should be hot along its entire length. A thermometer inserted into the center will read 80 °C (180F).

Remove the galantine from the heat and leave to cool in its poaching liquid. It will take a long time, therefore it is best to make this in advance. The galantine may be kept in its cooking liquid for 5-6 days.

Glazing and Decorating

Remove the cooled galantine from the stock and place it on a cooling rack.

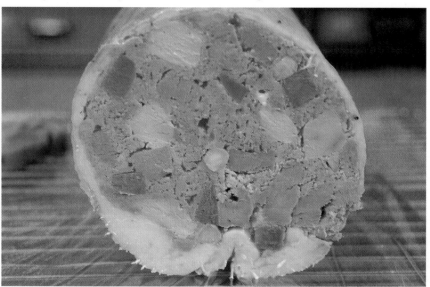

Cut the twine and unroll the bandage. Remove the cheesecloth and plastic wrap after cutting the ends. Carefully dry the outside of the galantine with a hand towel.

Put the galantine on a cooling rack and brush on a coat of aspic that has been stirred over ice until it thickens slightly.

Decorate the top of the galantine with designs made from various ingredients (blanched leek green, cooked egg white, truffles, pistachios, poached carrot strips).

Brush on a second coat of aspic to set the decoration and make the galantine shiny.

Presentation

The chicken galantine is lovely presented on a decorated platter or on a platter simply dressed with salad greens. It may also be sliced and presented on individual plates.

Storage

The decorated and glazed galantine should not be kept for more than 2-3 days. A new coat of aspic should be added daily to keep it looking its best. If the galantine is sliced, the slices should be tightly covered with a piece of plastic wrap.

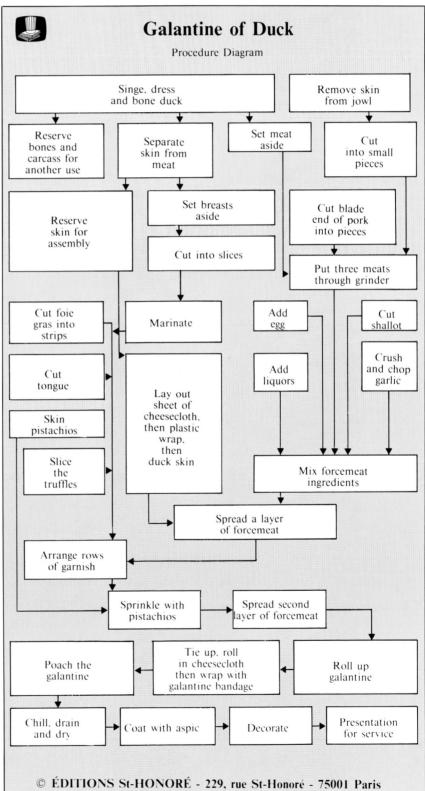

Galantine of Duck

Procedure Diagram

Singe, dress and bone duck

Remove skin from jowl

Reserve bones and carcass for another use

Separate skin from meat

Set meat aside

Cut into small pieces

Reserve skin for assembly

Set breasts aside

Cut blade end of pork into pieces

Cut into slices

Put three meats through grinder

Cut foie gras into strips

Marinate

Add egg

Cut shallot

Cut tongue

Add liquors

Crush and chop garlic

Skin pistachios

Lay out sheet of cheesecloth, then plastic wrap, then duck skin

Slice the truffles

Mix forcemeat ingredients

Spread a layer of forcemeat

Arrange rows of garnish

Sprinkle with pistachios

Spread second layer of forcemeat

Poach the galantine

Tie up, roll in cheesecloth then wrap with galantine bandage

Roll up galantine

Chill, drain and dry

Coat with aspic

Decorate

Presentation for service

© ÉDITIONS St-HONORÉ - 229, rue St-Honoré - 75001 Paris

Galantine of Chicken

Introduction

As stated earlier, the term galantine applies to large pieces. For this dish, be sure to use a fresh top quality chicken.

This is an excellent dish, with balanced flavors and elegant presentation, often served on a decorated platter.

Usually presented as part of a buffet or as a first course for a special dinner, it is always popular because of its visual appeal as well as its delicious taste.

Ingredients

For 12-15 portions:

1 chicken (1.8kg (approx 4lb))

Forcemeat

100g (3 1/2oz) sirloin tip of veal
100g (3 1/2oz) chicken meat
100g (3 1/2oz) jowl
Salt, pepper, saltpeter, allspice
30g (1oz) clarified butter
20g (2/3oz) shallots
90g (3oz) mushrooms
Few drops lemon juice
100g (3 1/2oz) purée of foie gras
1 egg
2cl (4tsp) cognac
3cl (2tbsp) sherry
20g (2/3oz) truffle

Garnish

75g (2 1/2oz) ham
75g (2 1/2oz) tongue
60g (2oz) fat back
30g (1oz) pistachios

Cooking Liquid

5-6L (about 6 quarts) chicken stock

Aspic Glaze

2L (2qts) chaud-froid sauce

Decoration

Truffle, egg white, chicken aspic

Equipment

Cutting board, cleaver, chef's knife, paring knife, flexible fine-bladed knife, palette knife, pastry brush, spatula, trussing needle, kitchen twine, skimmer, ladle, sauté pan with lid, mixing bowls, plates, hotel pans, measuring cup, meat grinder, fish poaching kettle, thermometer, hand towel, sheet pan, cooling rack, truffle cutter

Preparing the Chicken

Singe off any down and feathers from the skin to make it clean and smooth for use in wrapping the galantine.

Remove any bits of impurity from the skin.

With a chef's knife or cleaver, cut off the neck, wing tips and feet at the lower leg joint.

Boning the Chicken

Remove the wishbone, then cut along one side of the backbone and follow the contour of the bones to cut away the meat on either side. Take care not to pierce the skin, which must stay intact in order to wrap up the galantine.

Scrape all the meat from the carcass; reserve the carcass for making stock.

Carefully bone the wings and thighs. For the legs, loosen the cen-

tral bone by scraping the meat away from it, then cut it off halfway down, leaving the lower part of the bone attached to the skin.

Keep the prepared chicken chilled until ready to use. Add the bones to the carcass for use in the stock.

Preparing the Garnish

Trim the ham and tongue completely, then slice into strips.

Plunge the pistachios into boiling water for a few seconds, then rub off the skins.

Set aside each ingredient separately in the refrigerator.

Making the Mushroom Duxelles

Sort, trim, wash and drain the mushrooms, then sprinkle them with lemon juice and chop them.

Peel the shallot, cut it in half, then cut it into fine dice.

In a small saucepan, cook the shallot in clarified butter until it is soft but not brown. Add the mushrooms and season with salt and pepper. Cover the pan and cook for a few minutes to draw the liquid out of the mushrooms.

Remove the lid and continue cooking to evaporate the rendered moisture. When all the liquid has evaporated, transfer the mushrooms to a plate and leave them to cool.

Preparing the Forcemeat Ingredients

Trim the sirloin tip of veal and remove any tendons, then cut it into chunks.

Remove any bones and tendons from the chicken meat (this is in addition to the whole chicken), and cut it into chunks.

Remove the skin from the jowl and cut it into chunks.

Put the three meats through a meat grinder fitted with a fine disk and chill in a covered bowl until ready to use.

Preparing the Purée of Foie Gras

Stir the foie gras with a spatula until it is soft and creamy.

Break the egg.

Chop the truffle finely and reserve on a small plate.

Seasoning and Marinating the Forcemeat

Add the mushroom duxelles, purée of foie gras, egg and chopped truffle to the ground meat.

Season with salt, saltpeter, pepper and allspice. Add the cognac and sherry.

Mix the ingredients well with a spatula.

Cover and leave to marinate 3-5 hours maximum; this will allow the flavors to marry.

Assembling the Galantine

Lay the boned chicken flat on a work surface, spreading it out evenly.

Salt and pepper it lightly.

Spread the chicken with a third of the forcemeat (divide the forcemeat into thirds beforehand to make this easier).

Arrange the strips of fat back, ham and tongue in an alternating pattern on the forcemeat layer.

Sprinkle with pistachios.

Spread on a second layer of forcemeat, then arrange another layer of garnish strips, this time in reverse order so the cross-section of a slice will have a pretty pattern.

Sprinkle with more pistachios, then spread on the third layer of forcemeat.

Close up the chicken by bringing the edges of the skin together and pinching them slightly to form a seam that is sewn shut with kitchen twine.

Make sure the filling is packed in tightly.

Reshape the chicken and truss with kitchen twine so it keeps its shape (pass the twine under the thighs and wings).

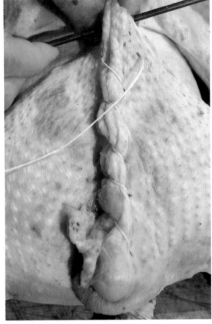

Cooking

The prepared chicken is placed in the poaching pan and covered with light chicken stock, containing a bouquet garni or aromatic vegetables, if you like.

Heat the stock to 75-85 °C (170-185F). Check the temperature with a thermometer.

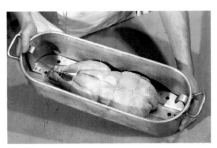

Estimate 50-60 minutes of poaching for an average size chicken.

Checking the Cooking

The chicken can be tested by touch, with a thermometer or by inserting a metal skewer to test the heat at the center (see explanation in Galantine of Duck recipe).

Remove the galantine from the heat and leave to cool in the cooking liquid. It will take a long time to cool, therefore it is best to make this at least one day in advance. The galantine may be kept in its poaching liquid for 4-5 days in the refrigerator.

Remove the galantine from the stock and drain on a rack. Dry with a hand towel and remove all the trussing strings.

Glazing

Place the galantine on a rack, back side down, to coat it with chaud-froid sauce that has been stirred over ice to thicken slightly.

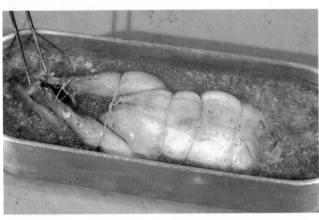

Note: a chaud-froid may be made of a mixture of mayonnaise and aspic, or a classic chaud-froid may be used, made from velouté or béchamel with aspic.

Brush on a thick coat of chaud-froid sauce.

Let this layer set, then pour over a thinner layer using a spoon or a ladle, to give the galantine a very smooth surface.

Decorating

Decorate the galantine according to your personal preference. In the example pictured here, the decoration of black truffles and white egg is simple yet effective.

Other colors can be added by using ingredients such as blanched leek greens or thin strips of poached carrot.

Brush the decorated galantine with a thin layer of clear aspic to secure the decoration and make the galantine shiny.

Presentation

Often presented on a decorated platter, it may also be set on a platter decorated simply with greens or diced aspic, or cut into slices, brushed with a thin layer of aspic and served on plates.

The glazed galantine should be kept no more than 1-2 days and should be reglazed on the second day so it keeps its shine.

If the galantine is sliced and arranged on plates, the slices should be covered tightly with a piece of plastic wrap to keep them from drying out and discoloring. This applies also to slices displayed in a specialty food shop.

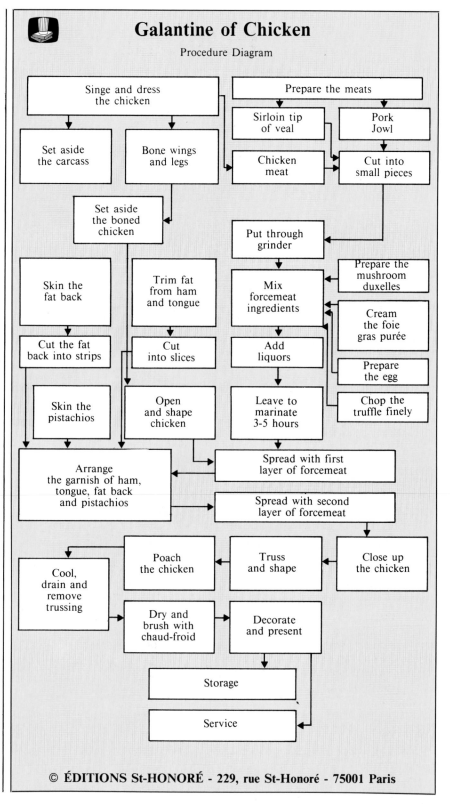

Galantine of Chicken
Procedure Diagram

Singe and dress the chicken → Prepare the meats

Set aside the carcass

Bone wings and legs

Sirloin tip of veal — Pork Jowl

Chicken meat — Cut into small pieces

Set aside the boned chicken

Put through grinder

Skin the fat back

Trim fat from ham and tongue

Mix forcemeat ingredients ← Prepare the mushroom duxelles

Cream the foie gras purée

Cut the fat back into strips

Cut into slices

Add liquors

Prepare the egg

Skin the pistachios

Open and shape chicken

Leave to marinate 3-5 hours

Chop the truffle finely

Arrange the garnish of ham, tongue, fat back and pistachios

Spread with first layer of forcemeat

Spread with second layer of forcemeat

Cool, drain and remove trussing

Poach the chicken

Truss and shape

Close up the chicken

Dry and brush with chaud-froid

Decorate and present

Storage

Service

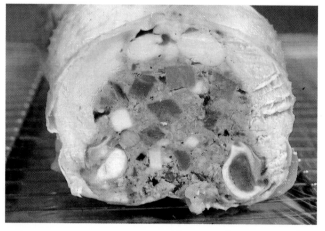

Ballotine of Squab

Introduction

This elegant dish can be made with quail or squab to create lovely ballotines.

Depending on the size of the bird, they are served whole or cut neatly in half and served on a plate with a simple decoration. They are served as a first course for a grand dinner or as a light main course at lunch.

Equipment

Cutting board, paring knife, chef's knife, flexible fine-bladed knife, palette knife, spatula, scissors, vegetable peeler, trussing needle, kitchen twine, plates, pastry bad and medium plain trip, measuring cup, large saucepan, mixing bowls, pastry brush, meat grinder, thermometer, sheet pan, cooling rack

Ingredients

3 suqabs weighing 400g (14oz) each

Garnish

75g (2 1/2oz) foie gras
20g (2/3oz) truffles

Cooking Liquid

2.5L (2.5qts) chicken stock

Aspic Glaze

Chicken aspic

Forcemeat

75g (2 1/2lb) chicken breast meat
75g (2 1/2oz) pork jowl
30g (1oz) squab liver
30g (1oz) purée of foie gras
1cl (2tsp) cognac
2cl (2tsp) sauternes
Salt, saltpeter, pepper, allspice

Aromatic Vegetables

200g (7oz) carrots
75g (2 1/2oz) leeks
20g (2/3 oz) celery
Bouquet garni (thyme, bay leaf, parsley stem)

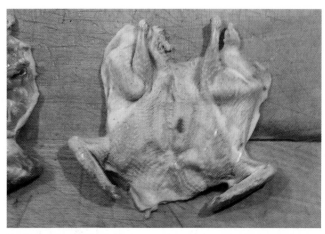

The procedure for making this ballotine of squab is very similar to the procedure for Galantine of Chicken.

Preparing the Squabs

Choose plump young squabs.

Pass the birds over a flame to singe off any remaining down and feathers; make sure the skin is clean and smooth, as it will wrap the ballotine and will show through the aspic glaze.

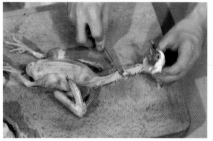

With a chef's knife, cut off the neck, the wing tips and the feet at the lower leg joint.

Cut around the wishbone and remove it. If the squabs still have their innards, remove them. Trim the livers and set them aside. Discard the bile sack and the rest of the innards.

Boning the Squabs

With a paring knife, make an incision along the backbone, then remove the meat from the carcass by scraping carefully away from the bones, taking care not to pierce the skin.

Carefully bone the thighs. Loosen the central leg bone and cut it off halfway, leaving the lower half attached. Remove the upper bone from the wing, but leave the

lower one attached to help the squab keep some shape. Reserve the carcass and bones to make the stock for the poaching liquid. Chill the prepared squabs until ready to use.

Preparing the Forcemeat

Remove the tendons from the chicken breasts (turkey breast may be used also), and cut the meat into 2cm (3/4in) cubes.

Skin the jowl and cut it into pieces the same size as the chicken pieces.

Combine the squab livers with the two meats.

Making the Forcemeat
Put the meats through the meat

grinder fitted with a fine disk.

Combine the ground meat in a bowl with the purée of foie gras, which will bind the forcemeat. Mix well with a spatula.

Season with salt, saltpeter, pep-

per and allspice. Poach or pan-fry a spoonfull of forcemeat, taste and adjust seasoning if necessary.

Add the cognac and sauternes. Mix and chill in the refrigerator for 1-2 hours so the flavors marry well.

Preparing the Garnish Ingredients

Use foie gras from a roll, terrine or can. Cut it into 1cm (3/8in) slices, then into matchsticks about 1cm (3/8in) across. Cut the truffles into 6mm (1/4in) matchsticks.

Filling the Squabs

Lay the squabs in a row with the skin side down.

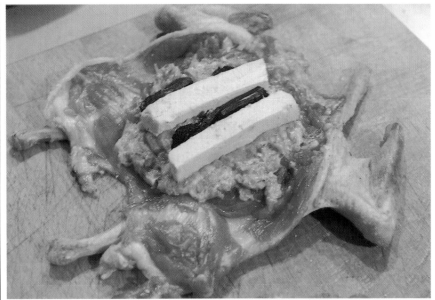

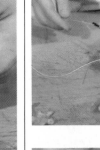

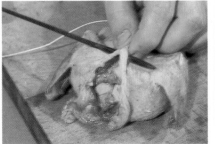

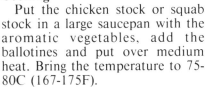

Spread them open and season lightly with salt and pepper. Divide the forcemeat into the number of portions equal to the number of squabs so you are sure to put an even amount into each ballotine. Spread the inside of each squab with half of the portion of forcemeat, using the pastry bag and tip.

Arrange the garnish to have two strips of foie gras placed lengthwise, with a row of truffle in the middle, as shown at left. Spread on the second half of the forcemeat.

Close up the squabs and shape them into their original form. Pinch the skin to form a seam down the back and sew it up with the trussing needle and twine, making sure to leave no gaps.

Truss the squabs to help them keep their shape during cooking.

Cooking

Put the chicken stock or squab stock in a large saucepan with the aromatic vegetables, add the ballotines and put over medium heat. Bring the temperature to 75-80C (167-175F).

Use the thermometer to verify the temperature. Estimate 20-25 minutes poaching time.

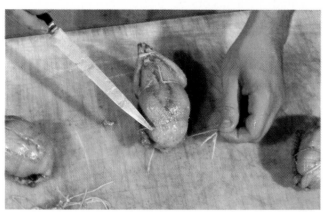

Checking the Cooking

Remove a squab. Insert a trussing needle through the center; leave

it in for a few seconds, then remove it and feel the temperature. It should be hot along its entire length. Leave the squabs to cool in the poaching liquid. Because this takes quite a while, it is best to perform this step at least one day ahead.

The ballotines can be stored 5-6 days in their cooking liquid at 6C (43F).

Glazing

Remove the ballotines from their cooking liquid, place on a cooling

rack to drain, then dry completely with a hand towel.

Remove the trussing strings and return the ballotines to the cooling rack. Coat them with the chicken aspic that is just at the point of setting. Chill until the first coat has set, then brush on a second coat for the best shine.

These squab ballotines are rarely decorated, as the brilliant aspic glaze is sufficient.

Presentation

These ballotines may be presented on a decorated platter, or

more simply on a plate or platter decorated with chopped aspic or a few salad greens.

Conservation

The squab ballotines may be kept 1-2 days; they should be brushed with a new coat of aspic the second day to keep their shine and freshness.

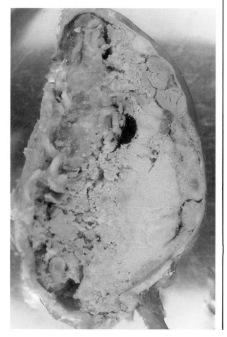

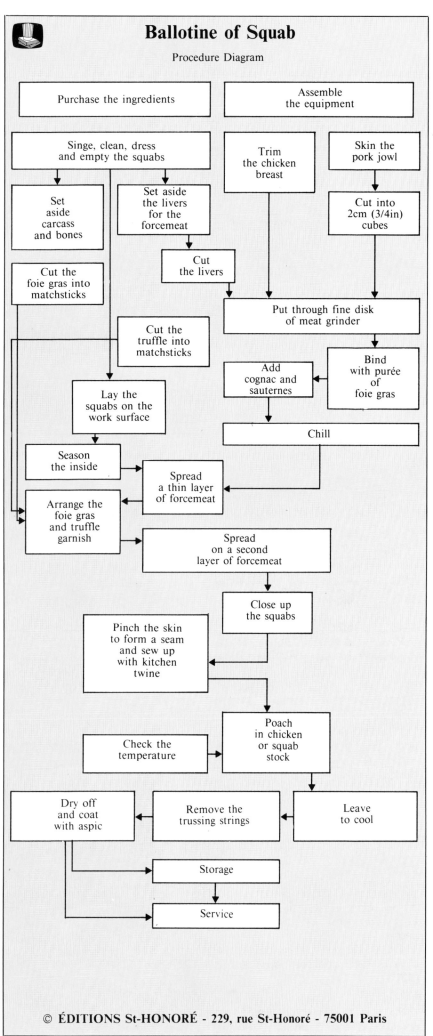

Ballotine of Squab

Procedure Diagram

Purchase the ingredients → Assemble the equipment

Singe, clean, dress and empty the squabs

Set aside carcass and bones

Set aside the livers for the forcemeat

Cut the livers

Trim the chicken breast

Skin the pork jowl

Cut into 2cm (3/4in) cubes

Cut the foie gras into matchsticks

Cut the truffle into matchsticks

Put through fine disk of meat grinder

Bind with purée of foie gras

Add cognac and sauternes

Lay the squabs on the work surface

Chill

Season the inside

Spread a thin layer of forcemeat

Arrange the foie gras and truffle garnish

Spread on a second layer of forcemeat

Close up the squabs

Pinch the skin to form a seam and sew up with kitchen twine

Check the temperature

Poach in chicken or squab stock

Dry off and coat with aspic

Remove the trussing strings

Leave to cool

Storage

Service

© ÉDITIONS St-HONORÉ - 229, rue St-Honoré - 75001 Paris

Galantine of Salmon

Introduction

This galantine is not made very often, yet it has many advantages for the caterer: it has a relatively low food cost for a fancy final product, it is fairly easy to make and its taste is delicious and out of the ordinary.

It rounds out the selection of galantines, and it is appropriate for service at many occasions: in a restaurant, as part of a cold buffet, as a first course for a special dinner.

It may be presented on a decorated platter or arranged on plates. A " green sauce " (mayonnaise flavored with fresh herbs) or mousseline sauce (hollandaise lightened with whipped cream) makes a delicious accompaniment. The galantine of salmon is different from meat or poultry galantines in this respect, as the latter are rarely served with a sauce.

Ingredients

For a galantine 32cm (13in) long and 8cm (3 1/4in) in diameter, yielding about 30 slices:

Forcemeat

2kg (4 1/2lb) salmon filets, 3/4L (3 cups) " Americaine " sauce (made with full flavored fish stock, tomatoes, coqnac, and herbs) reduced to 1/4L (1 cup)

" Panade " (Binding Ingredients)

120g (4oz) flour – 4 egg yolks
90g (3oz) melted butter
250g (1 cup) milk
Salt, pepper, nutmeg

Garnish

20 crayfish – 1 bunch sorrel
6 sole filets – 30g (1oz) pistachios

Cooking Liquid

6L (6qts) fish stock

Decoration

Egg whites – Truffle – Chervil

Aspic Glaze

Fish aspic

Equipment

Cutting board, paring knife, fish fileting knife, chef's knife, pastry brush, spatula, vegetable peeler, pastry scraper, palette knife, mixing bowls, plates, large saucepan, sauté pan, measuring cup, copper

bowl, colander, sheet pan, cooling rack, food processor, hand towels, cheesecloth, plastic wrap, galantine bandage, kitchen twine, fish poacher, thermometer, drum sieve

Preparing the Salmon

Use prepared boneless salmon filets or a whole salmon. For the whole salmon, rinse it, cut off the fins, scale it, rinse under running water, cut open the belly, remove the innards and wash the inside.

Using the paring knife or the fish fileting knife, cut off the filets.

Remove the skin and rinse the filets with cold water to make sure they are completely clean.

Lay the filets on a hand towel to dry them, then chill (at 4C (40F)) until ready to use.

Preparing the Panade

In a saucepan, combine the flour, the melted butter and the egg yolks.

Season with salt, pepper and a pinch of grated nutmeg. Mix with a spatula, then add the milk which has been heated in another pan.

Mix together well, put the pan over low heat and stir over the heat

for a few second to dry out the mixture (as for cream puff pastry). Transfer to a plate to cool. Cover with plastic wrap or rub a little butter over the surface to prevent formation of a skin.

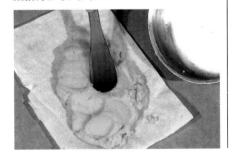

The Salt Water Crayfish

Remove the shells from the raw crayfish, rinse them under cold water and dry them on a hand towel. The shells may be used to make the fish stock.

The Sorrel

Remove and discard any tough stems, then wash the sorrel leaves carefully and drain them. In a large pan that conducts heat well, bring some salted water to a rolling boil. Prepare a bowl of ice water.

With the help of a skimmer, plunge the sorrel leaves into the boiling water; immediately remove them and put them in the ice water to stop the cooking process--do this leaf by leaf. Lay the chilled leaves out carefully on a hand towel to dry.

Roll up each crayfish in a prepared sorrel leaf and set aside in the refrigerator.

The Sole Filets

Trim the filets and with the flat side of the chef's knife or a cleaver, tap lightly to flatten the filets and break the thin tendons that would otherwise cause the fish to shrink and curl during cooking. Dry off the filets on a hand towel, then cut them in half lengthwise and chill

until ready to use.

The Pistachios

Plunge the pistachios in boiling water for a few seconds to loosen their skins, dry them off then rub off the skins. Set aside.

Making the Salmon Forcemeat

Cut the chilled salmon filets into pieces so it is easier purée them in the food processor. Process the salmon until it starts to hold in a mass, then gradually add the reduction of " Americaine " sauce.

Transfer the salmon mixture to a mixing bowl and add the panade.

Season with salt and pepper and mix thoroughly with a spatula. Poach or pan-fry a spoonful of

forcemeat and taste then adjust seasoning if necessary.

Assembling the Galantine

Lay a piece of cheesecloth on the

work surface and lay a piece of plastic wrap on top. Divide the forcemeat into three equal parts.

Spread the first portion of forcemeat on the plastic to form a rectangle approximately 28-30cm (11-12in) by 12-15cm (5-6in). Arrange

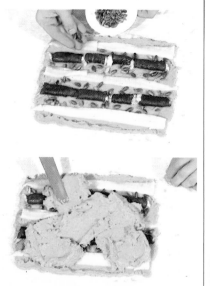

lengthwise rows of garnish, alternating the filets of sole and the sorrel-wrapped crayfish, as shown.

Sprinkle half the pistachios on top. Spread on a second layer of forcemeat.

Arrange another layer of garnish, reversing the order of the sole and crayfish rows so the garnish will form a pretty pattern when the galantine is rolled and sliced.

Sprinkle the rest of the pistachios on top.

Spread on the last portion of forcemeat.

Rolling the Galantine

With the help of the plastic wrap, roll up the galantine tightly. Twist the two ends firmly to seal. Roll the

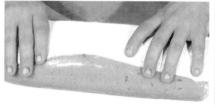

sheet of cheesecloth around the galantine securely to help the galantine keep its cylindrical shape.

Tie up the two ends with kitchen twine. Wrap the galantine carefully and fairly tightly with the galantine

bandage (a long cloth strip specially made for wrapping galantines; if not available, cut a hand towel into strips or use a whole towel).

Tie the galantine with kitchen twine as if it were a roast, as shown.

Cooking

Put the prepared galantine in a fish poacher and cover with fish stock. Put the pan over medium

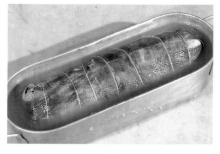

heat and bring the temperature of the stock to 70-75C (158-167F). Use a thermometer to monitor the temperature.

For a galantine the size of the one in this recipe, estimate 30-35 minutes poaching time.

Leave the galantine to cool in its poaching liquid. As with all preparations of this kind, allow plenty of time for cooling; it is best to cook

them at least one day in advance. They may be kept in the poaching liquid 4-5 days at 4C (40F).

Glazing and Decorating

Remove the galantine from the poaching liquid and set it on the cooling rack to drain. Remove the trussing strings, unwrap the galantine bandage, then cut the ends of the cheesecloth and plastic wrap and remove them. Dry the galantine with a hand towel. Set the galantine on the cooling rack and with a spoon or ladle pour over a coat of fish aspic that has been chilled until it is ready to set.

Decorate the top of the galantine with colorful ingredients such as leek green, carrot, pimentos, zucchini skin and eggplant skin.

Apply another coat of aspic with a pastry brush to fix the decoration and make the galantine shine.

Presentation

This galantine can be presented whole on a decorated platter or cut into slices arranged on a plate. The slices should be brushed with a thin layer of aspic to keep them from drying out. If slices are to be displayed in a refrigerated case, they should be covered tightly with a piece of plastic wrap.

The finished galantines may be kept 1-2 days and a new coat of aspic should be applied the second day. Serve the galantine with a green sauce or mousseline sauce.

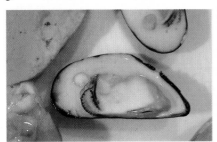

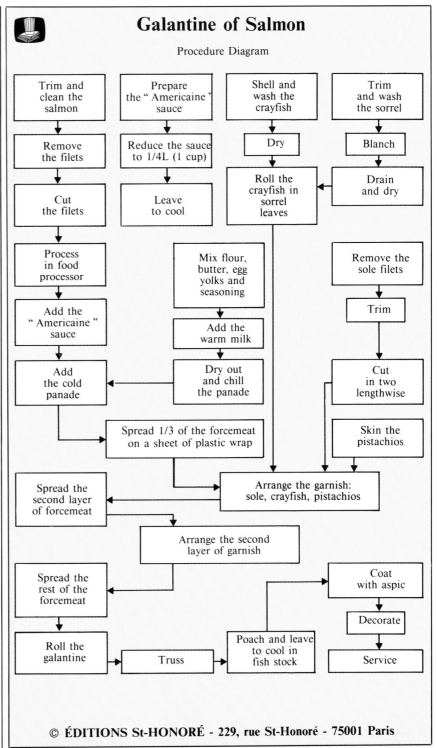

Galantine of Salmon

Procedure Diagram

Trim and clean the salmon → Remove the filets → Cut the filets → Process in food processor → Add the "Americaine" sauce → Add the cold panade

Prepare the "Americaine" sauce → Reduce the sauce to 1/4L (1 cup) → Leave to cool

Shell and wash the crayfish → Dry → Roll the crayfish in sorrel leaves

Trim and wash the sorrel → Blanch → Drain and dry

Mix flour, butter, egg yolks and seasoning → Add the warm milk → Dry out and chill the panade

Remove the sole filets → Trim → Cut in two lengthwise → Skin the pistachios

Spread 1/3 of the forcemeat on a sheet of plastic wrap

Arrange the garnish: sole, crayfish, pistachios

Spread the second layer of forcemeat

Arrange the second layer of garnish

Spread the rest of the forcemeat

Coat with aspic → Decorate → Service

Roll the galantine → Truss → Poach and leave to cool in fish stock

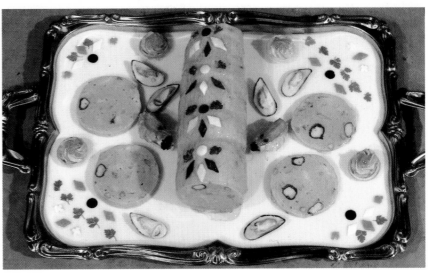

Chapter 5
Aspics

Aspics are a lovely addition to a dinner buffet. They can be made in many different shapes, and the caterer can vary the ingredients to reflect the season and the tastes of the customer.

The selection in this chapter shows the variety that is possible using different molds and ingredients.

Aspics made in rectangular shapes can be particularly dramatic when colorful leaves of cabbage are used to line the mold.

Since each ingredient is seen through the crystal clear aspic, it is important to shape and arrange all of the ingredients in an attractive way.

The selection in this chapter includes:

Chicken Aspic with Sherry

Seafood Aspic with Vegetables

Aspic with Foie Gras

Rabbit and Crayfish Aspic

Ham and Parsley in Aspic

General Advice for Making Aspic

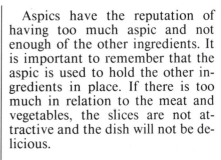

The Aspic

The aspic used to make these lovely dishes should have enough gelatin to be firm enough to slice neatly. Too much gelatin, however, gives the aspics a chewy consistency. You can test the aspic by pouring a little on a plate, chilling it to set and testing the texture.

The color should be an appetizing amber and the aspic should be crystal clear so that the neatly arranged, colorful ingredients are visible.

Different stocks and flavorings are used to make aspics that marry well with the other ingredients. For example, seafood aspics should be made from a fish stock.

Aspics have the reputation of having too much aspic and not enough of the other ingredients. It is important to remember that the aspic is used to hold the other ingredients in place. If there is too much in relation to the meat and vegetables, the slices are not attractive and the dish will not be delicious.

Assembly

The aspics are assembled in steps by arranging the garnish in layers, covering with aspic, chilling to set, then arranging the next layer.

The bottom of the molds are decorated with attractively shaped vegetables, egg white, meats, truffles etc. to make the aspic an eye-catching presentation when it is unmolded.

It is important to use a variety of colors in each aspic and arrange each layer of garnish neatly so that each slice is attractive.

Storage

Left in the mold and covered securely with plastic wrap, aspics will keep 3-4 days in the refrigerator.

They should be kept chilled at all times. It is recommended to have insulated containers to transport them. It is important to inform the customer to keep the aspic cold until ready to serve.

Presentation

For neat slices, use a very sharp knife that is heated before cutting each slice.

Aspics should always be served cold, however, they are best when allowed to sit unrefrigerated a little to " take the chill off ".

If it is necessary to arrange the slice well in advance, cover each plate with plastic wrap.

Present the slices of aspic on plates with a simple garnish of lettuce leaves.

Chicken Aspic with Sherry

Introduction

This aspic combines fresh tasting colorful ingredients, resulting in a delicious dish.

The chicken aspic is flavored with sherry in this recipe, however madeira or port would also be appropriate.

It is important to use a top quality chicken. The chicken is poached and cooled in the cooking liquid. The breasts are then coated with a chaud-froid sauce and the meat from the rest of the chicken is made into a light mousse. These two preparations make a lovely contrast of texture in this dish.

Equipment

Cutting board, fluted aspic mold, mixing bowls, chef's knife, thin-bladed flexible knife, cleaver, vegetable peeler, paring knife, palette knife, ladle, spatula, pastry scraper, drum sieve, pastry brush, trussing needle and kitchen twine, saucepans, plates, measuring cup, colander, fine-meshed conical sieve, hotel pan, egg slicer, pastry cutter, ice bath, food processor, cooling rack, sheet pan, round rack, round baking sheet, pastry bag and tip

Ingredients

(for 2L (2qt) molds)
1 large chicken, chicken stock
1 carrot
1 stalk celery
57g (2 1/2oz) onions
20g (2/3oz) shallots
3 cloves garlic
1 bouquet garni
9 quail eggs
30g (1oz) corn kernels
45g (1 1/2oz) green beans
75g (2 1/2oz) peas
100g (3 1/2oz) carrots
100g (3 1/2oz) turnips
Truffles
Chicken aspic

Preparing the Chicken

To prepare the chicken to be poached, cut off the feet, the neck, and the wing tips. To clean the inside of the bird, first loosen the lungs that are attached to the rib cage, then pull out all the innards. Truss the chicken.

Poaching the Chicken

The chicken is poached in chicken stock with an addition of aromatic vegetables to augment the flavor.

The carrots, onions and shallots and celery are cut into medium dice. The garlic is crushed, a bouquet garni is made with bay leaf, thyme and parsley tied together in a leek leaf. Add these ingredients to the stock.

Place the trussed chicken in the chicken stock and lay a hand towel on top to keep the bird moist during cooking.

Bring the liquid to a simmer (about 85 °C (185F)). Poach the chicken for about 1 hour depending on the size and quality of the chicken.

The flesh should be firm to the touch and the juice clear. (Prick the leg to test the juices.)

Leave the chicken to completely cool in the stock, then place on a rack to drain. It is best to prepare the chicken to this point several hours before assembling the aspic.

Cutting Up the Chicken

Remove the legs. Neatly cut around each breast, remove it, take off the skin and trim the breasts of fat if necessary. Set aside the carcass and the legs for the mousse.

Slice the chicken breasts in pieces as shown, cutting across the grain. Chill the chicken until ready to coat with chaud-froid.

Preparing the Chaud-froid

2/3 mayonnaise
1/3 chicken aspic

Melt the aspic, then set it over ice to cool and thicken slightly. (It should be the same temperature as the mayonnaise.)

Gently whisk the aspic into the mayonnaise, taking care not to incorporate any air which will create bubbles in the chaud-froid.

Set the chaud-froid over ice to thicken slightly. It should have the consistency of very thick cream.

Coat the chilled pieces of chicken with the chaud-froid using a spoon or pastry brush.

Chill to set and apply another coat of chaud-froid if necessary.

Making the Chicken Mousse

Take all the chicken meat off the bones of the legs and carcass. Remove the skin and trim away fat and tendons.

Ingredients

For 2 2L (2qt) aspics
150g (5oz) chicken meat
45g (1 1/2oz) goose liver mousse
7cl (approx. 1/4 cup) chicken aspic
1dl (1/2 cup) heavy cream, whipped
Seasonings (salt, pepper)

Purée the meat in the food processor and add the melted aspic in a steady stream.

Pass this mixture through a fine-meshed drum sieve to make it smooth, being sure to scrape the

underside of the sieve to recuperate all the purée.
Stir in the liver mousse until completely incorporated.

Fold in the whipped cream, working over ice if necessary.

Add salt and pepper to taste.

253

Preparing the " Macedoine " of Vegetables

The aspic includes a colorful assortment of vegetables cut in small pieces (" macedoine ").

Peel the carrots and turnips, remove the strings from the green beans, and shell the peas, then rinse all the vegetables in cold water.

Cut the green beans in even pieces (about the size of a pea), and cut the carrots and turnips in small dice about the same size.

Cooking the Vegetables

Cook all the vegetables separately in salted boiling water. As soon as they are cooked, drain and refresh in ice water to set the bright color and stop the cooking.

Drain all the vegetables well, then dry them on a hand towel.

Assembling the Aspic

Chill the molds to facilitate the assembly.

Set the molds in a pan with crushed ice so that the layers of aspic will set quickly and the aspic will not melt at room temperature.

Pour a thin layer of aspic in the bottom of the mold and chill in the refrigerator to set.

Place a decoration of egg whites and truffles, cut out with a pastry cutter, on the bottom of the mold.

Arrange a layer of the chicken coated with chaud-froid, placing

the more attractive side facing the bottom of the mold.

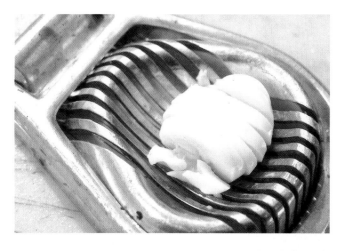

Cover the pieces of chicken with aspic and chill to set.

Add a mixture of all the vegetables in an even layer. Pour aspic to cover the vegetables and chill to set.

For the next layer, alternate slices of hard-boiled quail egg and rosettes of the chicken mousse, piped out with a pastry bag and star tip.

Cover these ingredients with aspic and chill to set.

Finish with another layer of pieces of chicken coated with chaud-froid.

Pour aspic to cover the chicken pieces completely and chill for several hours to allow the aspic to set completely.

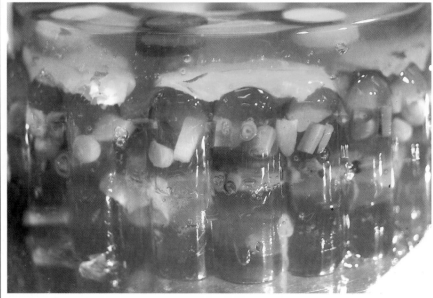

To unmold the aspic, set the mold in a basin of warm water for a few moments, then turn out onto a platter.

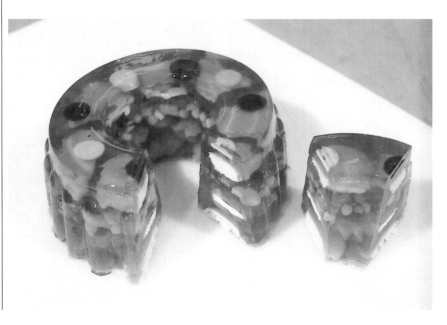

Storage

Once the aspic has set, cover the mold securely with plastic wrap. Left in the mold, the aspic will keep up to 48 hours in the refrigerator at 4 °C (40F).

Presentation

Aspics are always eaten cold, but for the best taste they should not be served directly from the refrigerator.

Slice the aspic with a very sharp knife dipped in hot water.

Decorate the plate or platter with some lettuce leaves.

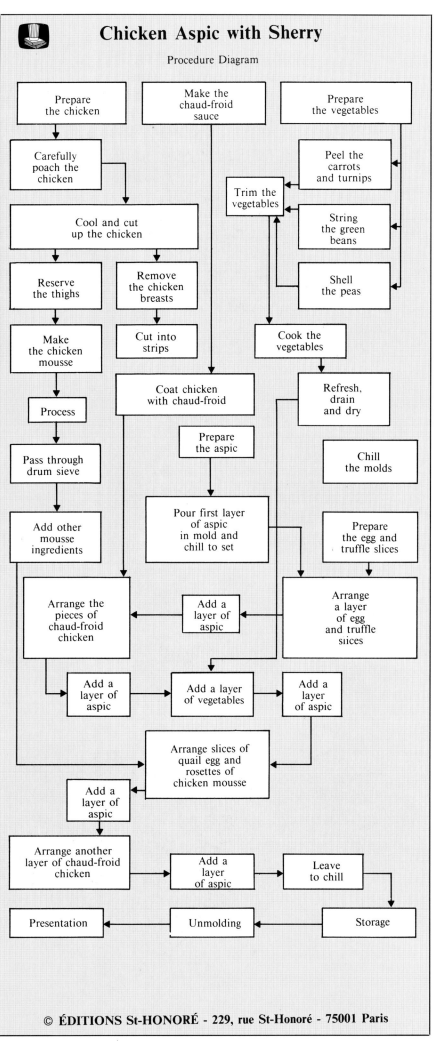

Chicken Aspic with Sherry

Procedure Diagram

- Prepare the chicken
  - Carefully poach the chicken
  - Cool and cut up the chicken
    - Reserve the thighs
      - Make the chicken mousse
        - Process
        - Pass through drum sieve
        - Add other mousse ingredients
    - Remove the chicken breasts
      - Cut into strips
- Make the chaud-froid sauce
  - Coat chicken with chaud-froid
  - Prepare the aspic
    - Pour first layer of aspic in mold and chill to set
- Prepare the vegetables
  - Peel the carrots and turnips
  - String the green beans
  - Shell the peas
  - Trim the vegetables
  - Cook the vegetables
  - Refresh, drain and dry
  - Chill the molds
  - Prepare the egg and truffle slices
  - Arrange a layer of egg and truffle slices

- Arrange the pieces of chaud-froid chicken
- Add a layer of aspic
- Add a layer of aspic
- Add a layer of vegetables
- Add a layer of aspic
- Arrange slices of quail egg and rosettes of chicken mousse
- Add a layer of aspic
- Arrange another layer of chaud-froid chicken
- Add a layer of aspic
- Leave to chill
- Storage
- Unmolding
- Presentation

© **ÉDITIONS St-HONORÉ - 229, rue St-Honoré - 75001 Paris**

Seafood Aspic
with Vegetables

Introduction

This aspic combines a delicious variety of seafood with a colorful garnish of vegetables.

The example shown here is assembled in a ring mold (used most often in pastry to make " savarins "). The lovely spirals of sole " paupiettes " are particularly attractive when arranged in this mold.

The aspic is made with fish stock that is carefully clarified. An infusion of fresh herbs such as tarragon and a few drops of anisette can enhance the flavor of this aspic.

Ingredients

For 2 ring aspics (1.5L (1 1/2qt)
  " savarin " molds)
6 filets of sole
6 salt water crayfish
10 medium shrimp
1/2L (1/2qt) mussels
Approximately 12 spinach leaves
1 lemon
1 lime
2 carrots (approx. 200g (7oz))
1 avocado
1/4 cup green peppercorns in
  brine
1 cup corn kernels
200g (7oz) red pepper
Fish aspic

Equipment

Cutting board, aspic molds, mixing
bowls, chef's knife, vegetable
peeler, paring knife, ladle, palette
knife, spatula, pastry scraper,
saucepans, plates, measuring cup,
fine-meshed conical sieve, hotel
pan, ice bath, cooling rack, sheet
pan, toothpicks, channel cutter

Preparing the Seafood

The variety of seafood for this
aspic includes: sole, crayfish, mussels and shrimp.

The Sole Paupiettes

These lovely spirals are made by
rolling filets of sole with leaves of
spinach and crayfish to make
" paupiettes ", then slicing them.

Bone the sole. Use the bones to
make stock and trim the filets to
make the paupiettes. Remove the
shells from the crayfish. Wash the
spinach ad remove the stems. Lay
the filets flat with the skin side up
and season with salt and pepper.

Place an uncooked spinach leaf
on each filet.

Place a crayfish at the end of
each filet and roll up to form a
paupiette. Secure the end with a
toothpick.

Poaching the Paupiettes

Poach the paupiettes in fish
stock or a court bouillon. Start the
cooking in cold stock, then bring
the liquid to a simmer and poach
gently.

Let the paupiettes cool in the liquid. When they are cool, drain
them on a hand towel.

Slice the paupiettes into medallions about 1/2cm (approx. 1/4in)
thick and set aside in the refrigerator until ready to assemble the
aspic.

The Shrimp

Remove the shells from the
shrimp and pull off the dark vein
that runs the length of the shrimp.
Cut them in half lengthwise and set
aside in the refrigerator.

The Mussels

Rinse the mussels in a basin of
cold water, changing the water sev-

eral times until all the sand is eliminated.

Cook them " à la marinière " by
steaming them open in a large pot

with white wine, shallots and parsley.

Remove the shells and pull off
the black rim or " beard ". Set the
mussels aside in the refrigerator.

Preparing the Vegetable Garnish

This step includes seven different preparations.

The Lemons and Limes

The lemon and lime are prepared in the same way, however, the zest of the lime is tougher and more bitter and therefore needs to be blanched twice.

Cut off the ends of the fruit and carefully pare the zest (not the white pith) with a vegetable peeler. Cut the pieces of zest into very thin strips (julienne).

Blanch the lemon and lime julienne separately. Place them in cold water and bring to a boil for 3-4 minutes, refresh under cold running water, then drain. Repeat the process for the lime zest.

Peel the white pith from the lemon and line and cut out each section of fruit with a thin-bladed stainless steel knife.

Cut the sections into small pieces and set aside in the refrigerator.

The Avocado

Choose an avocado that is ripe but not too soft. Cut in half, remove the pit and carefully scoop out the flesh and sprinkle with lemon juice.

Cut the avocado into small dice and sprinkle with lemon juice.

Set aside in the refrigerator.

The Red Pepper

You can use fresh red pepper or top quality pimentos sold in jars.

Cut the fresh pepper in half and remove the seeds. Blanch in boiling water, then peel away the skin and cut into small dice.

Set aside in the refrigerator.

The Green Peppercorns

Drain the green peppercorns, dry them on a paper towel and set aside.

The Corn

Drain the corn, dry on a paper towel and set aside.

The Spinach

The spinach used in the sole paupiettes is washed thoroughly and the stems are removed.

The Carrots

Choose vibrant carrots that are large enough to make attractive slices or "rondelles" to decorate the aspic.

Peel the carrots and rinse them.

Using a channel cutter, cut grooves the length of the carrot to make lovely fluted slices.

Slice the carrots about 2-3mm (1/8in) thick.

Cook the carrots in boiling salted water, making sure not to overcook them so they maintain their decorative shape.

Stop the cooking by plunging the carrots into ice water, and remove them as soon as they are cooled so they do not become watery. Drain them on a hand towel.

Set aside in the refrigerator.

Assembling the Aspic

Chill the molds.

To facilitate the assembly, set the mold in a pan with crushed ice, and set the aspic in a bowl of crushed ice as well.

Pour a thin layer of aspic in the bottom of the mold and chill in the refrigerator to set.

Arrange alternating slices of paupiette and fluted carrots.

Cover with aspic and chill to set.

Arrange dices of avocado, red pepper, lemon and lime mixed with corn and green peppercorns over the surface of the aspic.

Cover with aspic and chill to set.

Storage

Once the aspic has set, cover the mold securely with plastic wrap.

Left in the mold, the aspic will keep up to 48 hours in the refrigerator at 4 ^{0}C (40F).

Alternate the shrimp and mussels as shown and top them with a mixture of lemon and lime julienne.

Cover with aspic and chill to set.

Finish the assembly with another layer of medallions of sole paupiettes and fluted carrot slices.

Cover with aspic and chill the aspic for several hours to completely set.

It is recommended to make the aspic the day before it will be served.

Unmolding

To unmold the aspic, set the mold in a basin of warm water for a few moments, then turn onto a platter.

Presentation

Aspics are always eaten cold, but for the best taste, allow them to rest a few minutes out of the refrigerator to " take the chill off ".

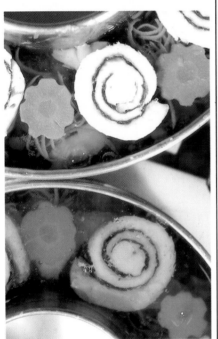

Seafood Aspic with Vegetables

Procedure Diagram

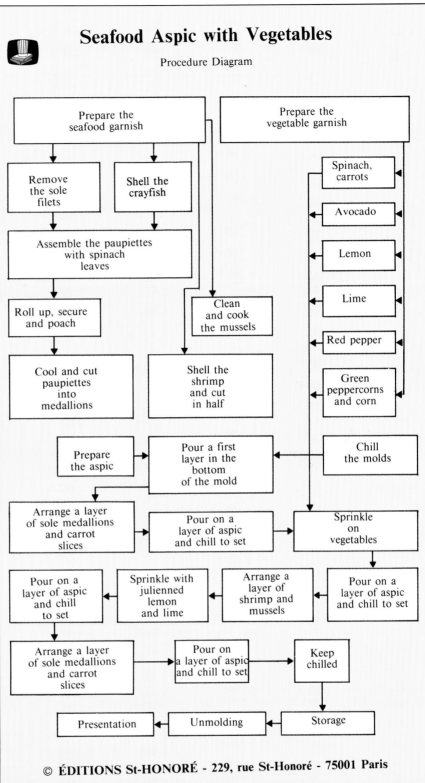

Prepare the seafood garnish	**Prepare the vegetable garnish**

Remove the sole filets → Shell the crayfish

Spinach, carrots
Avocado
Lemon
Lime
Red pepper
Green peppercorns and corn

Assemble the paupiettes with spinach leaves

Roll up, secure and poach → Clean and cook the mussels

Cool and cut paupiettes into medallions → Shell the shrimp and cut in half

Prepare the aspic → Pour a first layer in the bottom of the mold ← Chill the molds

Arrange a layer of sole medallions and carrot slices → Pour on a layer of aspic and chill to set → Sprinkle on vegetables

Pour on a layer of aspic and chill to set ← Sprinkle with julienned lemon and lime ← Arrange a layer of shrimp and mussels ← Pour on a layer of aspic and chill to set

Arrange a layer of sole medallions and carrot slices → Pour on a layer of aspic and chill to set → Keep chilled

Presentation ← Unmolding ← Storage

Slice the aspic with a very sharp knife dipped in hot water. Decorate the platter with halved fluted lemon slices.

© **ÉDITIONS St-HONORÉ - 229, rue St-Honoré - 75001 Paris**

Aspic with Foie Gras

Introduction

This is a very festive aspic that uses luxurious ingredients, therefore it is more expensive and is usually served for special occasions.

The foie gras and truffles are set in an aspic flavored with Sauternes, which enhances these ingredients.

Equipment

Cutting board, mixing bowls, aspic molds, small round pastry cutter, sharpening steel, paring knife, thin-bladed flexible knife, palette knife, ice bath, plates, ladle, pastry brush, saucepan, whisk, spoon, cooling rack

Ingredients

For 2 1 3/4L (1 3/4qt) molds
350g (11oz) foie gras " en bloc "
150g (5oz) foie gras mousse
4 hard-boiled eggs
1 truffle
45g (1 1/2oz) green beans
2 artichokes
Sauternes
Aspic flavored with Sauternes

Preparing the Vegetable Garnish

The Green Beans

Choose very thin, top quality green beans.

Remove the strings and rinse the beans. Cook the beans by plunging them into rapidly boiling salted water. Cook them until they are no longer crunchy but still firm. Stop the cooking by plunging them into ice water.

As soon as they are cool, drain them so they do not become watery, then dry them on a hand towel. Cut them into pieces about 3-4cm (1 1/4-1 3/4in) long.

The Artichokes

Choose large fresh artichokes.

Trim the leaves with a stiff-bladed stainless steel knife, as shown in Chapter 1.

Cook them in salted water with lemon added to keep them from darkening.

A "blanc" can also be used to keep the color. The "blanc" (which means "white" in French) is made with flour, olive oil, lemon juice, salt, pepper and a few coriander seeds, combined in a pot of water and heated before the artichokes are added.

Bring the liquid to a simmer and cook until tender but firm. Let the artichokes cool in the liquid.

Drain the cooled artichoke bottoms in a colander, then dry them on a hand towel.

Remove the "choke" and cut into slices about 3-4mm (1/8in) thick. Artichoke bottoms from a can or jar can be used, but the taste and texture is inferior to fresh ones.

The Eggs

Place the eggs gently in a pot of simmering salted water and cook for 10 minutes (for large eggs).

Cool them under cold running water, then remove the shells without damaging the whites.

Rinse them to remove any bits of shell and dry them on a hand towel.

The Truffle

Cut the truffle into thin slices. Use the largest slices for the decoration on the top of the aspic. Cut the slices into a circle or other shape with a pastry cutter. Cut the rest of the slices into matchsticks.

Preparing the Foie Gras

Stir the foie gras mousse until it is creamy and stir in Sauternes until the consistency is right for piping. (Smooth, soft but will hold its shape.)

Cut the "bloc" of foie gras in slices using a thin-bladed knife dipped in hot water.

Set aside in the refrigerator.

Assembling the Aspic

To facilitate the assembly, set the mold and bowl of aspic in a bowl of ice.

Pour a thin layer of aspic in the bottom of the mold and chill in the refrigerator to set.

Arrange decoratively-shaped truffle and egg white in an attractive pattern on the bottom. Cover with aspic and chill to set.

Next, place the slices of foie gras and pipe out rosettes of mousse between the slices as shown. Cover with aspic and chill to set.

Cover the surface of the aspic with a mixture of the artichokes, | green beans and truffles, as shown. | Cover with aspic and chill to set.

Arrange a second layer of slices of foie gras and rosettes of mousse.

Cover with aspic and chill for several hours to set completely.

Storage

Once the aspic has set, cover the mold securely with plastic wrap. Left in the mold, the aspic will keep up to 48 hours in the refrigerator at 4 °C (40F).

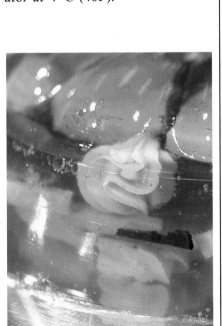

Unmolding

To unmold, dip the mold in a bowl of warm water for a few moments.

Invert the mold on a platter and shake it gently to help release the aspic from the mold.

Presentation

Aspics are always eaten cold, but for the best taste, allow them to sit at room temperature for a few minutes to "take the chill off".

Slice the aspic with a very sharp knife dipped in hot water.

Because the aspic is very decorative in itself, the only other decoration needed on the platter is a few salad greens.

Aspic with Foie Gras
Procedure Diagram

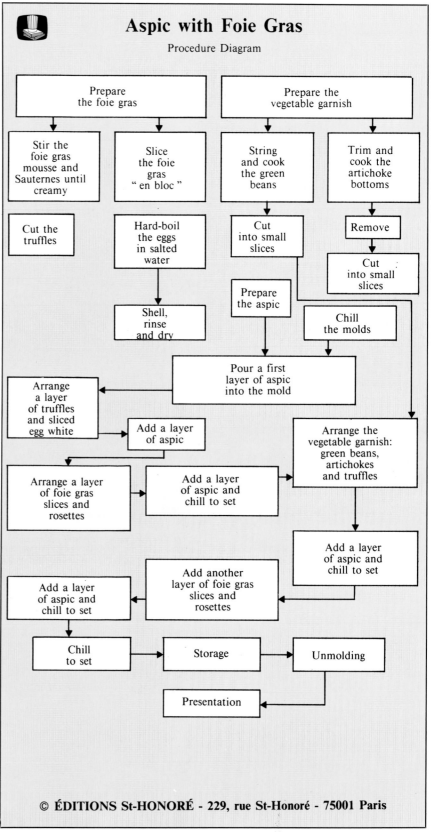

Prepare the foie gras → Stir the foie gras mousse and Sauternes until creamy → Cut the truffles

Prepare the foie gras → Slice the foie gras "en bloc" → Hard-boil the eggs in salted water → Shell, rinse and dry

Prepare the vegetable garnish → String and cook the green beans → Cut into small slices

Prepare the vegetable garnish → Trim and cook the artichoke bottoms → Remove → Cut into small slices

Prepare the aspic → Pour a first layer of aspic into the mold

Chill the molds → Pour a first layer of aspic into the mold

Pour a first layer of aspic into the mold → Arrange a layer of truffles and sliced egg white → Add a layer of aspic → Arrange a layer of foie gras slices and rosettes → Add a layer of aspic and chill to set → Arrange the vegetable garnish: green beans, artichokes and truffles → Add a layer of aspic and chill to set → Add another layer of foie gras slices and rosettes → Add a layer of aspic and chill to set → Chill to set → Storage → Unmolding → Presentation

Aspic of Rabbit and Crayfish

This dramatic aspic uses blanched cabbage leaves to line the mold and encase the other ingredients.

In this chapter, the recipe is made in a rectangular mold, however, it would be equally attractive assembled in a ring mold.

Rabbit and crayfish are both delicate and marry well together to make this delicious dish.

Equipment

Terrine molds, mixing bowls, cutting board, sheet pan, cooling rack, sharpening steel, paring knife, thin-bladed flexible knife, chef's knife, plates, sauté pans, skimmer, ice bath, saucepan, pastry brush, ladle, tablespoon, hotel pan, colander, fine-meshed conical sieve

Ingredients

For a terrine mold 29cm (11 1/2in) long by 10cm (4in) wide by 9cm (3 1/2in) high
1 rabbit, approx. 1.6kg (3.5lb)
1 green cabbage
1 small bunch chervil
1 small bunch chives
1 small bunch tarragon
30 fresh water crayfish
3 leeks (green part only)
180g (6oz) shallots
150g (5oz) spring onions
Rabbit aspic

Preparing the Rabbit

Bone the rabbit using the techniques described in the recipe for Rabbit and Hazelnut Tourte in Chapter 2. Be sure to work on a cutting board with a very sharp knife.

Remove the filets and hind legs. Bone the legs and remove the thigh meat.

This recipe does not call for the flank filets or the front legs, therefore they are not boned. Reserve them for another use.

Remove any tendons from the filets, then cut the filets and the thigh meat into strips about 2-3cm (about 1in) long and 8mm-1cm (about 3/8in) wide.

Reserve any bones for use in the stock.

Set aside in the refrigerator until ready to use.

Sautéing the Rabbit Strips

Salt and pepper the strips of rabbit.

Heat some clarified butter in a pan and sauté the rabbit over high heat, turning the pieces over to cook them evenly. The rabbit strips will cook quickly (about 1-2 minutes).

Drain them in a strainer to remove excess fat and set aside in the refrigerator.

The Aspic

Aspic made from rabbit stock will reinforce the flavor of the rabbit meat.

The Crayfish

Remove the dark vein that runs the length of the crayfish by holding the two middle segments of the tail flap, twisting and pulling the vein out. This should be done before cooking, as the vein will give a bad flavor to the crayfish.

Sautéing the Crayfish

Sauté the crayfish over medium-high heat in a pan with a little olive oil, shaking the pan and stirring the crayfish as they cook. They are cooked when the shell becomes bright red (about 1-2 minutes).

Removing the Shells

The shells are more easily removed when the crayfish are still warm. Be careful to remove the tail meat in one piece.

Set the shelled crayfish aside in the refrigerator.

The shells can be used to add flavor to a fish stock or to make an " Américaine " sauce.

Preparing the Vegetables

This recipe includes five vegetables that are prepared separately.

The Cabbage

Choose a firm round cabbage with bright green, unblemished leaves.

Detach the leaves and choose the most vibrant ones for this dish. Wash them thoroughly in a large basin of cold water.

Cooking the Cabbage

Plunge the leaves two or three at a time into rapidly boiling salted water, using a slotted spoon to keep them submerged. The cabbage should be firm but not crunchy, so that it will line the mold easily without breaking and will be pleasant to eat.

Stop the cooking by plunging the leaves into ice water. As soon as they are cool, drain them so that they do not become watery, then dry them on a hand towel. Turn them over so they are completely dry.

Cut out the central rib of the leaves with a paring knife.

Set aside in the refrigerator.

The Leeks

Choose leeks with bright green leaves.

Trim any damaged leaves and cut off the white of the leek; reserve for another use.

Wash the green leaves of the leek in a large basin of cold water, changing the water several times until all the sand is eliminated.

Cutting the Leeks

Line up the leaves so that neat slices can be cut from one end. Using a chef's knife, slice them thinly, making a lovely julienne of leek.

Cooking the Leeks

Plunge the prepared leeks into a pot of rapidly boiling salted water. They will cook very quickly.

Stop the cooking by plunging them into a basin of ice water and drain them immediately so that they do not become watery. Dry the leeks on a hand towel and set aside in the refrigerator.

The Onions

Pearl onions or spring onions can be used.

Trim them and rinse them.

Plunge the onions into a pot of rapidly boiling salted water. Test the onions with a skewer or the point of a knife; they should still be slightly firm.

Stop the cooking by plunging them into a bowl of ice water; drain them, and dry on a hand towel.

The Shallots

Remove the skin, rinse, then cut the shallots into very fine dice and set aside.

The Herbs

Pluck the leaves from the stem of the tarragon and chervil and chop finely with a chef's knife.

The chives are cut in very small pieces and set aside with the other herbs.

Assembling the Aspic

Set the mold in a pan with crushed ice to facilitate the assembly. Set the aspic over ice as well.

Line the mold with the cabbage leaves, overlapping a little so that there are no gaps and letting the ends hang over the sides to fold over the top of the aspic.

Pour a little aspic into the bottom of the mold, which will coat the outside of the leaves and ensure easy unmolding.

On the bottom, sprinkle a mixture of chopped shallots and herbs.

Cover with aspic and chill in the refrigerator until set.

Assembly continued

Arrange rows of rabbit strips and crayfish in the mold. Cover with aspic and chill in the refrigerator to set.

Cut the onions in half (if they are large) and arrange a row down the center of the aspic.

Place the prepared leek green on either side of the onions, cover with aspic and chill to set.

Arrange a second layer of rabbit and crayfish, alternating the order of the first layer to make the slices of the assembled dish more attractive.

Cover with a layer of aspic and chill to set.

Repeat with a third layer of rabbit and crayfish, cover with a layer of aspic and chill to set.

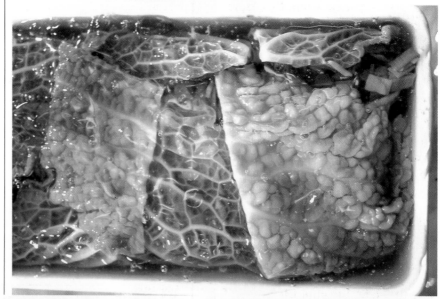

Finish with another layer of onions and leeks, then cover with a layer of aspic and chill to set.

Fold the leaves of cabbage over the top of the aspic. They should cover completely without overlapping too much; trim the leaves, if necessary, with scissors.

Pour a final layer of aspic on top to coat the leaves and seal the dish in aspic.

Storage

Left in the mold, covered securely with plastic wrap, this aspic will keep for 3-4 days in the refrigerator at 4 °C (40F).

Unmolding

To unmold, dip the mold in a bowl of warm water for a few moments. Invert the mold on a platter and shake it gently to help release the aspic from the mold.

Presentation

Aspics are always eaten cold, but for the best taste, allow them to sit at room temperature for a few minutes to " take the chill off ".

Because the ingredients in this aspic have different consistencies, slicing must be done very carefully with a serrated or very sharp thin-bladed knife. Arrange the slices neatly on a platter to serve.

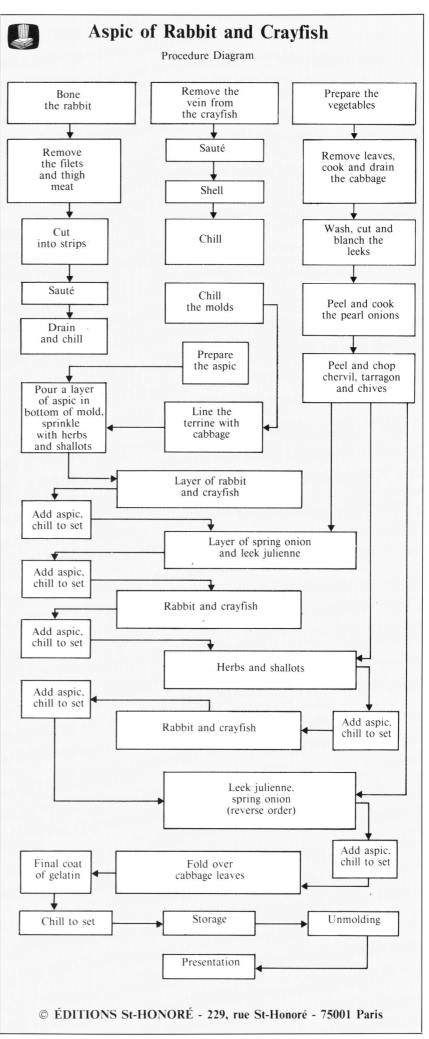

Aspic of Rabbit and Crayfish

Procedure Diagram

Bone the rabbit → Remove the filets and thigh meat → Cut into strips → Sauté → Drain and chill

Remove the vein from the crayfish → Sauté → Shell → Chill

Prepare the vegetables → Remove leaves, cook and drain the cabbage → Wash, cut and blanch the leeks → Peel and cook the pearl onions → Peel and chop chervil, tarragon and chives

Chill the molds

Prepare the aspic

Line the terrine with cabbage

Pour a layer of aspic in bottom of mold, sprinkle with herbs and shallots

Layer of rabbit and crayfish

Add aspic, chill to set

Layer of spring onion and leek julienne

Add aspic, chill to set

Rabbit and crayfish

Add aspic, chill to set

Herbs and shallots

Add aspic, chill to set

Rabbit and crayfish

Add aspic, chill to set

Leek julienne, spring onion (reverse order)

Add aspic, chill to set

Final coat of gelatin ← Fold over cabbage leaves

Chill to set → Storage → Unmolding

Presentation

© ÉDITIONS St-HONORÉ - 229, rue St-Honoré - 75001 Paris

Aspic with Ham and Parsley

Introduction

This is a regional favorite from Burgundy, traditionally prepared for Easter, that is appreciated throughout France. It is a rustic aspic that is at home as a dinner first course, light luncheon main course or as picnic fare.

The ingredients are not expensive and it is therefore affordable for all occasions. The ham poached in white wine and the parsley macerated in vinegar make this aspic very refreshing.

Calves' feet are used to add natural gelatin to the aspic.

Equipment

Cutting board, large stock pot, sharpening steel, boning knife, paring knife, vegetable peeler, slicing knife, chef's knife, thin-bladed flexible knife, palette knife, tablespoon, hotel pans, mixing bowl, fine- meshed conical sieve, skimmer, ladle, whisk, hand towel or cheesecloth, measuring cup, ice bath

Ingredients

3kg (6 1/2lb) ham
2 calves' feet
2L (2qts) white wine
6-8L (6-8qts) water

Clarifying Ingredients

3L (3qts) cooking liquid
8 egg whites
200g (7oz) leek green
12-20g (approx 1/2oz) gelatin per
  liter (per quart) of aspic

Aromatic Garnish

240g (1/2lb) carrots
120g (4oz) onions
60g (2oz) shallots
15g (1/2oz) garlic
200g (7oz) leeks
100g (3 1/2 oz) celery
2 sprigs thyme
1 bay leaf
10 parsley stems
2 cloves
15 black peppercorns
15 coriander seeds
Salt to taste

Preparing the Ham

It is recommended to use a fresh ham, and if possible, the fore-leg portion or "jambonneau". The large bone in the center of the fresh ham should be removed to facilitate cooking.

Degorge the ham in a basin of cold water for two hours, to draw out blood. Change the water a few times.

After it is degorged, blanch the ham by placing it in cold water and bringing it to a boil for 3-4 minutes, which will draw out more impurities.

Rinse the ham under cold running water until it is cool.

Preparing the Calves' Feet

The calves' feet will render more gelatin if the skin is cut and the bones are exposed.

Blanch them by placing them in cold water and bringing it to a boil for 3-4 minutes to draw out impurities, then rinse under cold running water.

Preparing the Aromatic Vegetables

Peel the carrots and rinse them.

Trim any damaged leaves from the leeks and celery and rinse thoroughly.

Peel the onions, shallots and garlic.

Make a bouquet garni with parsley stems, thyme and bay leaf wrapped in a leek green and tied with kitchen twine.

Seasoning

Add a little salt depending on the saltiness of the ham, more salt can be added later if necessary.

The coriander, peppercorns and cloves are tied in a piece of cheesecloth. The cloves may be inserted into the onion instead.

Cooking the Ham

Place all of the ingredients in a large pot and cover the ham with the water and wine. Cook over moderate heat, for about 15-20 minutes per 500g (1lb) of meat.

Checking the Cooking

When the ham is done, a skewer will insert easily and be hot when removed, and the juices will be clear. The doneness can be checked as well with a thermometer inserted into the center of the ham that should read 85C (185F).

Cooling

It is recommended to let the ham cool in the liquid. This will take quite a while so the ham should be poached the day before assembling the dish.

Drain the cooled ham before cutting it into cubes.

Pass the cooking liquid through a sieve to remove the bones and vegetables.

Preparing the Cooked Ham

Place the cooled ham on a cutting board and remove the skin. Cut away all the fat as well which could cloud the aspic.

Cut along the bone with a stiff bladed knife, turning the ham to free the bone on all sides; remove it.

With a very sharp knife, cut the meat into neat cubes about 1.5-2cm (approx. 1/2in) on each side.

The ham can also be shredded, but this will not be as attractive.

Clarifying the Cooking Liquid

Skim all the fat that rises to the surface of the cooking liquid.

Clean the leek greens and cut them finely, then mix them with the egg whites.

Stir in a little cooking liquid to make a pourable mixture, then add this to the cooking liquid.

Stir all of the ingredients together on high heat, stirring constantly at first so that the egg whites do not stick to the bottom.

Bring to a boil, then lower the heat to maintain the liquid at a simmer and stop stirring.

Cook the liquid with the egg whites for 1-1 1/2 hours.

The egg whites will absorb fats and impurities and the simmering action will bring them to the surface.

The chlorophyll also has a clarifying effect.

Carefully remove the impurities that rise to the surface and strain the clarified liquid through a fine cheeesecloth or hand towel.

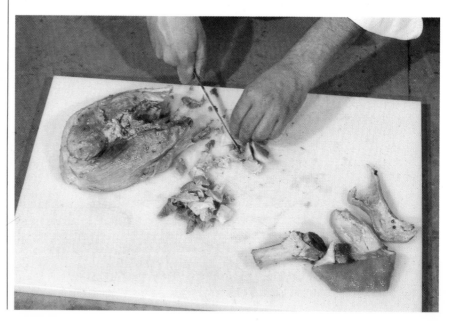

Adding Gelatin

Pour a little of the clarified liquid on a plate and chill in the refrigerator to set.

Taste the set aspic to determine how much gelatin needs to be added and if additional seasonings are necessary.

Soften the gelatin (leaves or powder) in cold water, then dissolve it in the hot liquid.

Test the aspic again for consistency and flavor.

Add more gelatin if necessary to achieve an aspic that is firm but not chewy.

Preparing the Parsley

It is recommended to use flat Italian parsley because it has more flavor.

Remove the leaves from the stems. Squeeze and wash thoroughly in cold water and then dry on a hand towel.

Chop the dry parsley finely with a chef's knife.

Macerate the chopped parsley in vinegar for about 15 minutes to give it a tangy flavor.

Stir the macerated parsley into the clarified liquid.

Assembling the Aspic with Ham and Parsley

Choose a mold to suit the occasion and method of sale.

This aspic can be assembled in a rectangular or round mold or in a traditional salad bowl, as shown.

Chill the mold in the freezer to facilitate the assembly.

Pour a little aspic into the bottom of the chilled mold and put in the refrigerator to set.

Spread a layer of ham over the set aspic, pour aspic to cover and chill until set.

Repeat this process to fill the mold, ending with a layer of aspic on the top to completely cover.

Chill several hours to set completely.

Storage

Left in the mold and covered securely with plastic wrap, this aspic will keep for 3-4 days in the refrigerator at 4 °C (40F).

Unmolding

To unmold, dip the mold in a bowl of warm water for a few moments. Invert the mold on a platter and shake it gently to help release the aspic from the mold.

Presentation

The aspic with ham and parsley is often presented whole on a bed of greens.

It may also be sliced and arranged on plates, with a few salad greens and perhaps some condiments such as cornichons (small sour gherkins) or pickled onions. Slice the aspic with a very sharp knife dipped in hot water.

Aspics are always eaten cold, but for the best taste, allow them to sit at room temperature for a few minutes to "take the chill off".

Aspic with Ham and Parsley
Procedure Diagram

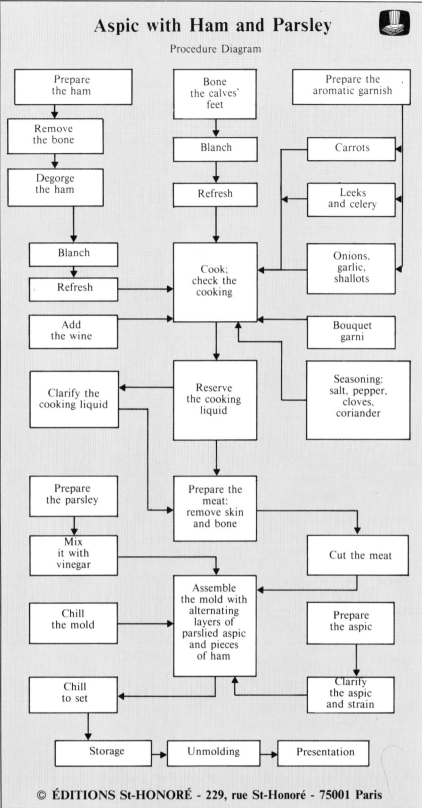

Prepare the ham → Remove the bone → Degorge the ham → Blanch → Refresh → Add the wine

Bone the calves' feet → Blanch → Refresh → Cook; check the cooking → Reserve the cooking liquid → Prepare the meat: remove skin and bone

Prepare the aromatic garnish: Carrots; Leeks and celery; Onions, garlic, shallots; Bouquet garni; Seasoning: salt, pepper, cloves, coriander

Clarify the cooking liquid

Prepare the parsley → Mix it with vinegar

Chill the mold

Cut the meat

Prepare the aspic → Clarify the aspic and strain

Assemble the mold with alternating layers of parslied aspic and pieces of ham

Chill to set → Storage → Unmolding → Presentation

© ÉDITIONS St-HONORÉ - 229, rue St-Honoré - 75001 Paris

Chapter 6

Pizzas and Quiches

Pizzas and quiches are included together in this chapter because they are both made with a bottom crust topped with ingredients that include vegetables, meats, seafood and cheese. Each pizza is first spread with a zesty tomato sauce and the quiche ingredients in each recipe are combined with a savory custard before baked.

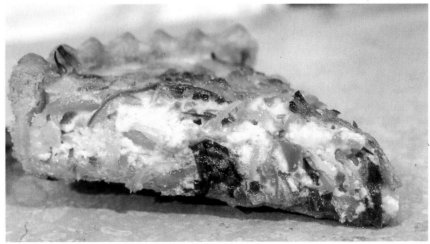

Introduction to
Pizzas and Quiches

This chapter includes variations of pizzas and quiches that reflect the imagination of the chef. These are versatile dishes that can feature seasonal ingredients and can be made to suit the tastes of the customer.

These pizzas and quiches may be made in large sizes to serve several people or in small individual portions.

Each variety is cooked differently, depending on the pastry base used, the choice of filling ingredients and the size.

To taste these dishes at their best, they should be eaten soon after they are made, sometimes within one day. They are always served hot.

These popular dishes may be served as a hot hors d'œuvre, as a first course for a lunch or dinner, or as a light main course on a restaurant lunch menu. These dishes also can round out the selection offered at a buffet.

Both pizzas and quiches can be loosely described as " pies " which are made with a bottom crust and topped with a selection of ingredients. Although there are similarities, the basic preparations are different:

For Pizzas: The bottom crust is made with bread dough or enriched " pizza dough " which is spread with a tomato sauce.

For Quiches: The bottom crust is made of basic pie pastry or puff pastry and is filled with custard.

General Advice for Quiches

In France quiches are sometimes called "flamiches" or "croustades" depending on the ingredients used and the origin of the dish. They are always savory tarts that are made with basic pie pastry and a custard filling. Puff pastry can be used for the bottom crust but has a tendency to become soggy quickly.

Tart pans or pastry rings are lined with the dough. You may use different heights and sizes.

For larger tarts, the pastry may require blind baking before filling so that the crust gets cooked properly. Smaller versions do not need blind baking because the pastry

base is rolled thinner and the oven temperature is hotter, so the crust bakes properly along with the filling.

The food cost will vary with the ingredients used, as there are countless variations of quiche, flamiche and croustade, many of which are addressed in Volume 3 of this series.

Storage times for these savory tarts is relatively short (1-2 days) in order to keep the pastry crisp and the filling fresh tasting.

These dishes must be reheated before serving in order to bring out the best flavors and textures.

General Advice for Pizzas

Pizzas are Italian in origin, but over the last 20 years they have become quite popular in France and have been adapted to French tastes.

The pizza base is made of bread dough or special pizza dough, a milk-enriched dough with extra salt and the addition of olive oil.

Onions and tomatoes are a frequent choice for a topping, along with a variety of other colorful and flavorful ingredients.

Pizza can be a light meal in itself, as it is quite nourishing.

The dough and filling are always cooked together in a hot oven (220 °C (425F)) until the crust is evenly browned and crisp.

The food cost is usually low, though of course the more elaborate toppings will cost more.

Pizzas are easy to make and their versatility makes them very useful for the caterer.

Pizzas: Basic Preparations

1 - Pizza Dough

Basic pizza dough is a raised dough enriched with milk. It may be made with water, which will make it less soft than the version using milk, and with all-purpose flour, because the dough does not need the added body it would de-

30g (1oz) yeast
1/2L (2 cups) milk
10g (2tsp) salt
1kg (2lb) flour
2 eggs
200g (7oz) melted butter or 1.5dl (2/3 cup) olive oil

Thickness of crust: 7mm (3/16in)
Weight of dough: 550g (1lb)
Weight of pizza sauce: 450g (15oz)
Weight of tomatoes: 800g (1lb 10oz)

2 - Pizza Sauce

Ingredients
4dl (1 2/3 cup) olive oil
5kg (11lb) onions
5kg (11lb) fresh tomatoes
1 bouquet garni (thyme, bay leaf, parsley stems, leek green, basil)
200g (7oz) garlic
500g (1lb) tomato paste
Salt, pepper, sugar

The pizza sauce, which is used in combination with a variety of other topping ingredients, may be made in large batches when tomatoes are in season, then frozen or canned for later use.

Procedure

Plunge the tomatoes into boiling water for a few seconds, then peel

rive from bread flour. Olive oil gives the dough more flavor than melted butter. It is best to make the dough one day in advance so it has time to rest.

The dough does not need to rise right away; it may be refrigerated immediately after kneading.

For approximately 1.4kg (3lb) dough, yielding 20 individual pizzas or 3 large pizzas with 8 portions each:

For a Small Pizza

Diameter of the crust: 14cm (5 1/2in)
Thickness of the crust: 5mm (about 1/4in)
Weight of the dough: 70g (about 2 1/2oz)
Weight of the pizza sauce: 60g (2oz)
Weight of the tomatoes: 100g (3 1/2oz)

For a Large Pizza (8 servings)

Diameter of the crust: 30cm (12in)

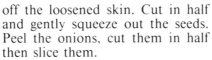
off the loosened skin. Cut in half and gently squeeze out the seeds. Peel the onions, cut them in half then slice them.

Peel the cloves of garlic, cut them in half and remove the green sprout. Crush the garlic and chop it finely. Set aside.

Heat the olive oil in a heavy-bottomed pan. Add the onions and cook over low heat until they are soft and golden. Add the prepared tomatoes, the garlic, the bouquet garni and some salt and pepper.

Cover the pan and cook the mixture in the oven at 180C (350F) for about 1/2 hour. Stir frequently with a wooden spoon so the mixture does not stick to the bottom. Taste the mixture during cooking and add tomato paste as necessary to obtain a rich tomato taste.

At the end of cooking, if the mixture is too watery, remove the lid and continue cooking to evaporate the moisture. This step may be done on top of the stove as well, but in this case, the mixture must be stirred constantly so that it does not burn on the bottom.

Taste and adjust seasoning, adding a little sugar if the tomatoes are very acid. Chill immediately.

Adding the Topping

Make the pizza dough at least one day ahead. Roll out the crust ahead of time so the dough has time to rise; it should double in bulk. Brush the rolled out crust with egg glaze before leaving to rise so that a dry skin does not form. Brush with glaze a second time before adding the topping.

Using a fork or a palette knife, spread on a layer of chilled pizza sauce. Leave a border of about 1cm (3/8in).

Cut some tomatoes into 4mm (about 1/8in) slices and lay them in an attractive pattern on the pizza. Season with salt, pepper and oregano.

Ingredients for Toppings

The caterer's imagination can have free rein when it comes to toppings. The recipes in this chapter are typical French combinations, but there is no limit to the number of delicious combinations to be made.

For example:

Sardines - Mackerel - Squid - Shrimp - Octopus - Clams - Baby eels - Ham - Prosciutto - Bacon - Mozzarella - Eggs - Fresh cheeses - Eggplant - Capers - Basil - Celery - Spinach - Cucumber - Onions

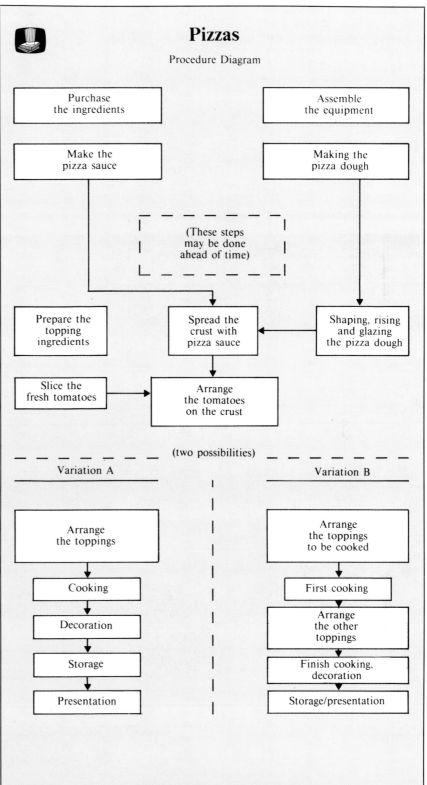

Pizzas

Procedure Diagram

```
Purchase                          Assemble
the ingredients                   the equipment

Make the                          Making the
pizza sauce                       pizza dough

            (These steps
            may be done
            ahead of time)

Prepare the      Spread the        Shaping, rising
topping          crust with        and glazing
ingredients      pizza sauce       the pizza dough

Slice the        Arrange
fresh tomatoes   the tomatoes
                 on the crust
```

(two possibilities)

Variation A	Variation B
Arrange the toppings	Arrange the toppings to be cooked
Cooking	First cooking
Decoration	Arrange the other toppings
Storage	Finish cooking, decoration
Presentation	Storage/presentation

1. Cheese, Mushroom and Olive Pizza

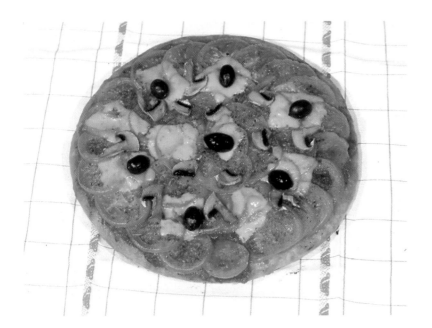

Ingredients
(for the topping for a large pizza)

10 slices of swiss cheese
  (60g (2oz))
Mushrooms (75g (2 1/2oz))
9 black olives (45g (1 1/2oz))

Preparation

Use a swiss cheese without too many holes.

Wash the mushrooms, slice them into 3mm (1/8in) slices and sprinkle them with lemon juice to prevent them from discoloring.

Choose flavorful, unpitted, plump black olives (olives marinated in oil and herbs are a good choice).

Assembly

Lay the slices of cheese on the unbaked pizza crust that has been spread with pizza sauce and topped with sliced tomatoes.

Distribute the sliced mushrooms evenly over the surface of the pizza. Sprinkle it with a little olive oil.

Cook the pizza on a heavy baking sheet or pizza pan in a hot oven.

When the pizza is cooked and the crust is crispy take it from the oven and add the olives. Brush the pizza with a little more olive oil to give it a nice shine.

2. Anchovy, Olive and Green Pepper Pizza

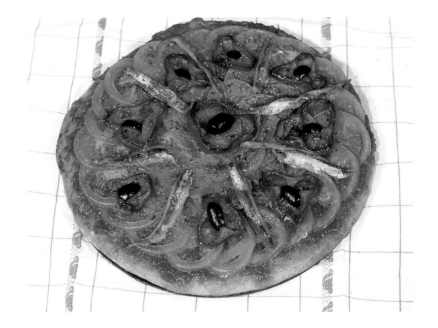

Ingredients

(for the topping for a large pizza)

1 green pepper (60g (2oz))
8 anchovy filets (45g (1 1/2oz))
9 black olives (45g (1 1/2oz))

Preparation

Cooking the Green Peppers

Cut the stem from the pepper and shake out all the seeds. With a thin-bladed knife, cut away the white ribs (which are bitter) on the inside of the pepper.

Cut crosswise slices about 3mm (1/8in) thick.

Sauté the pepper slices in olive oil to give them a little color and mellow their flavor. They should still be firm as they will cook again on the pizza.

Assembly

Lay the pepper slices on the unbaked pizza crust that has been spread with pizza sauce and topped with sliced tomatoes. Sprinkle the pizza with a little olive oil.

Cook the pizza on a heavy baking sheet or pizza pan in a hot oven.

When the pizza is cooked, take it from the oven and arrange the anchovy filets and olives in a neat pattern on top. (If these ingredients were cooked with the pizza, they would be too dry and salty.) Brush a little more olive oil on the pizza to give it a nice shine.

3. Artichoke, Asparagus, Fava Bean and Olive Pizza

Ingredients

(for the topping for a large pizza)

32 fava beans (130g (4oz))

3 artichokes (150g (5oz))

16 prepared asparagus tips (120g (4oz))

9 black olives (45g (1 1/2oz))

Use sliced artichoke bottoms or tiny purple baby artichokes, which make the pizza very attractive.

Preparation

If using whole baby artichokes, they must be pre-cooked before adding them to the pizza. Boil them in salted water until they are cooked but still firm, then refresh them immediately in cold water to stop the cooking. Drain well. Cut them in quarters (larger or smaller, according to the size).

Remove the hull from the beans and blanch them in boiling water to remove the skin.

Assembly

Arrange the artichokes and asparagus tips on the unbaked pizza crust that has been spread with pizza sauce and topped with sliced tomatoes. Sprinkle with a little olive oil and cook the pizza on a heavy baking sheet or pizza pan in a hot oven until it is 3/4 cooked.

Lay the beans on the partially cooked pizza, return it to the oven and continue cooking. When the pizza is cooked, take it from the oven and arrange the olives attractively on the finished pizza. Brush it with a little more olive oil to give it a nice shine.

4. Zucchini, Corn, Broccoli and Olive Pizza

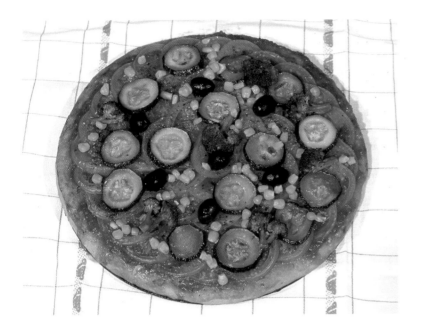

Ingredients
(for the topping for a large pizza)

broccoli flowerets (120g (4oz))
1 large zucchini (120g (4oz))
3 tbsp corn kernels (30g (1oz))
9 black olives (45g (1 1/2oz))

Preparation

Rinse the zucchini, but do not peel it. Cut off the two ends and slice the rest into 6mm (1/4in) slices.

Sauté the slices lightly in olive oil over high heat to give them a deep golden color; add only a few slices at a time to the pan so they brown well. Season with salt and pepper and drain.

Clean the broccoli; boil it in salted water. It should remain slightly crunchy as it cooks again on the pizza. Drain and separate into smaller flowerets if necessary.

Assembly

Arrange the pre-cooked zucchini slices and broccoli on the unbaked pizza crust that has been spread with pizza sauce and topped with sliced tomatoes. Sprinkle with a little olive oil.

Cook the pizza on a heavy baking sheet or pizza pan in a hot oven.

When the pizza is cooked, take it from the oven and sprinkle on the corn and black olives. Brush the pizza with a little more olive oil to give it a nice shine.

5. Hearts of Palm, Olives, Tuna and Fennel Pizza

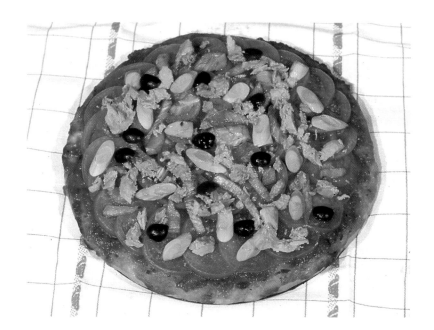

Ingredients
(for the topping for a large pizza)

2 hearts of palm (100g (3 1/2oz))
1 head fennel
Canned tuna, in oil or water
 (150g (5oz))
10 black olives (60g (2oz))

Preparation

Slice the hearts of palm on the bias. Break up the tuna into large flakes.

Peel the fennel, cut it in half and slice into thick slices. Sauté the fennel lightly in olive oil to give it a golden color.

Assembly

Arrange the hearts of palm and fennel on the unbaked pizza crust that has been spread with pizza sauce and topped with sliced tomatoes. Sprinkle a little olive oil on top.

Cook the pizza on a heavy baking sheet or pizza pan in a hot oven.

After the pizza is cooked, take it from the oven and add the tuna and black olives. Brush on a little more olive oil to give it a nice shine.

6. Zucchini, Mussels, Corn, Shrimp and Bay Scallop Pizza

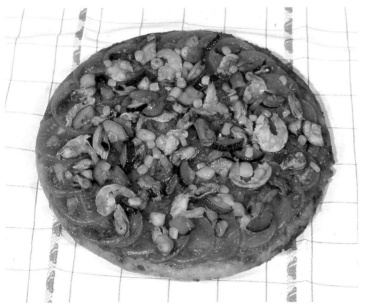

Ingredients
(for the topping)

16 bay scallops (150g (5oz))
24 mussels (250g (8oz))
8 medium cooked shrimp (110g (4oz))
2 tbsp corn kernels (60g (2oz))
1 medium zucchini (60g (2oz))

Preparation

Rinse the zucchini but do not peel it. Cut off the two ends and slice the rest into 6mm (1/4in) slices, then cut the slices into quarters. Sauté the zucchini slices in olive oil to give them color and to cook them. Drain the corn kernels.

Scrub and wash the mussels. Steam them open " la marinière " (in a little white wine, chopped onions and shallots, bouquet garni). Remove the shells and pull off the dark rim (the beard). Set aside.

Shell and wash the bay scallops, if they are not already prepared.

Peel the shrimp. If they are large, cut them in half lengthwise.

Assembly

Arrange the seafood on the unbaked pizza crust that has been spread with pizza sauce and topped with sliced tomatoes. Sprinkle with a little olive oil.

Cook the pizza on a heavy baking sheet or pizza pan in a hot oven. After the pizza is cooked, take it from the oven and add the zucchini and corn kernels. Brush on a little more olive oil to give the pizza a nice shine.

Before...and After Cooking

Quiche Lorraine

Ingredients

For a quiche 28cm (11in) in diameter and 3.5cm (1 1/2in) high

Introduction

This is a traditional quiche that originated in the Alsace-Lorraine region of France.

This delicious dish is made using a crust made from basic pie pastry or sturdier "pâté pastry", which should be pre-cooked if the quiche is large. There are many variations on the filling. The main ingredient is bacon, either fresh, lightly salted or smoked. If the bacon has a strong flavor, it may be blanched before adding to the quiche. The bacon may be cut into strips or cubes, and it is always browned before adding to the quiche, which eliminates some of the excess fat and gives the bacon a nutty taste.

Ham may be substituted for some of the bacon, which will yield a slightly less fatty dish and may reduce the overall food cost. Cheese is optional, but it adds smoothness and rich flavor. The quiche is bound with a custard made of heavy cream, milk, eggs and seasoned with salt, pepper and nutmeg.

This quiche is delicious any time of the year and it is sure to please any customer. It is fairly simple to make and the food cost is relatively low.

Filling

20g (2/3oz) clarified butter
100g (3 1/2oz) fresh or lightly salted bacon
100g (3 1/2oz) smoked bacon
100g (3 1/2oz) boiled or baked ham
130g (4oz) swiss cheese

Custard

2dl (3/4 cup) milk
3dl (1 1/4 cup) heavy cream
5 eggs
Salt, pepper, nutmeg

Procedure

Cut the ham, cheese and bacon into small cubes.

Blanch the bacon in boiling water, then refresh it in cold water and drain well. Sauté the blanched bacon in a little oil until brown and crispy, then drain thoroughly. Reserve the bacon grease, and brown the diced ham in it. Drain the ham.

Filling

Sprinkle the ham, bacon and cheese over the cooked crust.

Mix the custard ingredients thoroughly with a whisk and pass through a fine-meshed conical strainer. Pour the strained custard into the crust to cover the filling ingredients.

Quiche Lorraine

Procedure Diagram

```
Make the pastry          Cut the ham            Cut the bacon
                         and cheese             into cubes
     │                   into cubes                  │
     ▼                        │                       ▼
   Line                       │                     Sauté
 the molds                    │                    the bacon
     │                        ▼                       │
     │              Sprinkle the ◄───────────────────┘
     └─────────────► ham, cheese
                     and bacon on
                     the crust │
                        │          │
 Prepare                ▼          ▼
 the quiche         Fill the    Blind bake
 custard ──────────► crust with  the crust
                    the custard
                         │
                         ▼
 Check              Cook in a
 the cooking ─────► medium oven
                         │
                         ▼
 Presentation ◄─────── Cooling
```

Cooking

As the filling ingredients are already cooked, the aim is simply to cook the custard until lightly set and the crust until crisp and brown (if it has not been pre-cooked).

Pre-cooking the crust: 20-25 minutes.
Cooking the quiche: 25-30 minutes.
Temperature: 190-200 °C (about 375F)

Storage

Store the quiche lorraine at 4 °C (40F) for 1-2 days.

Presentation

Reheat the quiche in a low oven and present on a platter with a doilie or sliced on a plate.

Trianon Croustade

Introduction

Light and refreshing, this quiche, known as a croustade, can be made year-round and is always popular. The combination of cheese, mushrooms and tomatoes is delicious, with an agreeable melting texture.

The croustade is bound with a highly-seasoned custard made from heavy cream, milk and eggs.

Ingredients

For a quiche 28cm (11in) in diameter and 3.5cm (1 1/2in) high

Filling

650g (1lb 5oz) peeled, seeded and chopped tomatoes
3cl (2 tbsp) olive oil
60g (2oz) shallots
30g (1oz) garlic
1 bouquet garni (thyme, bay leaf, parsley stems, leek greens)
Salt, pepper, sugar
30g (1oz) clarified butter
350g (12oz) mushrooms
1/2 lemon
Salt, pepper
200g (7oz) swiss cheese

Custard

2dl (3/4 cup) milk
2dl (3/4 cup) heavy cream
5 eggs
Salt, pepper

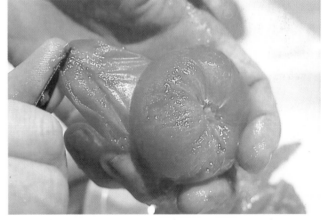

Procedure

The procedure for this croustade is simple and the food cost is low. Cook it in the same manner as the other quiches in this chapter. As the filling ingredients are already cooked, the aim is simply to cook the custard until lightly set and the crust until crisp and brown (if it has not been pre-cooked).

Peel the shallots, cut them in half, then cut them into fine dice. Peel the garlic, remove the green sprout from the center. Crush the garlic cloves and chop them finely. Cook the shallots in olive oil until they are very soft but not brown.

Add the prepared tomatoes, the chopped garlic and the bouquet garni. Season to taste with salt and pepper. Cover the pan and cook for a while on the stove, stirring occasionally. Remove the lid and continue cooking to dry out the mixture slightly, stirring frequently so it does not stick to the pan.

Wash the mushrooms and cut them into pieces. Sauté them in clarified butter. Cut the cheese into small cubes.

Note

As with other recipes in this chapter, it is best to blind bake the crust for large preparations. For this croustade, be sure the tomato mixture has been cooked long enough to evaporate the excess liquid, otherwise it will make the pastry crust soggy.

Use fresh tomatoes when they are in season; otherwise good quality canned tomatoes may be substituted.

Mix the custard ingredients with a whisk, then pass it through a fine-meshed conical strainer.

Assembly

Arrange the diced cheese and sautéed mushrooms on the crust. Spread the cooked tomatoes on top, then pour over the strained custard.

Cooking

Pre-cooking the crust: 20-25 minutes

Cooking the croustade: 25-30 minutes

Temperature: 190-200 °C (about 375F)

Storage

The Trianon croustade can be kept at 4 °C (40F) for 1-2 days.

Trianon Croustade

Procedure Diagram

```
Make the pastry          Peel and seed           Cut the
       |                 the tomatoes             shallots
       v                      |                      |
     Line                     |                      v
      the                   Cut the               Heat the
     molds --------+       cheese                 olive oil
       |           |       into cubes                |
       |           v          |                      |
       |         Blind        |                      |
       |         bake         |                      |
       |      the crusts      |                   Crush the
     Prepare       |          |                   garlic
      eggs         +----------+---> Pass the         |
       |                            custard through  |
       v                            a strainer <-----+
      Add                               |         Cut and sauté
      the                               |         the mushrooms
     filling                           |
   ingredients                          |
       |                                v
       v                          Pour the custard
     Season -------------------->  into the crust
                                        |
                                        v
   Presentation <--- Cooling <--- Cook in a medium
                                      oven
```

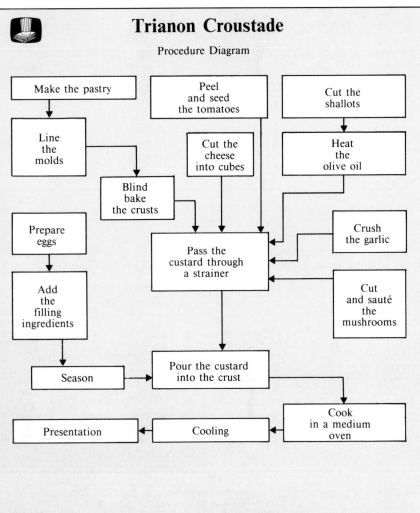

Onion and Roquefort Croustade

Ingredients

Filling

750g (1 1/2lb) onions
45g (1 1/2oz) clarified butter
Bouquet garni (thyme, bay leaf,
    parsley stems, leek greens)
Salt and pepper

Custard

125g (4oz) roquefort
2.5dl (1 cup) heavy cream
2dl (3/4 cup) milk
5 eggs
Salt, pepper, nutmeg

Introduction

This croustade is most appropriate for the fall or winter season as it is slightly heavier than the others because of the large quantity of onions. It is nonetheless delicious, especially the combination of onions and roquefort cheese.

As with all the recipes in this chapter, it is best to blind bake the crust to be used for large croustades.

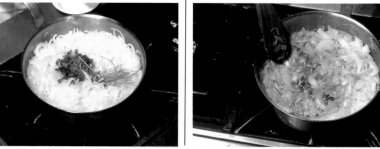

Procedure

Peel the onions, cut them in half, remove the stems and slice the onions crosswise.

Put them in a heavy-bottomed pan with the clarified butter or some oil.

Add the bouquet garni and cook in a low oven or over very low heat on the stove until the onions are very soft and deep golden. Taste and adjust seasoning if necessary. Drain off any excess liquid and remove the bouquet garni.

Pay close attention to the onions during cooking and make sure they cook down to a very soft, thick compote.

As onions are always an inexpensive ingredient, this croustade is very economical to make.

Choose a roquefort that is heavily " veined ", which indicates that it will have better flavor.

Assembly

Distribute the onion compote over the bottom of the crust.

Blend the cream, milk and eggs with a whisk. Pass the mixture through a fine-meshed conical sieve, season with salt, pepper and nutmeg and add the cheese (crumbled into small bits). Pour the custard into the crust.

Cooking

Pre-cooking the crust: 20-25 minutes - Cooking the croustade: 25-30 minutes - Temperature: 190-200 ^{0}C (about 375F)

Storage

The onion-roquefort croustade can be kept at 4 ^{0}C (40F) for 1-2 days.

Onion-Roquefort Croustade

Procedure Diagram

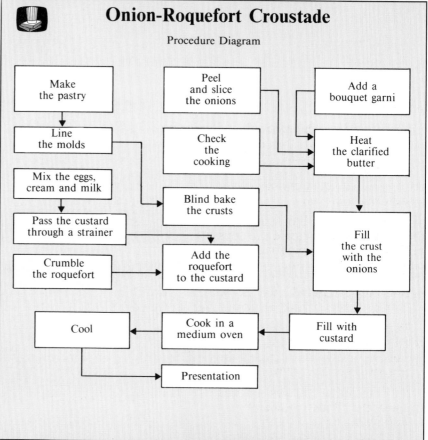

- Make the pastry
- Line the molds
- Mix the eggs, cream and milk
- Pass the custard through a strainer
- Crumble the roquefort
- Peel and slice the onions
- Check the cooking
- Blind bake the crusts
- Add the roquefort to the custard
- Add a bouquet garni
- Heat the clarified butter
- Fill the crust with the onions
- Fill with custard
- Cook in a medium oven
- Cool
- Presentation

Leek Flamiche

lengthwise so the concentric leaves can be opened out flat and cut into julienne with a chef's knife.

Ingredients

Filling

> 450g (1lb) leek whites
> 45g (1 1/2oz) clarified butter
> 1.5dl (2/3 cup) heavy cream
> Salt, pepper
> 15g (1/2oz) clarified butter
> 100g (3 1/2oz) fresh bacon

Custard

> 2dl (3/4 cup) milk
> 2dl (3/4 cup) heavy cream
> 6 eggs
> Salt, pepper, curry powder

Introduction

The name flamiche generally refers to a savory pie that is filled with a mixture of leeks that have been cooked in clarified butter until very soft, then enriched with a little heavy cream.

This delicious dish originated in the Burgundy and Picardy regions of France. Some crisply fried bacon cubes may enhance the filling, as well as a pinch of curry powder to season the custard, which is made with heavy cream, milk and eggs.

The dish is easy to make and depending on the price of leeks in the season in which it is made, the food cost is relatively low.

As with other recipes in this chapter, the filling ingredients are already cooked, so the aim is simply to cook the custard until lightly set and the crust until crisp and brown (if it has not been precooked).

Cook the sliced leeks in clarified butter in a covered pan over low heat until they are soft but not brown. After a while, remove the lid, add the cream and continue cooking for a few more minutes. Season with salt and pepper. Cook until the cream has reduced by 1/4 and the mixture is slightly thick.

Cut the bacon into small cubes and blanch it in boiling water, then

Procedure

Wash the leeks and trim them, using the white part only. Cut them in long chunks, then cut them

refresh in cold water. Drain well. Sauté the bacon in a little clarified butter until it is lightly crisp and brown.

Assembly

Distribute the leek mixture evenly over the bottom of the crust. Sprinkle the bacon on top.

Blend the ingredients for the custard with a whisk, pass it through a fine-meshed conical strainer and

pour the strained custard over the filling.

Cooking

Pre-cooking the crust: 20-25 minutes

Cooking the flamiche: 25-30 minutes

Temperature: 190-200 °C (about 375F)

Storage

The leek flamiche may be kept at 4 °C (40F) for 1-2 days.

Leek Flamiche

Procedure Diagram

```
Make the pastry          Trim                    Cut the
     │                   and wash                 bacon
     ▼                   the leeks                into cubes
   Line                      │                        │
the molds                    ▼                        ▼
     │                     Cut                     Blanch
     ▼                     into                   and sauté
 Blind bake              julienne                 the bacon
 the crust                   │                        │
                             ▼
 Combine                  Cook in
eggs, milk           clarified butter
 and cream             until soft
     │                       │
     ▼                       ▼
  Season                Fill the
     │                   crusts
     │
     ▼                                            Add cream
 Add the                                          to the
 custard                                          leeks and
                                                  reduce
     │
     ▼
Presentation  ◄──  Cool  ◄──  Cook in a
                              medium oven
```

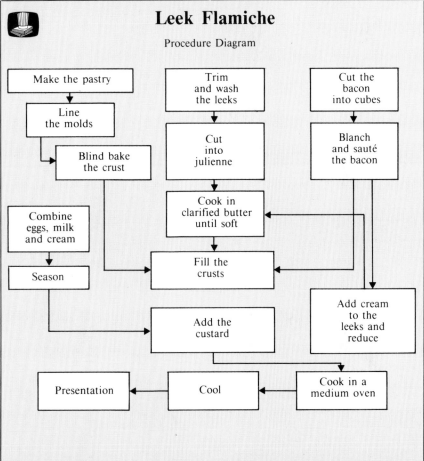

Croustade of Julienned Vegetables and Basil

Introduction

This refreshing croustade is delicious and versatile. It may be served in various ways depending on the style of sale and the needs of the customer. A large croustade serving many people may be presented whole or it may be cut into individual portions for sale. This dish may also be made in individual sizes or even as a mini-croustade to be served as part of a selection of hors d'oeuvres.

Spring is the best season for this dish, because basil is very fragrant and not too expensive.

Note

As with all the recipes in this chapter, the crusts for large preparations should be blind baked before the filling and custard is added in order to ensure a perfectly crisp golden crust. For smaller preparations, the crust and filling ingredients are cooked all at once.

Ingredients

For individual croustades, estimate 40-50g of filling ingredients and 4cl (about 3tbsp) of custard. For larger croustades, 80-100g (2 1/2-3 1/2oz) filling ingredients and 7cl (about 1/4 cup) custard per person. These proportions should be used as guidelines on which to base your own recipes.

Filling

75g (2 1/2oz) clarified butter
400g (14oz) carrots
300g (10oz) mushrooms
1/2 lemon
2 large leeks (about 400g (14oz))
15 basil leaves
Salt, pepper

Custard

1/4L (1 cup) milk
1/4L (1 cup) heavy cream
5 eggs
Salt, pepper

Equipment

Cutting board, paring knife, vegetable peeler, chef's knife, mandoline, mixing bowls, hotel pans, sauté pan with lid, whisk, fine- meshed conical sieve, 2-pronged fork, ladle, measuring cup

Making the Filling

Preparing the Leeks

Cut off the root end and cut off half the green part. Cut the leek in quarters down to the white part but

Preparing the Carrots

Peel the carrots with the vegetable peeler. Cut off the two ends, then rinse the rest. Cut the carrots into 5cm (2in) chunks, then cut 2mm (1/16in) strips on the mandoline. With the chef' knife, cut into julienne.

not all the way through the root end. Wash thoroughly, separating all the leaves.

Cut the leeks in 5cm (2in) chunks, flatten out the leaves, then cut into julienne with the chef's knife.

Preparing the Mushrooms and Basil

Use large white firm mushrooms. Trim off the stems, wash them and dry on a hand towel. Sprinkle them with lemon juice. Cut the mushrooms into 4mm (approx. 1/8in) slices, then cut into julienne. Wash the basil and pick off the leaves and dry them. Lay the leaves one on top of the other, then roll them up tightly and slice crosswise into strips.

Cooking the Vegetables

Heat the clarified butter in the sauté pan. Add the vegetables, season with salt and pepper. Cover and cook over medium heat.

Stir with the two-pronged fork from time to time to keep the vegetables from sticking together. Cook for about 10 minutes.

Add the julienne of basil just before the vegetables are finished. The vegetables should remain slightly firm.

Taste and adjust seasoning if necessary. Set aside.

Note

The vegetables should be cooked covered, which will draw out their natural moisture. Any remaining liquid should be drained off before the filling is added to the crust.

Making the Custard

Measure the ingredients, and combine the milk and heavy

cream. Add the eggs and whisk to combine thoroughly. Season with salt and pepper, then strain this mixture through a fine-meshed conical sieve.

Filling the Crusts

Fill the crust with the vegetable julienne, using a fork to distribute the vegetables evenly. Pour the custard into the crust.

Cooking

Cook the croustade in a medium oven (190 °C (375F)). The cooking time will vary depending on the size of the croustade. After cooking, remove the pastry ring or mold and leave to cool.

Storage

If all the components are prepared ahead (the vegetables cooked, the custard mixed and the pastry prepared), the croustade may be baked to order. The individual components may be kept at 4 °C (40F) for 4 days. Once they are cooked, the croustades may be kept at 4C (40F) for 2 more days.

Presentation

This croustade as well as the other quiches in this chapter should be warmed in a low oven before serving. Do not wrap it in aluminum foil to reheat because the steam will make the pastry crust soggy.

All of the quiches should be presented on a platter with a doilie or sliced on a plate.

Translator's Notes

Because these volumes were originally written for the French audience, some of the ingredients and equipment may need explanation.

Butter is always unsalted, unless otherwise indicated.

Clarified butter is obtained by melting butter, then pouring the pure fat portion off the top, and discarding the milk solids that settle at the bottom and which tend to burn at high temperatures.

Aspic is an important ingredient in catering as it gives a shiny finish to many cold items, as well as keeps the item fresh looking and tasting by sealing out the air. Basic aspic recipes are readily found in reliable cookbooks; top quality powdered aspic is a possible substitute for fresh.

Eggs are always large size (60g/2oz).

" Américaine " sauce is called for in several recipes. The main ingredients include fish stock, tomato, cognac and tarragon. Refer to a reliable source for a recipe.

Drum sieves have many uses in a French kitchen. The large size allows flour to be sifted quickly; meat and vegetable purées are forced through the mesh to obtain smooth mixtures.

Plastic pastry scrapers are an indispensable tool for the French chef, who uses them to scrape bowls clean, transfer mixtures efficiently, keep the work surface clean, as well as to mix pastry doughs.

Hand towels are an essential part of the French chef's equipment. Tucked into the apron, they are an ever-ready pot holder. They are often used to absorb moisture from draining vegetables or other foods; when dampened, they can be used to cover food to prevent drying. When they are in direct contact with food, the hand towels must be perfectly clean.

Sheet pans in France are made from heavy gauge iron that conducts heat evenly. Choose the heaviest sheet pans available.

Measurements are provided in both metric and U.S. units. Most U.S. conversions have been rounded off to the nearest half-unit, except for smaller quantities where accuracy is crucial.

Denis Ruffel:

A Widely-Respected Young Chef

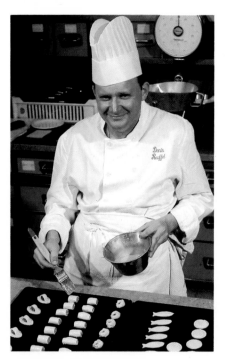

Very early in his career, Denis Ruffel made a name for himself as one of the most talented young chefs of the new generation.

Creative and skilled, meticulous and energetic, empassioned by teaching and always willing to share his knowledge, Ruffel is the ideal author for this series, The Professional Caterer.

After all, who could be more qualified than Denis Ruffel to cover such a field, which includes a wide range of dishes and varied and complex culinary techniques? From the simplest procedure to the most complicated " tricks of the trade " involved in these top-of-the-line recipes, Denis Ruffel offers food professionals a tool that will quickly prove itself indispensable.

For over fifteen years, I have had the pleasure of watching Denis Ruffel's remarkable professional development. Ever since his apprenticeship with Jean Millet, he has had a firm grasp of the fundamental techniques so essential to all top quality work.

Generous with his friends and devoted to his work, he is a paragon of dedication to our profession.

Through working with Denis Ruffel on several seminars, I came to know many of his qualities, including his wealth of knowledge, his modest nature, his friendly disposition, his constant smile and, above all, his outstanding talent for teaching.

His skills, which are equally strong in pastry, catering and cuisine, are limitless and without equal.

The Professional Caterer is the culmination of much hard work and planning, and it stands alone in the field of culinary cookbooks, offering recipes for appetizers to gala buffet fare, and covering the whole range of the catering repertoire.

In these books, Denis Ruffel unites simplicity with perfection. The professional as well as the newcomer to the field can choose from a wide variety of hors d'œuvres, canapés, appetizers, terrines and pâtés and quiches, as well as many other delicious preparations. The recipes are easy to follow, and they are made even clearer by excellent step-by-step photographs.

I would like to express my congratulations and thanks for this marvellous achievment. It is through the work of true professionals like Denis Ruffel--passionate, skilled and dedicated--that our profession will continue to grow.

M. A. Roux

Born in 1950, Denis Ruffel entered the field at the age of fourteen. He received his C.A.P. in Pastry at the Centre Ferrandi in Paris, with Jean Millet as his "maître d'apprentissage", who very quickly recognized his talents.

Passionate about cooking, Ruffel completed his training by receiving his C.A.P. in Cuisine, and worked, among other places, at La Bourgogne, under Monassier, and L'Archestrate, under Senderens.

Always striving for improvement, Ruffel received the Brevet de Maîtrise de Pâtissier-Confiseur-Glacier, and also studied at the Académie du Vin.

Since the late 1970s, he heads the kitchens of Jean Millet, maintaining the excellent reputation of Maison Millet, especially its prestigious catering department. Despite the heavy workload, Denis Ruffel finds time to participate in many other professional activities:

- Training classes at the Paris Chamber of Commerce
- Administrator for apprenticeship program at the Ecole Nationale de la Pâtisserie d'Yssingeaux
- Chef-instructor at Ecole de Cuisine La Varenne in Paris
- Winner of the Concours du Centenaire de la Saint-Michel
- Member of the Association Internationale des Maîtres Pâtissiers " Relais Dessert "
- Gold-medal winner 1985 of the Confédération Nationale de la Pâtisserie-Confiserie-Glacerie de France
- Honory member of the Confédération National de la Pâtisserie-Confiserie Japonaise
- Winner of the 1985 Culinary Trophy
- Winner of the Confédération Nationale de la Pâtisserie-Confiserie Espagnole (Salon Alimentaria en 1986)

The Professional Caterer is the product of Denis Ruffel's vast range of experience.

First published as *L'Artisan Traiteur* by Editions St-Honoré, Paris, France: copyright © 1987.
English translation copyright © 1990 by Van Nostrand Reinhold for the United States of America and Canada; by CICEM (Compagnie Internationale de Consultation *Education* et *Media*) for the rest of the world.
Van Nostrand Reinhold
115 Fifth Avenue
New York, New York 10003
Macmillan of Canada
Division of Canada Publishing Corporation
164 Commander Boulevard
Agincourt, Ontario MIS 3C7, Canada

ISBN 0-442-00140-1 (vol. 2)

CICEM, 229, rue St-Honoré
75001 PARIS (France)

© CICEM ISBN 2-86871-015-2
Dépôt légal 1er trimestre 1990
Imprimé en France par l'Imprimerie ❏ Alençonnaise

Library of Congress Cataloging-in-Publication Data

Ruffel, Denis :
Collective title: The professional caterer series / by Denis Ruffel (Born in 1950)

Contents:
Vol. 1. Pastry hors d'œuvres, assorted snacks, canapés, centerpieces, hot hors d'œuvres, cold brochette's.
Vol. 2. Individual cold dishes, pates, terrines, galantines, and ballotines, aspics, pizzas, and quiches.
Vol. 3. Croustades, quenelles, souffles, beignets, individual hot dishes, mixed salads, fish in aspic, lobsters, poultry in aspic.
Vol. 4. Meat and Games, Sauces and Bases, Planning, Execution, Display and Decoration for Buffets and Receptions.
1. Quantity cooking. 2. Caterers and catering. I.
Title : The professional caterer series.
TX820.R843 1990 641.5'7--dc20 89-22600
ISBN 0-442-00140-1 (vol. 2)